LEON URIS

Photo of Leon Uris by Jerry Bauer. Courtesy of HarperCollins Publishers.

LEON URIS

A Critical Companion

Kathleen Shine Cain

CRITICAL COMPANIONS TO POPULAR CONTEMPORARY WRITERS
Kathleen Gregory Klein, Series Editor

Greenwood Press
Westport, Connecticut • London

Library of Congress Cataloging-in-Publication Data

Cain, Kathleen Shine.
    Leon Uris : a critical companion / Kathleen Shine Cain.
      p. cm.—(Critical companions to popular contemporary
writers, ISSN 1082–4979)
    Includes bibliographical references and index.
    ISBN 0–313–30231–6 (alk. paper)
    1. Uris, Leon, 1924– —Criticism and interpretation.
2. Autobiographical fiction, American—History and criticism.
3. Historical fiction, American—History and criticism.   4. War
stories, American—History and criticism. I. Title. II. Series.
PS3541.R46Z62   1998
813'.54—dc21   97–52324

British Library of Cataloguing in Publication Data is available.

Library of Congress Catalog Card Number: 97–52324
ISBN: 0–313–30231–6
ISSN: 1082–4979

First published in 1998

Greenwood Press, 88 Post Road West, Westport, CT 06881
An imprint of Greenwood Publishing Group, Inc.

Printed in the United States of America

The paper used in this book complies with the
Permanent Paper Standard issued by the National
Information Standards Organization (Z39.48–1984).

10 9 8 7 6 5 4 3 2 1

In loving memory of
Catherine Mahoney Shine
1913–1997

"A mother is not a person to lean on
but a person to make leaning unnecessary."
—Dorothy Canfield Fisher

Contents

Contents

Series Foreword

The authors who appear in the series Critical Companions to Popular Contemporary Writers are all best-selling writers. They do not simply have one successful novel, but a string of them. Fans, critics, and specialist readers eagerly anticipate their next book. For some, high cash advances and breakthrough sales figures are automatic; movie deals often follow. Some writers become household names, recognized by almost everyone.

But, their novels are read one by one. Each reader chooses to start and, more importantly, to finish a book because of what she or he finds there. The real test of a novel is in the satisfaction its readers experience. This series acknowledges the extraordinary involvement of readers and writers in creating a best-seller.

The authors included in this series were chosen by an Advisory Board composed of high school English teachers and high school and public librarians. They ranked a list of best-selling writers according to their popularity among different groups of readers. For the first series, writers in the top-ranked group who had received no book-length, academic, literary analysis (or none in at least the past ten years) were chosen. Because of this selection method, Critical Companions to Popular Contemporary Writers meets a need that is being addressed nowhere else. The success of these volumes as reported by reviewers, librarians, and teachers led to an expansion of the series mandate to include some writers with wide critical attention—Toni Morrison, John Irving, and Maya Angelou, for example—to extend the usefulness of the series.

The volumes in the series are written by scholars with particular expertise in analyzing popular fiction. These specialists add an academic focus to the popular success that these writers already enjoy.

The series is designed to appeal to a wide range of readers. The general reading public will find explanations for the appeal of these well-known writers. Fans will find biographical and fictional questions answered. Students will find literary analysis, discussions of fictional genres, carefully organized introductions to new ways of reading the novels, and bibliographies for additional research. Whether browsing through the book for pleasure or using it for an assignment, readers will find that the most recent novels of the authors are included.

Each volume begins with a biographical chapter drawing on published information, autobiographies or memoirs, prior interviews, and, in some cases, interviews given especially for this series. A chapter on literary history and genres describes how the author's work fits into a larger literary context. The following chapters analyze the writer's most important, most popular, and most recent novels in detail. Each chapter focuses on one or more novels. This approach, suggested by the Advisory Board as the most useful to student research, allows for an in-depth analysis of the writer's fiction. Close and careful readings with numerous examples show readers exactly how the novels work. These chapters are organized around three central elements: plot development (how the story line moves forward), character development (what the reader knows of the important figures), and theme (the significant ideas of the novel). Chapters may also include sections on generic conventions (how the novel is similar to or different from others in its same category of science fiction, fantasy, thriller, etc.), narrative point of view (who tells the story and how), symbols and literary language, and historical or social context. Each chapter ends with an "alternative reading" of the novel. The volume concludes with a primary and secondary bibliography, including reviews.

The alternative readings are a unique feature of this series. By demonstrating a particular way of reading each novel, they provide a clear example of how a specific perspective can reveal important aspects of the book. In the alternative reading sections, one contemporary literary theory—way of reading, such as feminist criticism, Marxism, new historicism, deconstruction, or Jungian psychological critique—is defined in brief, easily comprehensible language. That definition is then applied to the novel to highlight specific features that might go unnoticed or be understood differently in a more general reading. Each volume defines two or three specific theories, making them part of the reader's understanding of how diverse meanings may be constructed from a single novel.

Taken collectively, the volumes in the Critical Companions to Popular Contemporary Writers series provide a wide-ranging investigation of the complexities of current best-selling fiction. By treating these novels seriously as both literary works and publishing successes, the series demonstrates the potential of popular literature in contemporary culture.

Kathleen Gregory Klein
Southern Connecticut State University

Acknowledgments

Before acknowledging anyone else involved in the writing of this book, I must thank Leon Uris himself for creating those memorable characters Conor Larkin and Atty Fitzpatrick. When I read *Trinity* for the first time in 1977, I finally understood what my grandparents had been talking about all those years ago, and the rebel music I had grown up with took on added meaning. In the past twenty years, the story of *Trinity* has become part of the ongoing family dialogue about "The Troubles." In order for me to do justice to Uris's work, I needed the help of a number of people. My parents, Dan and Catherine Shine, retold age-old stories of the Easter Rising. Jennifer Ferguson sent extensive E-mails about the rise of Nazism, the Warsaw ghetto Uprising, and the fall of the Third Reich. The staff of the United States Holocaust Memorial Museum provided a wealth of information about the Holocaust and the founding of Israel. Of invaluable assistance during the writing process were Kathy Klein, Barbara Rader, and my writers' group—MaryKay Mahoney, Al DeCiccio, and Mike Rossi. But my most heartfelt thanks go to my husband, Jim, and my daughter, Shannon. Home life is always a bit off center when one member of the family is living in another world; you guys kept things sane by reminding me that your world still had a place for me.

1

The Life of Leon Uris

To read Leon Uris's tenth novel, *Mitla Pass* (1988), is to read a thinly veiled biography of the writer's early life. Like Gideon Zadok in that novel, Uris was born in 1924 in Baltimore to an emotionally unstable mother, Anna Blumberg Uris, and a Communist Party organizer, Wolf Uris, who supplemented his income by working as a paperhanger. When Uris talks about his unhappy childhood, he might well be talking of Gideon: "I had a father who was terribly embittered. . . . His life was a series of failures. My mother was a little wacko" (Christy 1988, 70). One of the few joys in the author's early life was his relationship with his sister Essie, to whom *Mitla Pass* is dedicated. Uris temporarily severed his ties with his family, as does Gideon, at seventeen when he joined the Marines after dropping out of high school.

INFLUENCE OF MARINES

Uris's experiences in the Marines defined his life in several ways. First, the Marines offered him the sense of comradeship that he had never known in his family. Second, it established within him a sense of purpose and dedication to a cause. And finally, it provided him with the impetus to write his first novel. *Battle Cry* (1953) chronicles the lives of the men of the Sixth Marines as they train in San Diego and fight in the South

Pacific. Drawing from his experiences in the armed forces, Uris focuses on the dedication of the men to one another, their compassion for each other, and their bravery in battle. Uris served in the South Pacific and fought in the battle for Tarawa, an engagement that he re-creates graphically in his novel. Even more significant, however, is the tenderness that emerges among the men in times of need. When one of the men receives a "Dear John" letter, his comrades support him; and when many of the men fall ill in the tropics, the healthy ones care for the sick as would wives or nurses. These experiences depicted in his fiction clearly had a profound influence on Uris. The Marine Corps became for him everything that his family could not be.

After completing the novel, Uris discovered that the life of a writer is filled with frustration as well as triumph. *Battle Cry* was rejected by twelve publishers before finally seeing print and making the best-seller list. Critics called the novel authentic, claiming that it captured the gritty realities of war better than many previous war novels. Both critical and popular response to the book was such that Warner Brothers produced a film version in 1954, with Uris writing the screenplay. Although he has not commented a great deal on his experiences in Hollywood, Uris's depiction of its culture in novels such as *QB VII* and *Mitla Pass* suggest that he felt that he was prostituting himself when he worked for the movies.

LITERARY CAREER

From the first printing of *Battle Cry*, Leon Uris has never looked back. Each successive novel has achieved some measure of popular success, with a few becoming blockbusters. His second novel, *The Angry Hills* (1955), is loosely based on the wartime experiences of his uncle, who engaged in espionage in Greece for the British Army. Uris's interest in the European theater of World War II was apparently piqued in his research for *The Angry Hills*, for six of his next nine novels dealt at least in part with Nazism and the Holocaust. The first of these, *Exodus* (1958), focuses on the founding of Israel, where a number of the author's relatives lived. The critical and popular reception of this novel made Uris's name a household word.

More than forty years after its publication, *Exodus* remains the most famous of Uris's works, the novel for which he will be remembered. On the *New York Times* best-seller list for over a year (in first place for almost five months), the book has never been out of print and has sold over seven million copies. The research that went into it involved thousands of interviews, thousands of miles traveled within Israel, and more than two years of research and writing. In this novel Uris wanted to do for the Jews what he did for the Marines in *Battle Cry*. In a foreword to the second printing of the novel, Uris writes, "All the cliché Jewish characters who have cluttered up our American fiction . . . have been left where they rightfully belong, on the cutting-room floor. . . . *Exodus* is about fighting people, people who do not apologize either for being born Jews or the right to live in human dignity."

The astounding success of *Exodus* led to a film adaptation of the novel in 1960. Previously, films had been made of *Battle Cry* and *The Angry Hills*, but this project was monumental in scope. Directed by Otto Preminger, one of the foremost directors of the time, and starring such notable actors as Paul Newman, Eva Marie Saint, and Sal Mineo, the film became an instant classic. *Exodus* remains one of the most highly acclaimed films, both in critical and popular terms, in motion picture history.

In some parts of the world, the impact of *Exodus* went beyond merely educating the world about the history of anti-Semitism and the founding of Israel. Thirty years after the book was published, Edwin McDowell wrote of its impact on Soviet Jews for the *New York Times Book Review*. Rampant anti-Semitism within the Soviet government, coupled with the Soviets' support of Israel's enemies, meant that Uris's book was banned in the USSR. But Israeli embassy staff smuggled copies into the country soon after the book was published, and eventually it was translated into Russian by underground groups. "Because duplicating machines are illegal for the Soviet citizenry," writes McDowell, "the translations had to be typed page by page with as many carbon copies as could legibly be made at one time." *Exodus* is credited with raising the morale of Soviet Jewry, according to one of McDowell's sources: "It gave us hope and pride when we needed it." So damaging was the book to official Soviet pronouncements on the cowardice of Jews and the weakness of Israel, according to McDowell, that two dissidents sentenced to prison for anti-Soviet activities were convicted in part on the basis of distributing copies of *Exodus*.

Uris was so profoundly affected by his research for *Exodus* that he could not let the story alone. His next novel, *Mila 18*, was drawn from a segment of *Exodus* on the Warsaw ghetto Uprising. Continuing his research in the Israeli Memorial Archives and through interviews with survivors and a visit to the site of the ghetto, Uris used the novel to explore the origins of the fighting spirit that he found in recent immigrants to Israel. Although not as successful as *Exodus* (it would be almost impossible to match that success), *Mila 18* proved to further enhance Uris's stature among popular American novelists. As critic Midge Decter (1961) claimed, by 1960 Uris had "become the master chronicler and ambassador of Jewish aspiration not only to the Gentiles but to the Jews themselves" (358). By the time *Mila 18* was published, according to Decter, "it [was] unlikely that more than a handful of literate Americans [had] not either read one of his Jewish novels or been engaged in at least one passionate discussion about him with someone who [had]" (358).

Uris shifted his attention back to the aftermath of the war with *Armageddon* (1964), this time focusing on the Berlin crisis. What made this novel even more compelling to many Americans than its predecessors was the immediacy of the subject matter. By 1964 the Cold War with the Soviet Union was in full swing, and for most Americans Berlin was a living symbol of the possibility that the war might turn hot very quickly. Uris was able to capitalize on the highly publicized 1962 visit of President John F. Kennedy to West Berlin, where he announced to a cheering crowd, "Ich bin ein Berliner [I am a Berliner]." The assassination of Kennedy in November of 1963 only added to the mystique of that visit. Thus *Armageddon* appeared at a ripe moment in American history.

Topaz (1967), Uris's next novel, maintained his focus on the Cold War, specifically the Cuban Missile Crisis of 1962, with a corollary plot involving Soviet influence in France. Again the book was timely. The Missile Crisis had brought the world to the brink of nuclear war; five years later, with communist activity in a country called Viet Nam beginning to make the news, Americans were quite receptive to a novel that offered them the suspense of a spy thriller with the historical immediacy of the continuing threat of the Soviet Union. Charles DeGaulle's pulling France out of NATO military forces was still fresh in people's minds, as was the French president's apparent affinity for the Soviet Union. As with *Armageddon*, the American public was ready for this novel. Its popularity led Alfred Hitchcock, the master of the suspense movie, to make a highly successful film of the novel two years later.

In 1970 Uris turned his attention once again to the Holocaust. In *QB VII* he chronicles the story of a novelist, modeled after himself, who is sued for libel by a concentration camp survivor named in one of his books as a Nazi collaborator. Based loosely on a case in which Uris himself was sued, the novel explores the characters of Abraham Cady, the writer in question, and Adam Kelno, the physician who operated on inmates at the fictional concentration camp. A successful novel, *QB VII* was made into a miniseries for ABC television in 1974. As were adaptations of his other novels, the filmed version of *QB VII* received both popular and critical acclaim.

Leon Uris's next venture stunned his dedicated readers. Instead of further exploring the familiar topics of the Holocaust, World War II, and the Cold War, Uris set out in the 1976 blockbuster *Trinity* to tell the story of Ireland under English rule. Apparently Uris, accompanying his wife Jill to Ireland for a photography assignment, became intrigued by the history of the land and its people. What followed was the meticulous research for which the author had become well known, resulting in a sprawling story covering several generations. Readers of Leon Uris recognized in the characters of *Trinity* soulmates to those found in his Jewish novels. The same oppression, the same ethnic pride, and the same family tensions appeared in the hills and farms of Northern Ireland as they had in Israel, Poland, and Russia. And the struggles of the Irish produced the same kinds of heroes and traitors that readers had found in previous novels. *Trinity* remained on the *New York Times* best-seller list for almost two years, selling over five million copies. Its success in the United States can be attributed in part to the country's huge Irish-American population, who saw in this book what Jews saw almost twenty years earlier in *Exodus*.

After *Trinity* Uris did not produce another novel for eight years. In 1984 he returned his attention to the Middle East in *The Haj*, the story of *Exodus* as told from the Arab point of view. Although it was a popular success, *The Haj* received severe criticism for its portrayal of Arabs as thorough villains and degenerates. While all of his novels to date had been partisan, in *The Haj* many critics felt that Uris had crossed a line and characterized an entire ethnic group as treacherous, lazy, perverted, and fanatical.

Uris's next novel, *Mitla Pass* (1988), received similarly poor critical reviews, this time because the main characters seemed so unlikable. This criticism is interesting because *Mitla Pass* is by far the most autobiographical of all of Uris's books, and Gideon Zadok by far the character who most closely resembles the author. Some of the similarities between the author and his character are noted at the beginning of this chapter; other similarities include the Uris family's frequent moves, the author's poor performance as a student, his early job in the circulation department of a newspaper, his long but troubled marriage to his first wife, and his service as a war correspondent during the 1956 Sinai War. This book seems clearly to have been written to highlight the development of the writer; for although it is set, as are most of Uris's books, during a critical period in history, the setting is secondary to the main character's personal life.

Seven years passed between *Mitla Pass* and Uris's next book, his most recent. *Redemption* is a further exploration of the characters in *Trinity*. Although it covers much of the same ground as the earlier book, *Redemption* expands the scope of *Trinity* to include the story of Conor Larkin's emigrant brother Liam, who becomes a successful sheep farmer in New Zealand. It is through Liam's son Rory, who worships Conor as a hero, that the story of *Redemption* unfolds. Not only does this novel return readers to a work published almost twenty years earlier, but it also returns to Uris's roots, the graphic battle scenes of his first novel, *Battle Cry*.

At 74, Leon Uris is still working at his trade. Among his projects in the past several years has been a dramatic adaptation of *Trinity* that to date has not been produced. Given the dedication to his vocation that is evident in his autobiographical works as well as in his own words, it is doubtful that *Redemption* will be the last of his books.

MARRIAGES/ATTITUDES TOWARD WOMEN

As Uris's career developed, his treatment of female characters underwent significant change. This change can be attributed in part to his marital history. In 1945, at the age of 21, Uris married Betty Katherine Beck, with whom he had three children (Karen, Mark, and Michael) before being divorced in 1968. Uris has called that twenty-three-year marriage "disastrous" (Christy 1988, 70). Within a year of his divorce, he was married to Margery Edwards, who committed suicide within six months of the wedding. The author still feels somewhat responsible for Margery's death, having failed to notice precisely how deep her emotional problems ran. Two years later, Uris wed for the third time, to photographer Jill Peabody, when she was twenty-four and he forty-six. The couple was married for fourteen years before the birth of their first child, with another child following two years later. This marriage, which lasted for over twenty years before ending in divorce, often appeared to be a true partnership. Uris developed the idea for his 1976 novel *Trinity* while in Ireland with Jill on an assignment. Together the pair published *Ireland: A Terrible Beauty* (1975) and *Jerusalem, Song of Songs* (1981). Acknowledgments in several of his novels during their marriage speak to the respect he had for his wife's talents and her support of his literary aspirations. After living for more than a decade in Aspen, Colorado with Jill, Leon Uris moved to the New York City area before the publication of *Redemption* in 1995.

Uris's first and third marriages have clearly had an impact on his work, particularly on his treatment of women's roles in marriage. His troubled first marriage might well have influenced his characterization of Samantha Cady in *QB VII* (1970). Although she helps her husband with his writing when he is still an invalid, Samantha becomes downright shrewish as time goes on, adamantly refusing to understand the demands of a literary career. On the other hand, Val Zadok in *Mitla Pass* (1988) is treated more sympathetically. Gideon recognizes, as Abe does not, that his own self-absorption has contributed to the difficulties in the marriage. As Uris himself said in a 1988 interview, "One thing I found out in the marriage relationship is the necessity for respecting the wife as a unique individual, apart from the husband's aspirations" (Christy 1988, 70). This respect, which Gideon eventually develops, is precisely what is missing in Abe.

The portrayal of women in Uris's fiction seems to have become stronger after his marriage to Jill Peabody as well. In earlier works, women must often abandon their femininity if they are to be strong. Jordana Ben Canaan in *Exodus* (1958), for example, is the equal of any male in the kibbutz. But Uris explains her bitterness toward Kitty Fremont as the result of Jordana's inability to act upon such feminine urges as the desire to dress prettily. Unlike Jordana, the sensuous Juanita de Córdoba in *Topaz* (1967) sometimes appears to be more an ornament than the leader of the anti-Castro underground. In later novels, however, women's femininity does not conflict with their strength. Atty Fitzpatrick, Shelley MacLeod, and Caroline Hubble in *Trinity* (1976) and *Redemption* (1995) see themselves as equal to the men around them. They do not associate femininity with superficial things like clothing and cosmetics, but rather with intellectual as well as physical attractiveness. Georgia Norman in *Redemption* is also such a woman. This turn toward strong women may well be a result of the times; after all, Uris began writing more than a decade before the feminist movement arose and has continued to write throughout the feminist age. Nonetheless, the evolution of his female characters from superficial to substantial women corresponded to his marriage to a strong, professional woman.

THE ROLE OF THE WRITER

It is no accident that Abe Cady in *QB VII* and Gideon Zadok in *Mitla Pass* owe their troubled marriages in part to the conflicting demands of family and career. Leon Uris's conception of the writer's life, coupled with his dedication to his vocation, reflect his belief that writing is an all-consuming occupation. The fact that writers are prominent in each of his novels indicates his reverence for the profession. Among the secondary characters who share the author's occupation are Mark Parker (*Exodus*), Nelson Goodfellow Bradbury (*Armageddon*), and Franois (*Topaz*). Central characters who are writers include Marion Hodgkiss (*Battle Cry*), Mike Morrison (*Angry Hills*), Chris de Monti and Alex Brandel (*Mila 18*), Abraham Cady (*QB VII*), Ishmael (*The Haj*), Gideon Zadok (*Mitla Pass*), and Seamus O'Neill (*Trinity, Redemption*). In several novels, columns and stories produced by these fictional writers are used to further the plot.

Uris's attitude toward writing reflects that of his fictional authors. Both Gideon Zadok and Abe Cady describe writing as the most demanding of professions—lonely, gut-wrenching work that requires total honesty. Uris himself refers to writing as "a job you have to do all by yourself. The odds are all stacked against you." Although "it's a difficult road," he says, "it's the only road I ever thought I could travel" (qtd. in Christy 1988, 70). The personal price of writing can be high, according to Uris. There is a room inside everyone, he says, that houses "all the things you don't want to know about yourself." That room is usually kept locked, but "good writers have to confront the locked doors" (qtd. in Tischler 1995).

On the other hand, Uris says, writing offers freedom. "I've always wanted to be my own boss. . . . I have my freedom. I don't owe anybody anything" (qtd. in Christy 1988, 70). That sense of freedom, of being his own boss, is what causes Gideon Zadok to refuse to make the changes demanded by the editor of his first book. And it is what leads Gideon, Abe Cady, and Leon Uris to immerse themselves in the history of the Holocaust and the new state of Israel in order to tell the story of the Jews the way it must be told.

JEWISH IDENTITY

In writing *Exodus*, Uris said that he wanted to erase stereotypes of Jewish characters forever. In fact, throughout all of his Jewish novels

(*Exodus, Mila 18, QB VII, The Haj,* and *Mitla Pass*), as well as other novels in which Jewish people appear, the author has exceeded his goal. The historical accuracy of *Exodus* indicates the lukewarm commitment of the free world to finding homes for displaced Jews after the war. Both *Exodus* and *Mitla Pass* accurately illustrate the anti-Semitism that has permeated society in countries like Poland and Russia well into the twentieth century. And the banning of *Exodus* in the Soviet Union made it clear that the stereotype of the weak, cowardly Jew remained alive for decades after the Holocaust. The story of the underground popularity of *Exodus* in the Soviet Union through the 1980s is testimony to Uris's power of reversing such stereotypes. And his success in the United States is further evidence of that power. Midge Decter (1961) comments that Uris's books "by themselves have seemed to accomplish what years of persuasion, arguments, appeals, and knowledge of the events themselves . . . have failed to do" (360). In both the United States and the Soviet Union, *Exodus* has been credited with turning readers into avid Zionists, believers in the legitimacy of a Jewish homeland in Palestine.

Although Uris has been criticized for oversimplifying the situation in the Middle East, characterizing everything Jewish as good and everything Arab as bad, he does present a variety of Jewish characters in his novels. In *Mila 18* there are collaborators, traitors, and exploiters among the heroes of the Warsaw ghetto. In *Exodus* there are the terrorist Maccabees fighting for the same cause as the legitimate soldiers of the Haganah. And in *Mitla Pass* there are whining, greedy, and suffocating Jewish characters living alongside long-suffering Molly and heroic Lazar. What Uris has done for Jews is not simply to erase an unflattering stereotype, but to reveal Jewish characters to be essentially the same as characters from any other religion or ethnic group, with heroes as well as villains. In fact, when Uris creates his characters for *Trinity* and *Redemption*, the Irish are seen in much the same light as are the Jews in previous novels. The Irish suffer at the hands of the British in much the same way that the Jews suffer at the hands of organized anti-Semitism. And the Ireland of the two later books is populated by the same variety of characters as those who populate the Warsaw ghetto of *Mila 18* or the Israel of *Exodus*.

POLITICAL BELIEFS

One of the things that Uris's Jewish and Irish characters share is their fight against tyranny. Throughout his life and work, Uris has championed the cause of the underdog against a more powerful force. His hatred of fascism is understandable; his Jewish heritage makes the Nazi war against the Jews all the more reprehensible. But his disdain extends itself to communists as well. In *Topaz, Armageddon,* and *Mitla Pass,* communists are portrayed as despicable, treacherous villains. Whether they are Cubans, Soviets, or Americans, communists in Uris's fiction share one dream: total world domination. And they will exploit their own families, betray their friends, and undermine their own governments in order to accomplish their goals. While it is rather typical for Americans of Uris's generation to share an antipathy for communism, his feelings also arise from his childhood experiences. As he mentions on occasion in interviews, and as he details in depth in *Mitla Pass,* his father's communist activities contributed significantly to the family's unhappiness.

It is not only fascist or communist ideology that comes in for Uris's criticism, however. In *Trinity* and *Redemption,* and to a lesser extent in *Exodus* and *The Haj,* British imperialism is seen as the essence of evil. In his condemnation of the colonial mind-set that all but destroyed Ireland and that betrayed Palestinian Jews, Uris reflects what he learned in the Marine Corps. All people are equal, and while one power may be more dominant than another, no government has the right to impose its will on any population, even its own. Whether that government be fascist, communist, or capitalist does not matter; the freedom of the individual, the right of all people to self-determination, is paramount.

RECEPTION BY CRITICS

The political content of Leon Uris's work has a good deal to do with his popularity among the reading public. His ability to incorporate history into a fictional tale and to keep the action moving is also partly responsible for his popular appeal. Critical response to his work, however, has been mixed. While his storytelling ability is praised, critics consistently point to the partisan politics that dominate his tales. *Time* magazine says of *Exodus,* "Too often the author's flag-waving enthusiasm for Zionism diminishes rather than exalts the achievement of the Israelis" ("Bestseller" 1958). Evan Hunter (1984) echoes this sentiment in a review of *The Haj:* "When a view is so biased, it becomes impossible to accept even what appears to be impeccable research on past events" (7). Uris is also criticized for characters that are one- or two-dimensional and for dialogue that is wooden and contrived. According to the *Time* magazine review of *Mila 18* ("Back" 1961), "Uris' dialogue conjures up hours of bad movie time" (94). William S. Barrett (1964) uses another movie image when he complains that the characters in *Armageddon* appear to be "already prefabricated for the Hollywood movie in which they are bound to appear" (136).

A number of critics, however, praise Uris's storytelling ability. Even though Barrett criticizes the characterizations in *Armageddon*, he concludes that "despite these inadequacies, Mr. Uris turns out a gripping and compelling story" in which "he is able to evoke the atmosphere and tension of major events" (136). Pete Hammill (1976) offers the same criticism more forcefully in his review of *Trinity*: "Uris often writes crudely [and] his dialogue can be wooden. . . . None of that matters as you are swept along in the narrative" (5). And Quentin Reynolds (1961), calling *Exodus* "exciting both as a novel and as a historical document," claims that "*Mila 18* surpasses *Exodus* in every respect" (5).

Despite the mixed reviews received by all of his novels, critics agree that Uris connects with his audience. Given his belief that a good writer's "identification with readers has to be a strong one" (Christy 1988, 70), Leon Uris is true to his own critical standards. His satisfaction as a writer has always been closely related to how well his audience receives his work; and using that criteria, Uris is one of the most successful novelists of the late twentieth century.

2

Leon Uris's Literary Heritage

Every culture expresses itself more definitively through its artists
than through its historians.
—David Cowart

One of the things that critics find both frustrating and appealing about
Leon Uris's fiction is that often all that readers know about a particular
historical event comes from what they have read in one of his novels.
Uris is a storyteller, and in his stories he offers a version of history. The
tradition of historical fiction is a long and often illustrious one, particularly in the United States, where James Fenimore Cooper composed his
Leather-Stocking Tales during the early years of the Republic. Uris belongs in this broad tradition, but some of his works also fall into sub-
categories of historical fiction, such as war novels, thrillers, and political
novels. Understanding historical fiction can lead to a greater appreciation
of Uris's work.

THE TRADITION OF HISTORICAL FICTION

Nineteenth Century

Before the advent of writing, a people's cultural heritage was passed down orally by storytellers. The tradition of telling stories is so strong that even after thousands of years of literacy, stories often remain the primary means by which people define themselves and their culture. In the words of literary critic David Cowart (1989), "History and fiction . . . have affinities, and in many languages the words for story and history coincide" (17). Myths and legends of great heroes and momentous events rarely correspond exactly to factual accounts, but within those myths and legends are truths about the culture that are often missed by the historian. According to Cowart, "Artists provide the myths by which any cultural body defines itself, the myths that historians mistakenly seek to unravel" (25). In Western culture, historical novels were popularized by French Romantic writers such as Victor Hugo. In *The Hunchback of Notre Dame* (1831) Hugo explored medieval life in Paris, and in *Les Misérables* (1862) he delved into the Paris underworld of the early nineteenth century.

According to literary critic Lion Feuchtwanger, historical fiction became popular in the United States during roughly the same period, when James Fenimore Cooper began publishing his Leather-Stocking Tales. These novels featuring wilderness scout Natty Bumppo have been called "the first genuine historical novels in America" (Feuchtwanger 1963, 87). In novels such as *The Last of the Mohicans* (1826) and *The Deerslayer* (1841), Cooper captured "the greatness and decline of the Indians" (Feuchtwanger 1963, 87) during the wars with colonists in what is now the Northeastern United States and Southeastern Canada.

Cooper was followed by great writers such as Nathaniel Hawthorne and Herman Melville. Hawthorne's *The Scarlet Letter* (1850), as well as many of his short stories, reveal what everyday life was like in Puritan New England. Hawthorne's focus on the conflict between Puritan notions of guilt and the emerging colonial notions of personal freedom help readers better understand the Puritan era. Melville's *Israel Potter: His Fifty Years of Exile* (1855) chronicles the American Revolution by fictionalizing the story of an actual person who served in the Continental Army. Based loosely on Potter's autobiography, the novel features such historical figures as Benjamin Franklin, John Paul Jones, and Ethan Allen, and explores issues of bravery in battle and loyalty.

Feuchtwanger also considers Samuel Clemens (Mark Twain) to be a historical novelist. Although Twain does not focus upon specific historical events, his fiction chronicling the pre–Civil War era in the United States includes biting social commentary. His faith that individuals can overcome the oppression of an evil society, as seen in *The Adventures of Huckleberry Finn* (1884), is akin to Uris's faith in his heroes' ability to triumph over evil. In fact, Feuchtwanger's characterization of Twain as essentially "a reporter" but also "a romantic who becomes sentimental at the sight of human suffering and angry in a poetic and prophetic way in the face of injustice" (97) might well be said about Uris. Another author whose influence is evident in Uris's work is Stephen Crane, whose *The Red Badge of Courage* (1895) is similar to *Battle Cry* in that it depicts war from the point of view of the ordinary soldier. While Crane's novel questions the very notions of courage that Uris's celebrates, the two writers both explore warfare from the trenches rather than from the distant perspective of the generals.

Twentieth Century

In the twentieth century the American historical novel continued to focus on social commentary. Theodore Dreiser's *An American Tragedy* (1925), based on an actual murder case, roundly criticized both the American legal system and the materialism that drove many poor Americans to crime. In *The Financier* (1912), Dreiser created a fictional character based on the wealthy transportation magnate Charles T. Yerkes in order to criticize the unscrupulous business practices prevalent in early twentieth-century America. Dreiser, like Uris, has been criticized for stylistic awkwardness; but like Uris, his ability to tell a story has never been questioned.

Perhaps the most famous historical novel of the first half of the twentieth century is Margaret Mitchell's *Gone with the Wind* (1936). Set in the South during and immediately following the Civil War, this novel's memorable characters, who find themselves in the midst of a major conflagration, resemble those in several of Uris's novels. Mitchell has been accused of harboring a "nostalgia for the past [that] almost blinds her" (Feuchtwanger 1963, 115) in much the same way that Uris is accused of sentimentalizing Israel and Holocaust victims. But as with Dreiser and Uris, Mitchell is also praised highly for her storytelling ability.

The 1930s also saw the publication of John Dos Passos's *U.S.A.* trilogy, consisting of *The 42nd Parallel* (1930), *1919* (1932), and *The Big Money* (1936). A bitter critique of American society, this trilogy employs many of the same techniques used by Uris. Dos Passos intertwines the stories of his fictional characters with newspaper headlines, biographical sketches of historical characters, and popular songs. His sprawling narrative, covering the history of both his fictional and historical characters, captures the essence of early twentieth-century America in much the same way that Uris's fiction captures the essence of Israel and Ireland.

HISTORICAL FICTION IN THE AGE OF ANXIETY

The kind of historical fiction written in the United States prior to World War II certainly includes political commentary. But the war, particularly the event that ended it, changed human history forever. The advent of the nuclear age plunged humanity into what has been called the age of anxiety, a time when we are acutely aware of our capacity to destroy ourselves and our planet. In the words of critic David Cowart (1989), "A sense of urgency—sometimes even an air of desperation—pervades the historical novel since midcentury, for its author probes the past to account for a present that grows increasingly chaotic" (1). Leon Uris's fiction falls into the category that Cowart calls "The Turning Point—fictions whose authors seek to pinpoint the precise historical moment when the modern age or some prominent feature of it came into existence" (8). For many authors, of course, that moment occurred at some point between 1939 and 1945.

The World War II Novel

Authors who focus on World War II include James Jones, whose novel *From Here to Eternity* (1951) is based on his own wartime experiences in the military. Like Uris, Jones tells the story of military life from the point of view of the ordinary serviceman. Herman Wouk, whose novels *The Winds of War* (1971) and *Of War and Remembrance* (1978) chronicle the war from beginning to end, has been compared to Uris in his tendency to write sprawling commentary covering enormous territory. Perhaps the wartime novel that comes closest to Uris's *Battle Cry* is Norman Mailer's *The Naked and the Dead* (1948), which was highly praised for its realistic account of American soldiers in the South Pacific. Mailer's technique of using flashbacks to provide background on his characters is similar to that used later by Uris. All of these works explore the nature of twentieth-century warfare, including questioning the purpose of the war, facing an enemy who sometimes seems no different than oneself, and contemplating the impact of global conflagration.

The Holocaust Novel

If the atomic blasts in Hiroshima and Nagasaki signaled the advent of the age of anxiety in one respect, the Holocaust signaled it just as clearly in another. The bomb revealed to us that we were capable of total self-destruction; the Holocaust revealed that we were capable of total evil. The most famous literary work to emerge from the Holocaust is not a fiction at all: Anne Frank's *The Diary of a Young Girl* (1947), the true account of one family's years of hiding from the Nazis. Among novels dealing with the Holocaust are William Styron's *Sophie's Choice* (1979), in which the story of a Polish Catholic woman's experiences at Auschwitz are revealed in flashback. Styron's tale focuses on the guilt of survivors as well as on the overwhelming evil of the Nazis and raises questions similar to those raised in Uris's *QB VII*. Questions of collaboration with the Nazis also arise in Kurt Vonnegut's *Mother Night* (1961), featuring an American broadcaster in Germany who works as a double agent. Despite their effectiveness in furthering the Allied war effort, the broadcasts are also immeasurably valuable to the Nazis, raising the question of precisely whom the agent is working for. Less ambiguous than either of these novels is John Hersey's *The Wall* (1950), often compared favorably to Uris's *Mila 18*. Hersey's novel, like Uris's, uses fictional characters and diaries to recount the story of the Warsaw ghetto Uprising. Through this single event, both authors comment on the atrocities of the Nazis, the unspeakable suffering of European Jews during World War II, and the indomitability of the human spirit.

The Political Novel: The Cold War

The Allied victory in World War II was bittersweet: Nazism had been crushed and the concentration camps had been closed, but the threat of the bomb remained, and with it a new threat, the Soviet Union. No sooner was the global conflict over than a new, far more threatening conflict emerged between the United States and the Soviet Union. Combined with the knowledge that both countries possessed nuclear capabilities, the fears engendered by the Soviet threat produced fiction that posed questions probing into the very heart of human existence. Several popular novels in the 1960s capitalized on the threat of communism or nuclear war, among them Alan Drury's *Advise and Consent* (1961), Fletcher Knebel and Charles W. Bailey's *Seven Days in May* (1962), and Eugene Burdick and Harvey Wheeler's *Fail Safe* (1964). Drury's novel, focusing primarily on the confirmation hearings of a controversial appointee for secretary of state, features a Soviet landing on the moon that threatens U.S. security. *Seven Days in May* chronicles a military takeover of the U.S. government. While it does not directly involve a Soviet threat, the threat of dictatorship is clear. And *Fail Safe* explores the possibility of an accidental nuclear strike resulting in global disaster. These novels treat the Soviet and nuclear threats in rather superficial ways, focusing on impending disaster. What Uris does in novels such as *Topaz* and *Armageddon* is to explore the implications of the Cold War on international relations and the security of the free world. In this regard, his novels are closer to one of the most significant novels of the postwar period, George Orwell's *Nineteen Eighty-four* (1949). In that novel the evils of totalitarian government are illustrated in the story of Winston Smith, an Englishman in a futuristic dictatorship fashioned after the Soviet Union. The implications of a government taking over not only the physical freedom but also the minds of its subjects are chilling. Literary critic Irving Howe (1957) states that the terror of *Nineteen Eighty-four*, "far from being inherent in the 'human condition,' is particular to our century" (236). That terror lends what David Cowart (1963) calls an "apocalyptic tinge" to such fiction, stemming from its authors' understanding "that life under the gun . . . is now the condition of existence for humanity at large" (29). There is similar terror in Uris's Cold War novels, although Uris tends toward endings in which fears are resolved. Nonetheless, the vigilance necessary to ward off the threat of either tyranny or nuclear annihilation is a prominent feature in much of the political fiction of the late twentieth century.

The Espionage Novel

Closely related to the political novel of the postwar period is the espionage novel, normally featuring an Allied spy squaring off against his or her Soviet counterpart. One of the most prolific writers of such literature is John Le Carre, whose trilogy featuring British agent George Smiley includes intrigue, mortal danger, and continual struggle between communism and the free world. Another spy novelist, Tom Clancy, began writing traditional Cold War novels and then moved on, after the fall of the Soviet Union, to novels featuring the IRA and South American drug dealers. Uris's *Topaz* is traditional in the sense that the central conflict in the novel involves the power struggle between the United States and the Soviet Union. Uris, however, is less interested in action and adventure than he is in the implications of that power struggle for the world. Issues such as the origins of the Cold War in World War II, the strategic importance of relatively small powers such as Cuba and France, and the delicate balance maintained between the two superpowers feature more prominently in *Topaz* than in other espionage novels.

LEON URIS AND THE HISTORICAL NOVEL

Leon Uris's fiction draws heavily from the traditions of the historical novel. His settings, his characters, and his emphasis on action all reflect the more popular forms of historical fiction. While much historic fiction is set within a specific time period, Uris usually focuses even more narrowly on a particular event in history: the Warsaw ghetto Uprising, the Cuban Missile Crisis, or the Sinai War, for example. In setting his novels so specifically, Uris is able to explore the ramifications of particular historical events rather than simply illustrate life during a certain period. In this sense, his novels are typical of Cowart's (1989) "turning point fictions," addressing the question, "When and how did the present become the present?" (10). Uris is more interested in the context of and impact of particular historical events than in the details of the events themselves. Thus when he examines the Warsaw ghetto Uprising in *Mila 18*, Uris places it in the context of the history of Jewish settlement in Poland, the pervasiveness of anti-Semitism in Eastern Europe, and the covenant between the Jews and their God. Similarly, when he writes of the battle of Gallipoli in *Redemption*, he explores the notion of empire by focusing on the arrogance of the British leaders who allow colonial troops from Australia, New Zealand, and Palestine to become cannon fodder for the Turks. This focus on oppressed people and their oppressors is one of the distinguishing features of Uris's historical fiction. Like Mark Twain, Uris makes no pretense of being objective; he presents events from a biased perspective, illustrating Cowart's contention that the "lessons of history seem always to admit of radically different interpretations, and simple historical truth remains forever obscure" (25).

Uris's characters reflect that same bias with which he approaches historical events. His characters represent types rather than fully realized human beings; they exist to humanize the impact of historical events. Some of his characters are mythic, larger than life: Ari Ben Canaan of *Exodus*, Andrei Androfski of *Mila 18*, and Conor Larkin of *Trinity* and *Redemption* are all heroes cut from the same mold as a Ulysses or a Moses. Other characters are stereotypical: The peasants of Greece in *The Angry Hills*, the rural farmers of Ireland in *Trinity* and *Redemption*, and the Jewish settlers of Palestine in *Exodus* and *The Haj* reflect a pastoral view of the essential nobility of those who live simply and close to the land. On the other hand, the Hollywood executives and agents in *QB VII* and *Mitla Pass* and the New York businessmen in *Armageddon* represent the shallowness of American materialism. These characters are, as many of Uris's critics note, one-dimensional and rather flat. The same criticism was made in 1949 of Orwell's characters in *Nineteen Eighty-four*. Of this criticism, and of criticism about the drab style of the novel, Irving Howe (1957) argued, "The last thing Orwell cared about when he wrote *1984*, the last thing he should have cared about, was literature" (237). The same might be said of Leon Uris: The primary purpose of his novels (with the possible exception of *Mitla Pass*) is not to delve into the lives of his characters but to explore the impact of historical events upon them. As Dan Wakefield (1959) writes in a review of *Exodus*,

> The characters are firmly type-cast, but their main function is to carry along the plot that history has already written, and in that service they do quite well. The plot is so exciting that the characters become exciting too; not because of their individuality or depth, but because of the historic drama they are involved in. (318–319)

It is the history and not the characters that matters in Uris's fiction.

Because events rather than people constitute the focus of much of

Uris's work, it is not surprising that his novels feature locales that are sometimes more individualized than the characters living in them. Much like another contemporary novelist, James Michener, Uris invests in many of his locales a personality and a spirit that make the places come alive. Israel in *Exodus* might be considered the main character of the novel, as might Ireland in *Trinity* and *Redemption*. To a lesser extent, New Zealand in *Battle Cry* and *Redemption* and the Greek countryside in *The Angry Hills* exert such power over the characters that the places themselves seem humanized. Even the rubble of bombed-out Berlin in *Armageddon* has a profound influence on the lives of its inhabitants.

As a historical novelist, Leon Uris creates those stories that define the culture about which he writes. It was stated at the beginning of this chapter that for many readers, their only knowledge of the history featured in Uris's work comes from the work itself. Thus the role of the historical novelist is significant indeed, for an understanding of the culture is passed on through his or her words. Perhaps David Cowart (1989) captures the significance of the historical novelist best when he writes,

> The novelist invades the historian's domain more often and more successfully than vice versa. The reader, then, who wants to know what really happened at the Battle of Waterloo may learn more from [novelists] Hugo, Stendahl, or Thackeray than from [historians] Michelet or John Keegan, for the novelist routinely transcends imagined material to speak with great authority about the past. (20)

3

Battle Cry
(1953)

Hailed as the first novel ever to depict accurately life in the Marine Corps, *Battle Cry* is a rather unwieldy story of innocent boys who are transformed into fighting men. The novel alternates between first-person narrative, a technique in which a character speaks directly to readers, and an omniscient narrator, one who knows what each character is thinking, in telling the story of Danny Forrester and his fellow soldiers during boot camp, training, and battle in the South Pacific during World War II.

PLOT DEVELOPMENT

As he would later do with his other epic novels (novels that celebrate heroic achievement), Uris divides this book into several parts, each one telling the story of one stage of the soldiers' development. The glue that holds these men together is the sergeant known only as Mac, who opens the book with a prologue that establishes his character as a lifelong Marine. His monologue recalls the hard-boiled detective novels of the 1930s and 1940s: "I've sat behind a machine gun poked through the barbed wire that encircled the International Settlement when the world was supposed to have been at peace, and I've called Jap bluffs on the Yangtze Patrol a decade before Pearl Harbor" (1). Setting the tone for the novel,

Mac wonders at the assortment of kids, none of them seemingly Marine material, who show up to train as radio operators in the Sixth Regiment in the early days of American involvement in World War II.

Each subsequent part of the book opens with a similar prologue in which Mac reestablishes the tone: Through his eyes we see new lands, the hold of a troop ship, the aftermath of battle, and the gradual loss of innocence of the boys in his regiment.

The rigors of basic training, the vast array of types thrown together in the armed forces, and the bonds that form between men make up the first two parts of the book. Each young novice goes through a maturing process in basic and further training. Danny Forrester, the all-American boy, has a torrid affair with an officer's wife and later impulsively marries his high-school sweetheart. Constantine "Ski" Zvonski, the destitute city boy, receives a "Dear John" letter from his girl and attempts suicide. Spanish Joe Gomez, the Regiment's Bad Boy, is beaten at boxing and becomes the lifelong friend of his opponent, Marion "Sister Mary" Hodgkiss. Hodgkiss, the intellectual, sees his first short story published and falls in love with Rae, the stereotypical "hooker with a heart of gold." Finally, the regiment learns that their pal in basic, "Professor" Milt Norton, has died at Guadalcanal.

Part 3 takes place in New Zealand, where the regiment awaits battle orders, and on Guadalcanal, where they fight the Japanese. The beauty of a foreign land is seductive to Andy Hookans, who falls in love not only with a New Zealander war widow but also with the land itself. The appeal of this New World to a Westerner forms an integral part of two later novels, *Trinity* and *Redemption*, when Liam Larkin, exiled from his native Ireland, finds peace and founds a family in the rolling hills of New Zealand. The feel of a land without its men, playing host to foreign men, is established in this section. Uris touches here on one of the ironies of global conflict: While New Zealanders are entertaining the Americans and British who are going to protect them against the Japanese, their own men are fighting in Europe and North Africa against the Germans.

When the men ship out to retake Guadalcanal, Uris reveals to readers why Mac, in the prologue, contends that the Marines were shortchanged by the high command in World War II. Engaging in a bit of Army bashing, Uris bemoans the fate of the Marines sent in to clean up the messes produced by the other armed forces. It is in this part of the book that Uris achieves what critics applaud as an accurate depiction of the gritty reality of war. The descriptions of battle are without romance—every detail of the filth, disease, terrible food, and lack of sanitation is re-counted here. When Mac allows the men to remove their boots for the first time after a ten-day march, "a terrible smell arose over the bivouac. We hadn't seen our feet in over a week . . . they were turning green with fungus growths" (239).

Not only are the marches endless, but the battles themselves seem interminable. Retaking Guadalcanal is a sporadic venture, with no victory for weeks. Machinery breaks down, men break, luck plays a great part, and loyalty and devotion to each other fortifies men. The young Danny kills his first Japanese soldier here, wondering, "Why does he want to kill me? Maybe he has a girl, a Jap girl like Kathy. I'm not mad at him" (242). The revulsion Danny feels almost makes him crazy; as he finishes off the Japanese soldier, he is appalled that the man's eyes will not close and so he bashes the soldier with the butt of his rifle "until there were no eyes or face or head" (242). Uris does not present such graphic accounts of life in the trenches as an anti-war commentary, however. He hails the courage of men in impossible circumstances, and he does not question their cause. Later, in *Redemption*, Uris will sharply criticize the political leaders and generals for the carnage at the battle of Gallipoli in World War I, but here the war is a just one.

With the Guadalcanal Battle over, the squad enjoys a little rest and relaxation before battle training resumes. Major "Highpockets" Huxley works the men hard, turning them into a crack fighting machine. But the competition for glory among regiments is keen—the soldiers of the Sixth feel inferior because they are always cleaning up after the initial on-slaught. Through Huxley's hunger for the glory of his own campaign, Uris illustrates the mystique that leading a charge holds for military men. During the downtime, Uris also illustrates a number of other peculiarities of Marine life. The deep-seated racial and religious prejudice of some soldiers, for example, is seen when draftee Jake Levin replaces Ski, who has died on Guadalcanal. Speedy "Tex" Gray, otherwise sympathetic, reveals bigotry first toward Jake and then toward medic Pedro Rojas when the latter wins a medal. At one point Pedro, drunk, rails agains American racism and praises the openness of the New Zealanders. His descriptions of his home, a Mexican enclave in San Antonio, will be echoed later in descriptions of Jewish ghettoes in *Exodus* and *Mila 18* and Irish villages in *Trinity* and *Redemption*. Babies dying of disease, families living in shacks, people restricted from doing anything but low-paying fieldwork, and all because of ethnicity or religion—these images will return in subsequent books.

Uris also uses this interlude to acquaint readers with other, less-understood, features of a soldier's life. When the entire regiment comes down with malaria, for example, the men care for each other like mothers and wives. In a comic episode tinged with sentimentality, L.Q., the tough Los Angeles native, is adopted by a suburban New Zealand family. A more serious look at local color is provided when Seabags, the Iowa farm boy, learns about native New Zealand life when he becomes involved in the life of a Maori town.

The reality of war, however, also includes the desire to desert. Uris handles this issue adeptly when Andy, having finally found peace with his new wife Pat, contemplates desertion rather than risk losing her—and her losing another husband to the war. While Mac and Pat are finally able to convince him to do his duty, his questions about the unfairness of war are treated sympathetically.

Their rest and relaxation ended, the Sixth once again plays cleanup in Part 5 when the soldiers move in for the final attack on Tarawa after two other regiments are all but decimated in the battle to take the beachhead. Uris's own experiences in the Marine attack on this atoll contribute significantly to the credibility of the battle scenes. The carnage left by days of fighting is nauseating, as Mac describes his wade to the shore through a lagoon "filled with bobbing bodies." Some of the corpses, "whose eyes had been eaten away by the salt, had running, jellied masses over their faces and holes where eyes had once been" (382). And yet amid the devastation, the common humanity of soldiers is seen as Danny and the others offer water and a final smoke to a dying young Japanese soldier, seeing in him "just another poor guy doing what he was ordered to do" (380). These and other visions of the horrors of combat testify to the author's experience. Like Danny, Uris was only a teenager when he joined the Marines and fought in the battle for Tarawa.

The eventual victory, costing eight thousand lives, is in part credited to the efforts of the irreverent Captain Max Shapiro, a known trouble-maker in whom Major Huxley places his faith. Huxley's hunch about the man's leadership capacity is rewarded in the cleanup operation. Although the more traditional officers cannot see beyond Shapiro's unprofessional behavior, Huxley recognizes that in battle it sometimes takes unorthodox methods to get the job done.

As the men march across the atoll looking for retreating Japanese, Uris provides a brief glimpse of the idyllic life of such places. The men meet Calvin MacIntosh, a half-breed philosopher who has forsaken the civilized world. Innocent natives gladly join the marching Americans. When the Japanese are finally engaged, missionary nuns help with the wounded. Huxley's faith in the unorthodox Captain Shapiro again pays off, underscoring the importance of leaving battle strategies to those in the trenches. The battle brings out the best in the men, as Tex, the anti-Semite, reverently carries off the body of Levin, who has sacrificed his life for his comrades.

Just as Uris demonstrates how battle can prove men's strengths, he illustrates the price of a battle hard won when the men languish in inactivity after the Japanese are routed. Corruption, high jinks, and general lack of morale prevail once the battle is over. While the chapters detailing this interlude feature some humor, the sudden respite causes Andy Hookans's anguish to erupt again. Andy's questions about the ways of civilization are echoed in an incident in which Danny's near-fatal dengue fever is cured not by Western medicine but by the primitive remedies of the local chief.

In the battle for Tarawa the Sixth may have earned its share of glory, but the entire novel has been building to the battle in which the Sixth will lead the charge. The men get their chance in Part 6, when Huxley threatens to resign unless his squad gets to take the lead. His reward is one of the bloodiest and costliest fights in the war, the battle for Saipan, as the Allies make their final move in the impending invasion of Japan. The tensions that plague soldiers on the night before a battle are palpable as the men ponder their fates in the ship's hold. Marion Hodgkiss somehow knows that he is going to die; and as all hell breaks loose on Saipan, he does, along with Huxley, L.Q., Seabags, Joe, and Pedro. Taking command, the invincible Shapiro himself dies, but the men fight on, stopping the Japanese against all odds. The Sixth, at last, has proved itself.

In the aftermath of battle, Mac once again brings Andy, who has lost a leg, out of despair. Only Andy, Mac, Tex, and Danny have survived the war. Mac and Danny return home to visit the families of their fallen comrades. But with his war over, Danny is no longer a Marine; he will resume his life in Baltimore with Kathy. At the end of the book, Mac ponders the different paths their lives will now take: "For me, just a cruise was over. For me there would be another station, another batch of kids to train, another campaign. Our two lives, which had once been so important to each other, were now a long way apart" (474). As the two part ways at the Baltimore train station, yet another group of young men is departing for basic training, as Danny did three years earlier. For Mac, the story will continue.

CHARACTER DEVELOPMENT

In an epic, characters exist to illustrate certain human qualities. In Homer's *Odyssey*, for example, Odysseus represents strength, courage, and wisdom. Similarly, the characters in *Battle Cry* are more representatives of certain qualities than they are fully realized human beings. Furthermore, because it is a war novel, the female characters in this book are marginal—they exist solely to either try the men's souls or to wait patiently until they return.

During the period between World Wars I and II, the United States embraced isolationism, a belief that this country had no stake in the problems of other parts of the world. This isolationist fervor had reduced the U.S. armed forces significantly by the time of the attack on Pearl Harbor. The career sergeant Mac's chagrin at the amateur force he must lead is well founded; the soldiers in this book represent almost every type of volunteer and draftee found in the service during World War II. As such, the characters in *Battle Cry* also represent a cross section of the American population in the early years of the war. Danny Forrester is an eighteen-year-old all-American boy just out of high school, who gives up his college football career in order to serve his country. While in basic training Danny develops from a naive schoolboy into a trained soldier. He also undergoes a sexual and moral awakening during an affair with the wife of an overseas officer, later realizing his error and marrying his high-school sweetheart. Danny's evolution from innocent teenager into seasoned warrior may be seen as a metaphor for the American public. Hopelessly naive about its global responsibilities, Americans believed in the possibility of neutrality as war raged in Europe and Asia. It took the bombing of Pearl Harbor to awaken the nation. The wholesome Danny's awakening into the harsher realities of life mirrors that of his nation as the problems of the European and Asian nations refused to submit to local solutions. Just as basic training transformed Danny from a boy into a man, so too did entering the war transform citizens of the United States into citizens of the world.

As the boy-soldier, Danny also represents the new fighting man in World War II. Unlike career soldiers whose identities are forged by combat, Danny is an ordinary American whose fighting sense is fueled by idealism. He is fighting to preserve precisely that peaceful way of life that he has given up in order to wage war. Thus at the end of the novel he returns to his wife, his family, and his home town.

In contrast, Mac and Sam "Highpockets" Huxley are career soldiers. Both are appalled at the sight of the men they are expected to train, both convinced that the war is hopeless if placed in the hands of these amateurs. What distinguishes these "lifers" from the recruits is their sense of duty—while they cannot imagine how the boys presented to them will emerge into a fighting force, they nevertheless engage the young recruits in rigorous training. Mac and Huxley provide the framework in which the young soldiers will fight. While Huxley has a wife waiting stateside for him, his real home is in the armed forces. And in fact, his final request that the Sixth be given a front-line assignment is effectively a suicide wish. His dedication to his men outweighs his love for his family. Mac, without a family, is the quintessential soldier. While the boys fighting under Mac and Huxley live on ideals and the dream of a peaceful future, the sergeant and the major are always preparing for the next battle.

Among the other types in the regiment are Milt Norton, a university professor who befriends Danny and is killed early in the war. The death of this intellectual is the first indication that this war is being fought by men who have had to learn to become soldiers. Milt's dedication and ability to put aside academic pursuits to serve his country are all the more admirable when contrasted with the behavior of another professor, Lieutenant Bryce. Bryce's elitism, cowardice, and eventual madness reveal the uselessness of pure intellectuals in combat. Also fighting this war is Connie "Ski" Zvonski, representing the poor city dweller who hopes to use the Marines to make a life for himself. Ski goes on to become a hero after his girl leaves him. Andy Hookans, a Northwest lumberjack, is the honest soldier constantly questioning war and longing for a normal life. The iconoclast who proves that it is not the generals who win the war is seen in Captain Max Shapiro, whose unconventional strategies turn the tide of several battles and who dies firing his last shot at the enemy.

The varied ethnic and cultural makeup of the country is seen in other soldiers in the Sixth: Shining Lighttower, an American Indian; L.Q. Jones, a tough guy from Los Angeles; Speedy "Tex" Gray, a Texan whose prejudices are washed away by the blood of battle; "Spanish Joe" Gomez, a con man who finds the hero in himself; "Seabags" Brown, an innocent Iowa farm boy; and Brooklynite Jake Levin, the victim of anti-Semitism, who sacrifices his life for his comrades.

One of the most sympathetic characters in the novel is the one probably closest to the author himself, Marion "Sister Mary" Hodgkiss, who

keeps a written account of life in the platoon. Hodgkiss's literary aspirations and his love of classical music and literature make him the regiment's resident philosopher. His last words to Danny before battle are
haunting: "This much I can say, Danny: don't let anybody tell you that
you were a sucker. Something better has got to come from it all, it has
to. . . . It can't be for nothing" (456).

The Marines of World War II occupied a man's world. Thus the
women in *Battle Cry* exist almost exclusively in the background. However, just as the soldiers in the Sixth represent the American male population in the early 1940s, the women represent the things those men
were fighting for. Kathy, Danny's high-school sweetheart and wife, is
the all-American girl waiting for her soldier to return. Elaine Yarbor-
ough, the lonely officer's wife with whom Danny has a brief affair, is
the weak female who cannot stand by her man. Equally weak is Susan,
Ski's girl, who leaves him while he is still in basic training. On the other
hand, the love of a good man can save a fallen woman, as illustrated by
the character of Rae, the prostitute whose love for Marion reforms her.
Perhaps the closest to a fully realized female character in the novel is
the New Zealander Pat. Having been widowed earlier in the war, Pat is
wiser than many of the men around her; and while she loves Andy and
fears being widowed again, she also recognizes that he will be useless if
he shirks his duty.

Some reviewers criticize Uris for creating characters who are more
memorable as illustrations of certain qualities than as complex human
beings. But the emphasis in *Battle Cry* is not on character but on action;
the Marine Corps is the true central character of the book. In this sense,
then, Uris's characters serve their purpose well by reflecting the types of
men who served in the Corps and the women they left behind.

THEMATIC ISSUES

Just as the characters in *Battle Cry* are not complex, neither are the
themes—loyalty, patriotism, and courage under fire form the backbone
of the Marine Corps. Written from a fighting man's perspective, this
novel explores the gritty reality of war and battle. The Marines of *Battle
Cry* are alternately terrified and exhausted, bored and restless, depending
on what is happening in the war. The stamina it takes to fight a battle
is itself complex—it is not always bravery, but sometimes simply logic
and reason that make a man a hero. Jake Levin, for example, a draftee

with no particular reason to be loyal to a squad harboring anti-Semites, takes on a suicide mission during the battle for Tarawa. He does so not out of idealism or loyalty to the squad, but simply because there is no other way for the mission to succeed. His comrades may look upon his sacrifice as heroic, but Levin sees his final duty as would any military strategist: it is the only option. That such heroic decisions can be made for such practical reasons is one of the things that makes the book so insightful about the workings of a war machine.

While Uris treats military matters from the perspective of the trained soldier, he does not shy away from social commentary. For example, he highlights the irony of fighting for a country that does not afford you equal status, particularly in the persons of Jake Levin and Pedro Rojas. Both men know what it is to be ostracized in their own land, and yet both become war heroes. The treatment that the two receive at the hands of bigots like Tex, along with the recollections they share about prejudice back home, serve to remind readers that although the cause may be just, the country for which these men are fighting does not always treat its citizens justly. In fact, some of the soldiers openly criticize their country's bigotry; Rojas, for example, talks of how different life is for him in New Zealand, where he is accepted as an equal rather than shunned as a "Spic."

In this novel Uris does not seem to recognize the complexity of male-female relationships as clearly as he does relationships between fellow soldiers or between whites and people of color. Love relationships are presented rather stereotypically in this novel: the women either betray their men or stand by and wait for them. War is a man's activity; families and lovers must be put on hold while the real work goes on. The betrayal by women like Elaine and Susan stems from their inability to recognize this reality, while the steadfast loyalty of women like Kathy and Pat emerges from their ability to give selflessly to the cause. Nonetheless, Uris does allow Andy Hookans to question the sense of all this fighting, especially when the war seems to take on a life of its own.

In the end, however, Uris does not question the legitimacy or the meaning of war. Despite the disruption in family relationships and despite the carnage, he accepts the necessity of war and explores its impact on human relations, particularly relationships among men. If *Battle Cry* can be said to have one central theme, it would be that there is a beauty in war, a beauty born of loyalty to comrades, belief in a cause, and dedication to duty.

A NEW HISTORICIST READING OF *BATTLE CRY*

New historicists, like critics of other current schools, believe that the context in which a literary work is written is significant to an appreciation of the work. Jerome McGann, for example, argues that understanding the sociological context of a work is essential to a meaningful analysis of that work. In particular, new historicism considers the social, political, cultural, and economic implications of any literary work.

New historicists consider the literary work a part of the culture that produced it; for the new historicist, the literary work is both influenced by social and other forces and exerts influence on those forces. In part because of these mutual influences, new historicists consider history itself as open to interpretation. Dismissing a linear, fact-based view of history, new historicists insist that writers and critics alike must be aware of the perspective from which they view historical events, understanding that their own situation will color their view of history. Heavily influenced by French philosopher Michel Foucault, new historicists also believe that nothing in history is the result of only one cause; rather, many forces— political, social, philosophical, religious, economic, sociological, and even personal—combine to influence history. Considered from a new historicist perspective, *Battle Cry* is a reflection of several converging cultures during World War II: post-Depression United States, the military, and 1940s family life.

A new historicist reading of *Battle Cry* would most likely begin with an analysis of the American response to the war in Europe and Asia in 1941. At this time most people in the United States wanted nothing more than to stay out of war. The country was finally beginning to emerge from the Great Depression, Franklin Delano Roosevelt's New Deal had Americans feeling proud and hopeful again, and those old enough to remember World War I had no desire to become involved in foreign conflicts again. The bombing of Pearl Harbor on December 7, 1941 changed all that. Young men who had thought previously of nothing but their own futures suddenly felt a responsibility to their country. As Danny Forrester explains to his father, "It just doesn't seem right. Me going off to college to play football with a war going on" (16). The entry of so many boys like Danny into the armed forces had a profound impact not only on the country but on the services themselves. Mac, the sergeant who sees the Sixth Marines through its Pacific battles, is appalled when he first looks over these young volunteers, calling them "the most ill-aligned, saddest-looking excuse for a Marine squad" he has ever seen (4). In *Battle Cry*, however, Uris convinces readers that these "beardless babies of eighteen and twenty" (5) transform themselves into a tight-knit squad of soldiers devoted to their country, the Allied cause, and each other.

What Uris's novel uncovers for readers are the inner workings of a military unit with a clear purpose, with support from back home, and with the resources to accomplish its mission. The United States in World War II stood solidly behind its armed forces. The war in Europe was being fought to rid the world of the evils of Nazism. Although there was no such ideological demon to fight in the Pacific, American racial prejudice, coupled with news of Japanese atrocities in China, served to strengthen the population's resolve to liberate Asia from the stranglehold of the Japanese aggressors. The Sixth Marines, like every other military unit in the Pacific, focused their attention not on Japanese soldiers but rather on "Japs," refusing to think of the enemy in human terms. In fact, the only time Danny Forrester wavers in his dedication to battle is when he begins to recognize a kinship with his enemy: "Maybe he has a girl, a Jap girl like Kathy" (242). And yet even though Danny is sympathetic to the soldier here, he still uses the derogative term "Jap." This apparently racist attitude, presented without apology by Uris, seems at first to contradict the author's condemnation of racial and ethnic prejudice within the ranks. Pedro Rojas, for example, praises the New Zealanders for their lack of prejudice, contrasting them with their bigoted American counterparts. Jake Levin is seen as a hero for enduring anti-Semitic slights, and in fact becomes a hero when he sacrifices his life for the squad. Why, then, would Uris sympathize with racial prejudice against the Japanese?

The answer lies in the historical context of the book. *Battle Cry* presents readers with a country at war. Success in any war effort is built upon hatred of the enemy, and that hatred is easier to maintain if the enemy is seen as something—not someone—entirely different from oneself. The enemy is the Other. One's fellow soldiers, however, are essential to survival. In battle, each member of the unit must be totally dedicated to every other member. Thus prejudice within the squad is dangerous; it could lead to the deaths of individual soldiers or even the failure of the squad's mission. Prejudice against the enemy, on the other hand, fuels the fighting spirit of the squad, making it more likely that the soldiers will work together for victory.

This unity within the squad is also demonstrated in the way the men take care of one another. Having come to the Marines from a society in which sex roles are clearly delineated, these men find themselves living in a "family" of one gender. Thus they eventually adopt roles found in a typical American family of the early 1940s, whether those roles are traditionally masculine or not. In boot camp, for example, Professor Milt Norton acts as a father to Danny, trying to keep him from straying from his moral center. Marion "Sister Mary" Hodgkiss acts in a maternal role throughout the book, providing the squad with culture in the form of good literature and music. Even his name suggests his feminine role. Danny and several of the others in the squad play the roles of children, with Danny representing the dutiful son. Such behavior is necessary for these men to survive in a world that is both geographically and culturally foreign to them.

The squad would not survive, however, if the men were unable to recall what they are fighting for. They are reminded of this during their rest and relaxation in New Zealand. A former British colony similar to the United States in its social and cultural makeup, New Zealand provides the men of the Sixth with a glimpse of what life was like, and could be like again, back home. It is easy for a military unit in the throes of battle to lose a sense of civilization. When soldiers are unable to wash for days, when they cannot remove their boots and socks, when they are bitten by mosquitoes and burned by a tropical sun, it is easy to forget the ideals for which they are fighting. When they relax in New Zealand, the men of the Sixth are reminded of the lifestyle that they are fighting to preserve. When L.Q. is "adopted" by a suburban New Zealand family, he teaches the neighborhood children to play baseball, the Great American Pastime. Andy Hookans carries his domestic inclinations even further, falling in love and eventually marrying the war widow Pat. Through the New Zealand interlude and other flashbacks to life in the States, Uris reminds his characters and his readers that it is not the battle itself that is important, but the ideal for which it is fought.

It is unlikely that a novel like *Battle Cry* will ever be written about the Viet Nam War or even the Gulf War. World War II represents the last time in American history that the country found itself united in a military cause that it considered just. The justice of that cause is illustrated in the behavior of the soldiers in *Battle Cry*. It is difficult for the contemporary reader to understand the innocent patriotism, the hatred of the enemy, and the devotion of the squad portrayed in this novel. That difficulty is the result of over fifty years without a major global conflict, as well as a culture that questions the legitimacy of war as a means of solving political problems. But for the time in which it was written, *Battle Cry* captured perfectly the dedication of an entire military unit to a country, a cause, and the individual soldiers who fought the battle.

4

The Angry Hills
(1955)

A fast-paced novel, *The Angry Hills* contains enough plot twists to keep the most ardent suspense fans enthralled. Set in Nazi-occupied Greece, the story revolves around American writer Mike Morrison, a young widower with two children, doing business in Athens on the eve of the German invasion. The plot is a familiar one for a suspense novel: The innocent Morrison agrees to carry a paper to England for a Greek attorney. It turns out that the paper contains the names of Greek double agents ostensibly working for the Nazis; and when Morrison finds the attorney dead, he becomes the target of the Gestapo leader Konrad Heilser. What ensues is a constant race to outwit the Germans and a constant struggle to determine whom to trust.

PLOT DEVELOPMENT

As in other novels, Uris uses a specific point in history as the setting for his story: in this case, the Nazi invasion of Greece. Like *Battle Cry*, *The Angry Hills* also has at its core some personal history of Uris's. The author's uncle, who had fought in Greece, left a diary recounting various captures and escapes from the Nazis. The action of the story is loosely based on these adventures.

Although the novel is historical, its primary focus is Mike Morrison's odyssey after he acquires what comes to be known as the Stergiou list. Thus plot devices include many standards of the suspense/spy genre: In addition to the unwitting hero, we have a cat-and mouse-game played out aboard a British troop train, a long march to escape the pursuing Nazis, troubled love affairs, and cases of mistaken identity. In Part 1 Mike twice falls into Nazi hands and escapes both times. Finally, after collapsing in a small village, Mike awakens in the hut of a sympathetic villager, Christos Yalouris. Believing that he must conceal his identity, Mike calls himself Jay Linden, a New Zealander.

Part 2 finds Mike falling in love with the village. The peace and tranquillity of Paleachora is contrasted with the madness of modern urban life, especially during wartime. As he recovers from injuries sustained during his ordeal, Mike is cared for by Christos's niece, Eleftheria, a passionate young peasant who is quite willing to lose her virginity to the handsome stranger. But the peaceful interlude is shattered as the Nazis advance through the countryside, burning every village suspected to be harboring enemy British soldiers. When Paleachora is burned, Eleftheria brings Mike to her cousins in an even more remote village, a place reminiscent of those inhabited by Irish Catholics in *Trinity* and *Redemption* and by Palestinians and Jews in *Exodus* and *The Haj*. Kaloghriani is a hard, barren place, and working the land is tortuous. But the nobility of the peasants is inspiring.

A father-son relationship develops between Mike and his host, Barba-Leonidas, who does not want the young man to return to a hostile world. For his part, Mike wonders at the changes this place has wrought in him and longs to live out his days among these people. But his reverie is broken as the seventeen names on the Stergiou list march through his head. Accepting his duty, Mike sends Eleftheria to Athens to contact the Resistance. Part 2 ends with Mike's contact initiating plans to bring him in.

Part 3 opens as a female Underground operative, Lisa Kyriakides, is sent to Kaloghriani to bring Mike to Athens. As the American says farewell to his Greek friends, particularly the heartbroken Eleftheria, Lisa wonders if he might represent a solution to her dilemma. Lisa's collaborator husband has allowed her children to come into the hands of Konrad Heilser, the Nazi in charge of finding Mike Morrison. She has agreed to feed the Nazis information in return for visits with her children, but she is quickly running out of excuses for coming up empty handed at each meeting. Unaware yet of precisely how valuable Mike is, she considers the possibility of turning him over to the Nazis in exchange for her children. Her wavering between loyalty to the cause and to her children causes a number of plot twists.

Once the pair arrives in Athens, Mike's own attempts at escaping Greece are complicated when he falls in love with Lisa. Here we have the early version of the Romeo-and-Juliet theme so prevalent in Uris's novels: While both Mike and Lisa share political loyalties, she comes from a different world, and remaining with Lisa jeopardizes not only Mike's safety but his chances of returning to his own children.

The action escalates in Athens for a more important reason: Konrad Heilser and Greek collaborator Zervos are trying to capture Mike and the Stergiou list. Uris uses the interactions between Zervos and Heilser to establish the despicable nature of collaboration with the enemy during wartime. Solely to increase his own wealth and position, Zervos provides the Nazis with services ranging from prostitutes to intelligence, always at the expense of his fellow Greeks. Heilser's depravity is demonstrated in his lust for Lisa; if he followed his orders rather than his carnal desires, she would never be able to spirit Mike out of Athens. Despite his own weakness, however, Heilser is contemptuous of Zervos, illustrating the more general Nazi contempt for the people they had conquered. The contrast between the Heilser-Zervos conflict and the Lisa-Mike conflict is clear: Lisa may consider betraying Mike, but only out of love for her children. And Mike refuses at all costs to collaborate with the Nazis. Heilser and Zervos, on the other hand, both operate from the basest of motives.

Uris explores the conflicting loyalties that plague good people during wartime as Heilser offers Lisa safe passage to Egypt for herself and her children if she can find Mike Morrison. Until this point Lisa has not known the true identity of her charge, although she suspects that he is an American. Now, with the offer of freedom for her sons, she agonizes over betraying not only Mike but her comrades in the Underground as well. That the Nazis suffer no such moral dilemmas is clear when Lisa leaves the meeting with Heilser and Zervos. The Greek asks the German whether or not he plans to keep his promise to Lisa of safe passage. "Of course not" is Heilser's reply (166).

Tension mounts when Lisa decides to turn Mike over to the Nazis. Fittingly, her resolve to go through with the betrayal abandons her as she and Mike look out over the Acropolis by the light of a full moon. Mike has pondered the significance of Greece as the cradle of human freedom before, and now he thinks, "The very soul of his own country was born on this hill" (173). He and Lisa forge a bond as she leads him back to his hiding place, but he also begins to believe that he will have to escape without Lisa's help.

The plot thickens when Lisa sends Mike to meet the contact who will arrange his escape. Mike is greeted instead by an offensive man who implies that the contact has been arrested. Neither Mike nor the reader knows whether this man, calling himself Chesney, is friend or enemy. But Mike has no choice but to trust him. Pursued by the Gestapo after the meeting, Mike is saved by a prostitute, Ketty. Both of these encounters will be familiar to readers of suspense fiction. Also familiar is the now desperate love affair between Mike and Lisa. Part 4 of the novel ends as Mike finally decides that he must escape without Lisa's help and makes arrangements with the unsavory Chesney. The man's final words to Mike send a chill up the American's spine: Chesney not only knows who Mike is, but he is aware of the Stergiou list as well.

Mike's quandary deepens when the boat on which he is to escape is seized by the Nazis. More alone than ever, he wonders who has betrayed him. Mike's description of his cell in Averof Prison will be echoed in later works such as *Exodus*, *Mila 18*, and *QB VII*: "Their cell couldn't have held forty men properly. It contained ninety. . . . There were no bunks, no heat, no toilet facilities, no water. . . . Lice swarmed everywhere. Mammoth rats roamed" (218). Desperate, he smuggles a note to Lisa.

In a daring maneuver worthy of the most exciting action movie, the cars carrying Mike and a fellow prisoner to Gestapo headquarters are assaulted by Greek Resistance forces and Mike escapes the Nazis yet again. Further complications arise when Mike refuses to turn the Stergiou list over to the Underground until he, Lisa, and her two children are spirited out of Greece. The final pages of the novel are among the most exciting in suspense fiction, as the reader wonders who is behind which plan, who is working for whom, who is the enemy and who the ally, and ultimately, whether or not the escape plan will succeed. The final scenes keep the reader guessing; the character who sets up the escape may or may not be a double agent; it is not until the final lines that we realize he is—although not for the purest of motives—on the side of right. As Lisa and Mike view the coast of North Africa from the deck of a British submarine, Konrad Heilser, Zervos, and their entire Gestapo force find themselves surrounded by Greek Resistance fighters. True to the genre, Uris pulls his heroes from danger and punishes his villains in the final scene.

This tidy ending reveals *The Angry Hills* as a product of a relatively immature writer. Both Uris and his characters know that the execution of Konrad Heilser will result in the massacre of hundreds of Greek civilians. In later novels, Uris will acknowledge that winning battles like this one often result in later, and greater, losses. He also acknowledges in later works that heroes die. But in his more mature works (e.g., *Exodus, Mila 18, Trinity*) Uris focuses less on the adventures of his heroes and more on political and social conditions. *The Angry Hills* is a suspense novel rather than a historical novel, and thus lacks the complexities of Uris's later work. Exciting it may be, but the work is ultimately less satisfying to the discerning reader than the novels that follow it.

CHARACTER DEVELOPMENT

The distinction between hero and villain is clear in *The Angry Hills*: Mike Morrison, the innocent American who risks his life to help a foreign people regain their freedom, contrasts starkly with Konrad Heilser, the vile German who kills indiscriminately in order to conquer that people. Mike, of course, does not set out to become a hero. He agrees to deliver the Stergiou list to London simply as a favor. When his eyes are opened, however, he becomes determined to carry out his mission. His heroism is all the more admirable because of his, and his country's, neutrality. Although he has no use for the Nazis, he shares the common American opinion of the war in early 1941: "It simply wasn't America's affair" (6). But when Stergiou is murdered and the Nazis begin their pursuit, the war quickly becomes Mike Morrison's affair. At first, Mike's intent is simply to stay alive; but as he witnesses Nazi brutality and comes to appreciate the integrity of simple Greek life, he becomes determined to fight for those seventeen names and their occupied country.

Mike's decency is illustrated in his resistance to the advances of the voluptuous Eleftheria. Hopelessly in love with Mike and sexually innocent, Eleftheria throws herself at the American. It would be easy for Mike to take advantage of this young, eager, inexperienced girl. But his sense of honor prevents him from indulging in his physical passion for Eleftheria. Similarly, when he finds himself falling in love with the more worldly Lisa, he worries about the consequences of their affair, unable to simply revel in the sensual pleasure it offers the two in this turbulent time.

Mike's sense of honor is contrasted with Konrad Heilser's depravity. While Mike appreciates Lisa's conflicts, Heilser exploits them. It is he who holds her children hostage in his quest to possess Lisa, and it is he who makes false promises to her if she will consent to become his mistress. Unlike Mike's feelings for the woman, Heilser's are described purely in terms of lust: "His emotions began to boil at the thought of having her in bed with him" (150). Mike, in contrast, thinks of her in more romantic terms: "Lisa was an enchanted dream" (194).

Heilser's evil is no more a product of an individual personality, however, than is Mike's goodness. The good and evil represented by these two characters can be attributed almost entirely to their nationalities and political positions. In this novel, as in most of his work, Uris portrays sympathizers with anti-democratic ideologies (Nazis, communists, British imperialists) as the epitome of evil. Those who sympathize with democratic ideologies, particularly Americans, are essentially good. Even more despicable than the tyrants, however, are those who curry favor with them. The collaborator Zervos is described not only as politically evil but personally depraved as well: He arranges orgies for German officers and extorts money from wealthy Greeks suspected by the Nazis. He is so despicable that even Heilser can barely tolerate his presence. Zervos is the prototype of Franz Koenig, the ethnic German Pole in *Mila 18* who betrays his Jewish compatriots in order to further his own ambitions.

In contrast, those Greeks who remain true to their country are portrayed as saintly. Christos Yalouris and his fellow villagers "consider it a sacred duty to shelter escapees. Other men vowed to burn their wheat fields before giving the Germans a kernel of grain" (105). Indeed, these peasants watch the Nazis burn their villages one by one for sheltering British soldiers. Christos himself dies at the hands of the Germans rather than give Mike up to them. Even the love-struck Eleftheria helps Mike escape to Athens, knowing full well that it means she will never see him again.

Those Greeks involved in the Underground are more complicated, but no less noble, than their peasant counterparts. Understanding that the cause is more important than any individual life in such times, the Underground leaders instruct Lisa to kill Mike rather than allow the Germans to capture him. At the same time, when Lisa admits to losing Mike and confesses her relationship with the Nazis, her compatriots agonize over their decision of whether or not to eliminate her. The Underground leader Michalis warns the others, "We cannot let sentimentality rule us" (206). In reply, the priest, Papa-Panos, warns that "by her execution we place ourselves on the same level with the Nazis" (207). Their decision to spare Lisa's life is motivated as much by this sentiment as it is by their hope that she might still lead them to Mike and the Stergiou list. The difference between these people and the Nazis in this book is that while the Nazis kill for power—and often for sheer sport—the Greek patriots kill only when they have no choice, and then they do so reluctantly.

Other than the several Nazis, collaborators, and patriots discussed above, the characters found in this novel exist primarily to further the plot. For example, the little man with glasses who appears to be stalking Mike early in the book surprises both Mike and the reader by turning out to be Soutar, a partner of Stergiou's. And the likable Australian soldier Mosley, whom Mike meets in a bar before discovering Stergiou's body, turns out to be a German agent. The Palestinian couple, Yichiel and Elpis, who try to escape by boat with Mike late in the book, suffers the fate of many Jews at the hands of their Nazi captors. In later novels, minor characters like these will become more complex. All of the characters in *The Angry Hills*, minor and prominent alike, represent prototypes of characters who will appear in Uris's later, more sophisticated novels.

THEMATIC ISSUES

Although *The Angry Hills* is rather straightforward suspense fiction, it nevertheless introduces several themes that will be central to Uris's later, more complex novels. Perhaps the most recognizable theme in the book involves the tragically innocent American. Even in *Battle Cry* the innocence of American boys wholly unprepared for the ravages of war emerges as a subtheme. Here, however, Uris explores the serious consequences of innocence bordering on ignorance. Like many Americans of his day, Mike Morrison believes that the war is none of America's business. The last time battles were fought on American soil was almost eighty years earlier; only a few ancient American citizens can still remember the Civil War. Thus Mike is wholly unprepared for what befalls him in Greece. His mourning the death of his wife in an automobile accident, his longing to return to his children, his wistful thoughts of San Francisco—all of these things represent the global insignificance of typical American concerns in the face of the Nazi onslaught. Later, in *Exodus*, Kitty Fremont will come to postwar Greece and then Palestine, mourning the deaths of her husband and child. Like Mike, Kitty will have to create an entirely new context in which to view her world. Both

Americans, all Americans, no longer have the luxury of isolating themselves from political problems half a world away.

Like Kitty, Mike believes that tragedy is personal. His wife's death
does not represent a threat to others in the United States; it was an
accident. In Europe, on the other hand, there is no such thing as accidental death any more, nor is the death of a young person an extraordinary occurrence. Death has become all too common on the continent;
deaths are measured in hundreds, and not just battlefield deaths. The
simple rules of life that have comforted Mike at home do not apply in
Greece in 1941. In fact, it seems to him that there are no longer any rules
of human conduct.

In contrast to the theme of global conflict is that of the nobility of
pastoral life. As he recovers from his wounds in Paleachora, Mike wan-
ders through the "sloping vineyards," smelling "the sharp tang from the
huge sacks of goats'-milk cheese" and watching "the stalks of wheat
bend their golden heads." He gazes in the evenings at "the shepherd-
esses, their crooks of office in hand," as they return from the pastures
with their flocks (102). These same pastoral images, of which readers
saw a few in *Battle Cry*, will return in *Exodus, Trinity*, and *Redemption*. In
Uris's fiction, the peace and quiet of such places are always disrupted
by the forces of tyranny—political/ethnic tyranny in the form of Nazism,
religious/nationalistic tyranny in the form of Islam, or economic/impe-
rialist tyranny in the form of British capitalism.

If pastoral life is threatened from within Europe itself, then where will
the hope of the human race come from? In *Battle Cry*, American soldiers
were seen as the last hope of the Allies. Here too it becomes clear that
the torch has passed from the hands of the old European powers. Mike
may be neutral and innocent, but he holds the key to successful resistance in Greece; in his head are the seventeen names from the Stergiou
list. Just as the inexperienced boys of the Sixth Marines retook Tarawa
and Guadalcanal, so too will the unwilling, inexperienced American spy
help keep the Greek Resistance alive. Later, in *Armageddon* and *Topaz*,
Uris will portray the United States as the only force capable of halting
communist world domination. When Konrad Heilser bemoans his fate
at having to pursue an amateur, he may well be issuing a prophecy.
"There was nothing worse to contend with in this business than a desperate amateur" (80), he thinks, realizing that Mike Morrison has been
drawn into the fray unwittingly. After the war, communist forces in Berlin, Cuba, and France might well echo Heilser's sentiment. In subsequent
novels Uris will play out this theme of reluctant Americans saving the

world from dictatorship. The villain's cape will shift from the shoulders of the Nazis to those of the communists, but the hero will still carry the American flag.

Despite the turmoil of the times, however, human relationships, particularly sexual ones, endure. *Battle Cry* saw relationships between unlikely lovers—the intellectual Marion and the prostitute Rae, for example, or the Swedish-American Andy and the New Zealander widow Pat. In *The Angry Hills* Uris introduces the star-crossed lover theme that will recur in his later works. Lisa, caught up in both the Underground and Konrad Heilser's trap, is an unlikely mate for middle-class businessman Mike. Circumstances almost dictate that the pair, even if they do survive this adventure, will never see one another again. Indeed, when Mike pledges that he will return to Greece for her after the war, Lisa replies, "Let us be grateful for these few hours and not think of something a century from now" (193). Lovers in later books will whisper these same words, but none of them will enjoy the fairy-tale ending awaiting Lisa and Mike.

The personal conflicts that Lisa and Mike face before they are finally liberated also constitute a common theme in Uris's work. Lisa is tortured by conflicting loyalties: if she remains loyal to her compatriots and to Mike, she risks the lives of her children; but if she capitulates to Heilser and saves her children, she risks not only the lives of Mike and her fellow Resistance fighters, but the lives of hundreds of other Greeks as well. For his part, Mike longs to relinquish his unsought-for role of spy in the Greek countryside, longing to simply disappear and live out the pastoral life. But the names on the Stergiou list haunt him, and his sense of self-preservation succumbs to his sense of common humanity. In contrast, those who collaborate with the Nazis avoid such conflicting loyalties. The price, however, is high, as Zervos and others in future books discover at the hands of Resistance fighters.

The fate of collaborators, and their portrayal in this and other books, underscores a final common theme in Uris's work, that of clearly defined good and evil. Nazis, and in later books Arabs, communists, and British industrialists, not only espouse unsavory political and social views, but they are also characterized as slovenly, perverted, and thoroughly treacherous. Zervos and Heilser, along with other minor Nazi characters in *The Angry Hills*, revel in the degradation, torture, and killing of their victims. Off duty, they engage in perverse orgies and indulge their greed. Such behavior will recur in subsequent novels as well. Conversely, the heroes, while succumbing to the occasional human frailty, are almost always pure, innocent, and loyal—like Mike Morrison and Lisa Kyriakides. Readers of Leon Uris learn very quickly that his vision of the world includes very few gray areas.

A PSYCHOANALYTICAL READING OF *THE ANGRY HILLS*

In order to understand psychoanalytic criticism, one must first understand the basic tenets of Sigmund Freud's theories of the inner workings of the mind. Much of Freud's work is based on two premises, the first of which posits that the mind operates on both conscious and unconscious levels. While we may believe in our conscious minds that we have rational reasons for our behavior, that behavior is often influenced heavily by our unconscious, the repository of our deepest, unspoken fears and desires. The second of Freud's premises involves the familiar three-part construction of personality. The *id* functions on the unconscious level, seeking pleasure at any cost. The *ego*, representing reality, and the *superego*, representing society and conscience, function on both the conscious and the unconscious levels. Put simply, the ego serves to curb the desires of the id when those desires conflict with reason or logic, and the superego imposes the constrictions of authority and society on the id and the ego.

Infants, according to Freud, are all id. But as the expectations, first of the parents and later of others in the child's culture, begin to intrude on the child's desire to fulfill his or her needs, the ego and the superego begin to emerge. When the demands of the id are seen as inappropriate, sometimes even dangerous, the ego and superego work to push those desires back into the unconscious mind. Such desires do not disappear, however. They remain repressed, and at times emerge—in a slip of the tongue, in erratic behavior, or in dreams. Freud believed that dreams function symbolically to allow an outlet for unconscious desires. Thus, the interpretation of dreams can help a person understand a particular conflict that he or she is experiencing.

It is in Freud's theories of dream interpretation that literary critics found an intriguing new approach to analyzing literature. Freud himself applied his theories to literature, and since his time a number of psychologists and critics have refined his approach. A psychoanalytic critic looking at a literary work considers the surface story as the *manifest content* of the work, just as the psychoanalyst looks at details of the dream. What both the critic and the analyst are really looking for, however, is the *latent content*, or the underlying meaning, of the story. In both psychoanalysis and literary criticism, such meaning comes through in symbols, either through *displacement* or *condensation*. Displacement occurs when a related object or person represents the real subject of the dream or literary work. Condensation involves consolidating a number of subjects into one image.

Recognizing that readers often interpret works differently from the way the author intended and from the way other readers do, critics such as Norman Holland focus attention on the interaction of reader, author, and text. This analysis of the unconscious motivations of all three has become the hallmark of traditional psychoanalytic criticism.

The nightmare quality of *The Angry Hills* makes it an ideal text to examine from a psychoanalytical perspective. Just as our ordinary lives are sometimes invaded by bad dreams, Mike Morrison's normal existence is shattered twice: first when his wife is killed in an automobile accident and then when he comes into possession of the Stergiou list. Having begun to emerge from his first nightmare, Mike soon finds himself plunged into another, complete with the typical features of such a dream. He runs through dark alleys ending in brick walls, he leaps from moving trains, he escapes from his pursuers only to find himself trapped again, he is lulled into complacency in peaceful fields, and he meets people who represent the ultimate in evil and heroism. This nightmare can be viewed as symbolic of Mike's inner turmoil at the time. Threatened both by his own grief and the real dangers stalking him, Mike's id tells him to remain hidden in the villages of the Greek peasants. There he will never have to worry about Nazis, secret agents, or the complexities of the modern world. In Barba-Leonidas Mike even has a kindly father figure to care for him, and in Eleftheria he has a loving mate. But his superego, his sense of responsibility to the names on the Stergiou list, as well as his responsibility to fight the evil of Nazism, struggles with his id. His ego, recognizing the reality of the situation, negotiates between the two. He probably cannot hide out forever; the Nazis have pursued him relentlessly. And he still has two children at home, whom he desperately wants to see again. Mike thus represses the desires of his id and proceeds to contact the Underground.

The nightmare is also representative of the American psyche when the book was published. Having just emerged from a war that destroyed their innocence, Americans were being forced to consider how to realign their lives: first by coming to terms with the evils they had witnessed and second by determining how to deal with their fears of the new world order. Like Mike, Americans might understandably have longed to escape to a quieter, simpler life. But in the first decade of the Cold War, they suddenly found themselves in possession of their own Stergiou list, responsible for saving the world from the communist menace. In this sense, both readers and Mike Morrison are like the adolescent who suddenly realizes that adulthood means recognizing one's responsibility to—and often for—others. Growing up is a frightening, sometimes nightmarish, business.

Growing up means not only recognizing the demands of the present—getting the Stergiou list to British intelligence or halting the march of communism; it also means confronting the evils within ourselves. In this book, both for Mike and for readers, that evil is symbolized by Nazism. In displacing fears about our own evil tendencies onto the Nazis, we are able to explore the reasons behind such horrors as the Holocaust. In this regard, readers of *The Angry Hills* are able to characterize the perpetrators of such evil as the Other: Konrad Heilser is a depraved, sadistic man with no morals, and the Nazis running the prison are monsters. Readers encountering such characters can take comfort in their Otherness; these beasts bear no resemblance to the reader of the novel. Even the ordinary citizen who becomes caught up in the evil, represented by the collaborator Zervos, is gross, obese, indulgent, and devoid of any moral sense. In this way Uris, Mike, and readers are all able to understand the horrors of the Holocaust; the perpetrators of this evil are creatures unrelated to ordinary people. *They* did this; *we* could never do it.

But for Mike, as well as for readers, part of the nightmare is that evil is not always so readily recognizable. As Mike struggles to determine whom to trust, he discovers that it is sometimes impossible to distinguish friends from enemies. His initial trust in the affable Mosley is shattered when he discovers the man to be a Nazi; conversely, his fear of the sinister-looking bespectacled Soutar is revealed to be groundless when he discovers that the man is Stergiou's accomplice. Mike even wonders about Lisa's loyalties, and readers join him in wondering about Chesney's. For readers in the 1950s, this inability to distinguish friend from foe would be familiar. The ally who helped win the war, the Soviet Union, was now the enemy. The enemy, Germany, was now an ally. Internally, fears of communism had engendered an atmosphere of suspicion within the government, business, and the entertainment industry. Readers of *The Angry Hills* would be familiar with the sense of isolation plaguing Mike Morrison; the resolution of his fears at the end of the book would be comforting.

Fears of internal demons focus attention on the past; fears of external demons focus attention on the present. If a person is to avoid being trapped by such fears, attention must be focused on the future. As children grow up, the integration of the personality teaches them to defer gratification: By allowing the ego and the superego to repress the wishes of the id, children hope for eventual satisfaction of their desires. For example, by refusing the instant gratification of remaining in the village of Kaloghriani, Mike hopes to eventually find his way to home, safety, and his children. Similarly, Lisa learns that she must forego the immediate gratification of being with her children in order to ensure that they will be together safely in the long run. On the other hand, characters like Zervos are walking illustrations of instant gratification. Zervos gives no thought to the ramifications of his behavior for his country, his people, or the world. He indulges his greed, lust, and gluttony purely for the pleasure of the moment. Readers can recognize in these characters symbols of their own need to defer gratification of their desires. In the 1950s, this meant placing their hopes for the future in their children. Just as Mike and Lisa recognize that their salvation lies not simply in escaping the Nazis but in making the world better for their children, so too would readers of *The Angry Hills* see their roles as providers of a secure, prosperous future for their children. That Mike and Lisa are able to do this, and that the despicable Zervos dies as a result of his behavior, reassures readers that the domination of the ego and superego over the id is worthwhile.

The struggle of Mike Morrison to reintegrate himself into the world is representative of the struggle of all individuals to integrate themselves into their own worlds. It is significant that when he is hiding from the world, Mike must assume a false identity; he cannot be himself and succumb to the desire to remain in childish ignorance. Following Mike's odyssey, readers in the 1950s could be comforted in the knowledge that their vigilance against communism and their investments in their children's futures would pay off. Readers in any age can find in the novel reassurance that integrating the personality, leaving childhood behind and taking on the responsibilities of adulthood, is worth the struggle.

5

Exodus
(1958)

Loosely based on the true story of a ship filled with illegal immigrants to Palestine, *Exodus* recounts the story of the founding of Israel after World War II. Opening the novel on the island of Cyprus, Uris establishes the central characters and conflicts early. Kitty Fremont, an American nurse widowed in the war, works in the refugee camps where thousands of Jews, many of them children, await word on the Palestinian Mandate that will or will not allow them to settle in Israel. Kitty's humanitarianism is tempered by a hint of anti-Semitism, making her an apt representative of the world's reaction to the plight of displaced Jews after the war. She is involved in a love/hate relationship with the Zionist Ari Ben Canaan, an agent for Mossad Aliyah Bet, an organization intent on creating a Jewish state in Israel. Ari is assisted in his plot by the young Jewish Palestinian David Ben Ami, Cyprus commander of the Palmach, the secret Palestinian Jewish army. The pair are planning to draw world attention to the British blockade of Palestine.

PLOT DEVELOPMENT

Book 1, "Beyond Jordan," opens with Kitty Fremont's agreeing to work in a Jewish refugee camp. She becomes enamored of fourteen-year-old Karen Hansen Clement, whose gentle manner chips away at Kitty's aversion to Jews. Uris uses Karen's story to provide readers with a look at what the war years were like for Europe's Jewish population. Karen's father, a secular Jew assimilated into German life, represents those Jews who forgot their heritage and who turned a blind eye to Nazi atrocities until it was too late. Readers will see a more fully drawn character like this in Paul Bronski of *Mila 18*. It takes so long for men like Johann Clement and Paul to appreciate the Nazi threat that by the time they become aware, resistance is futile.

Sent to Denmark early in the war for safety, Karen finds love in a new family and witnesses the courageous resistance of the Danes to their occupiers. Readers learn of Danes following King Christian's lead, donning the yellow Star of David when the Nazis order all Jews to wear one. Karen's story also reveals the strength of Denmark's Underground Resistance movement, its continual sabotage of Nazi rule, and the brave people of its flotilla who spirit Jews away to the safety of Sweden. This image of a humanitarian country reaching out to Holocaust victims is contrasted later in the story of Dov Landau, survivor of the Warsaw ghetto and Auschwitz. Dov's story characterizes the Poles as historically anti-Semitic, willing collaborators with the Nazis. The story of the ghetto, and of the Polish betrayal of the Jews, will be played out in great detail in *Mila 18*. After the war, Karen feels compelled to search for her only surviving relative, her father. Her quest is symbolic of the hundreds of thousands of survivors who tried desperately to renew family ties after the devastation of the war. Karen's search leads her to the refugee camps of Cyprus, and eventually to Ari Ben Canaan.

Ari's plan is to fill a ship, christened *The Exodus*, with refugee children. As he correctly anticipates, world opinion will force the British to allow the ship to sail to Palestine. A zealot, Ari is willing to see the children suffer and perhaps die in order to further the cause. On the ship are Ari, Karen, Dov, Kitty, and sixteen hundred children engaged in a hunger strike until the British allow the ship to leave Cyprus. The British commander, Bradshaw, finds himself playing the role of Pharaoh, keeping the Jews from their Promised Land.

Book 2, "The Land Is Mine," opens with Ari's story, which, like Karen's, provides readers with historical background, this time focusing on Russia. Through the story of the Rabinskys, readers see the pogroms in Russia that destroyed Jewish villages and killed Jewish people. Generations of enduring discrimination and violence led many European Jews to embrace Zionism, the movement to build a Jewish homeland in

Palestine. In 1897 a convention in Switzerland called for a Jewish state; two decades later the Balfour Declaration promised a Jewish homeland. In the present time of the book, 1946, this hope remains unrealized. But Zionists continue to settle in Palestine, and Ari is born to Jossi Rabinsky, who has renamed himself Barak Ben Canaan, during the Turkish invasion in World War I.

The historical background that Uris provides in Book 2 makes the obsession of men like Ari Ben Canaan understandable. Born to a people who have been persecuted for centuries, learning about the string of broken promises to resettle in the Holy Land, and emerging from a Holocaust like none other the world has ever seen, the Zionists after World War II would not be stopped.

In placing blame for the postwar turmoil in Israel, Uris sees England and France dancing to an Arab tune once the value of Arab oil becomes clear and characterizes Arabs as treacherous cutthroats in league with the Nazis. But the Palestinian Jews themselves are also criticized when Akiva, Barak Ben Canaan's brother, helps form the Maccabees, a terrorist offshoot of the Haganah intent on offensive as well as defensive action. The Maccabees' reign of terror against the British in retaliation for what they see as British betrayal is, in Barak's eyes, both counterproductive and dishonorable. More productive is the settlement of kibbutzim in strategic places to fend off Arab attacks. These new kibbutzim strengthen the Jewish position in Palestine, but the price is high: representative of Arab brutality is the butchering of Dafna, Ari's fiancée and fellow freedom fighter.

The metaphorical butchering of the Jews by the British is illustrated in the story of the White Paper, which effectively ended Jewish immigration to Palestine just as Germany was becoming dangerous. British treachery is again illustrated when the British fail to recognize the contribution of the Palestinian Jewish forces, the Yishov. In retaliation for such betrayals, the Maccabees blow up British Headquarters at the King David Hotel.

Uris enhances the historical significance of the present story by ending this section with the arrival of the *Exodus* in Israel on the second day of Chanukah, the celebration of Judah Maccabee's liberation of Jerusalem from the ancient Greeks.

Book 3, "An Eye for an Eye," provides background on the early struggles leading to the British evacuation of Israel and the United Nations vote to partition Palestine. As Ari proudly shows Kitty his homeland, readers sense the omnipresence of British soldiers and the constant threat of Arab attack. Curfews and tension interrupt their sightseeing. Upon settling in, Karen, Kitty, and Dov find themselves at the strategically located kibbutz Gan Dafna, named for Ari's murdered fiancée.

The personal toll taken by years of undeclared war is demonstrated in relationships between characters. Akiva, long estranged from Ari's father, Barak, because of the Maccabees, seeks reconciliation through Ari. Barak refuses. Tension erupts as well between Kitty, with whom Ari is falling in love, and his sister Jordana, born a child of struggle. Jordana resents the domestic influence that Kitty has on her brother: In such times, femininity and domesticity are luxuries that warriors can ill afford. Kitty, for her part, is gradually becoming mesmerized by Israel, its history, and its ghosts.

The aftermath of the Holocaust still haunts some of the characters, as Karen finally finds her father, driven insane by grief and torture, unable to recognize her or respond to her. Dov, his ability to trust destroyed by his experiences in the ghetto and the concentration camp, loves Karen but feels unworthy of her. He flees and joins the Maccabees, to whom his forgery skills are invaluable. Through these two characters Uris illustrates the lingering impact of the Holocaust on an entire generation of Jewish children.

But while the war against the Nazis may be over, the struggle of the Jews continues. As tensions in Palestine escalate, the British become more brutal, resulting in a temporary unity between the Haganah and the Maccabees as they attack British records, railroads, and pipelines. When the British capture Maccabee leaders, including Akiva and Dov, the international outrage over the secrecy of the trials resembles that over the trial of Conor Larkin and his fellow IRA fighters in a later novel, *Trinity*. Ari, at the request of his father, frees Akiva and Dov from a prison fortress. Ari is wounded and Akiva dies during the escape. Over Akiva's unmarked grave Ari vows that someday "it will be a shrine of all Jews" (431).

Against the backdrop of imminent war as the United Nations announces partition of Palestine, Ari is saved by Kitty's medical skills. The contrast between these two reluctant lovers is sharpened as Ari's dedication to the cause comes up against Kitty's desire for deep human relationships. The price of Ari's dedication is too exorbitant for Kitty, who renews her determination to leave Palestine with Karen. But on returning to Gan Dafna, she takes one last look at the children of the Holocaust. This section ends with Kitty's acknowledging that Gan Dafna, Israel, "is where I belong" (451).

Book 4, "Awake in Glory," opens with a scathing criticism of the United Nations' handling of the rising tensions in Palestine. While political maneuverings result in a vote to partition Palestine and give the Jews a homeland, the Arab rioting that breaks out continues unchecked by either United Nations or British forces. Uris portrays the Israelis as lone fighters facing overwhelming odds. The stories of Jews protecting cities and kibbutzim take on epic proportions, as Uris weaves tales of cunning manipulations designed to make the cowardly Arabs believe that areas are far better defended than they really are. And the evacuation of children from Gan Dafna—achieved by drugging the children and carrying them bodily through treacherous mountain areas—is presented as the stuff that Bible stories are made of. This section in fact echoes many of the heroic battle stories found in the Old Testament. The author's repeated references to Biblical quests underscores his belief that the founding of Israel was more than a human endeavor. Kitty discovers early in her stay, as she looks at Ari and David Ben Ami, "This was no army of mortals. . . . It was the army of Israel, and no force on earth could stop them for the power of God was within them!" (357). Later, Bruce Sutherland, the sympathetic British military officer, declares that while his military training tells him that the Jewish cause is hopeless, "when you see what they have done with this land you are not a realist if you do not believe in miracles" (447).

And yet these soldiers are not gods. The war takes on a human face in Ari's agonizing over orders to take Abu Yesha, the village of Taha, his Arab friend from childhood. While Ari finds himself incapable of leading the attack on the village, he issues the order to destroy it. His heartbreak over this ultimate sin against his friend tends to humanize him—he has never shown such emotion before, even when the children on the *Exodus* were dying of starvation.

As the war rages, Uris establishes a position that he will later elaborate on at length (in *The Haj*) when he blames the Palestinian refugee tragedy entirely on the Arab nations. Claiming that Palestinian Arabs had always wanted to live in peace with the Jews, Uris insists that they were betrayed by their leaders. In the form of a report by Barak, he describes how Arab leaders are using peasants to fight Israel and using the refugees for political reasons. He cites in the report the fact that no Arab nation will provide the refugees a permanent home. While Uris's interpretation of the situation may be overly simplistic, most historians acknowledge that Arab countries did little to accommodate Palestinian refugees.

Book 5, "With Wings as Eagles," is fittingly the briefest in the novel. The war with the Arabs temporarily halted, Israel embarks on postwar settlement. Jews flock to Israel, tame the desert, establish an army, and bring into the world a new generation of Jews born in their own nation. The death of the old order is symbolized when Barak dies and is buried next to Akiva. But tragedy will remain with Israel, and its brightest children will be sacrificed. *Exodus* ends with hope for the nation but grief in the home as Karen is killed by Arabs on the land she calls "the bridge between darkness and light" (589).

CHARACTER DEVELOPMENT

Most of the characters in *Exodus* are fleeing, either from something or to something; some characters are doing both at the same time. Readers are introduced to the primary characters in the novel early, as hordes of refugees from Hitler's death camps are interned in camps of a different sort on Cyprus. It is on this island that readers are first introduced to the American nurse Kitty Fremont.

Kitty has been fleeing grief throughout the war. Shortly after her husband died on Guadalcanal, her daughter succumbed to polio. Burying her grief in work, Kitty arrives on Cyprus just as the Mossad Aliyah Bet plans to create an international incident. Kitty serves as a symbolic American. Like Mike Morrison in *The Angry Hills*, she has endured personal tragedy. But like Mike, she has never found herself immersed in an international tragedy like the Holocaust. She also represents prevailing American attitudes toward Jews. Not rabidly anti-Semitic, Kitty is nonetheless uncomfortable around Jews. "I suppose Jewish children are pretty much like any others," she tells her old friend Mark Parker, "but I'd just rather not get mixed up with them" (18), later explaining that she has "worked with enough Jewish doctors to know they are arrogant and aggressive people" (52). Kitty's resolve is shattered, however, when she meets Karen.

If ever a fictional character approached perfection, that character would be Karen Hansen Clement, the sixteen-year-old German Jewish girl who draws Kitty Fremont into the drama of Israel. Sheltered in Denmark during the Holocaust, Karen is nonetheless haunted by what has happened to her people. Like Kitty, she plunges into work to ward off grief, but unlike Kitty, she must contend with a tragedy of incomprehensible magnitude. Kitty may have lost a husband and daughter, but

Karen, like so many Jews, has lost an entire extended family. Her only hope is that her father remains alive. And yet, despite the horrors she has witnessed, Karen maintains a hope in humankind and a heart that embraces all whom she meets. She is running toward Eretz Israel, the Promised Land, where she hopes to find not only a home but also the father she has not seen since she was a child.

If Karen represents the Jewish spirit that would not be broken by the Holocaust, Dov Landau stands for the hatred bred in the ghetto and the camps. Only ten years old when the Germans invaded Poland, Dov has spent his adolescence in the Warsaw ghetto and Auschwitz. The brutality he has endured has left him bitter, angry, and filled with an indiscriminate hatred. Even after the liberation of Auschwitz, Dov cannot conceive of a world without "depravity and torture" (143). Dov is neither running away from nor to anything—he is simply running.

As Karen and Dov wait in the Caraolos detention camp, their savior plans a daring move to rivet the world's attention on Palestine. News correspondent Mark Parker claims that Ari Ben Canaan "could be mistaken for a movie leading man" (177), but his appearance hides a nature almost as cynical as Dov's. When David Ben Ami defends the Greek sympathizer Mandria, Ari warns him against being deceived by such men: "When the final battle comes we will stand alone. . . . We have no friend except our own people" (24). His cynicism does not prevent Ari from using Mandria, however; unlike Dov, Ari has channeled his anger and hatred. His goal is nothing less than to break the British blockade of Palestine and hasten the birth of the Jewish nation in Israel.

What Ari has not counted on in this mission, however, is meeting Kitty Fremont. Kitty is not one of "our own people," nor is she an active sympathizer like Mandria. Nonetheless, Ari finds himself drawn to Kitty; and throughout the novel the pair struggle with the conflict between their personal feelings and Ari's political commitment. The one great love of Ari's life was his fellow Haganah soldier Dafna, brutally butchered by the Arabs at age seventeen. The feelings he has for Kitty cannot match those for Dafna, for Kitty will never be able to share the passion for a Jewish homeland at the core of Ari's being. He longs to be able to explain his people's fanatical love of this land to Kitty, but she is an outsider and always will be. His journey seems fated to be a solitary one.

Ari's love of the land is natural, since he is a *sabra*, a Jew born in Palestine. His father, Barak, emigrated from Russia fifty years earlier. Leaving behind a tortured history of persecution, pogroms, and death, Barak has become a legend in Palestine, one of those fierce young immigrants who tamed a rugged, unforgiving land and made it flourish. Barak prides himself on his ability to coexist peacefully with Arabs; and with land bought from his Arab friend Kammal, he builds Yad El, "the Hand of God," from a swamp. Barak's dedication to his adopted land takes the form of negotiation and compromise. His brother Akiva is more impatient. Horrified by the British blockade of Palestine just as the Nazis begin closing in on European Jews, Akiva and a small band of soldiers break away from the Haganah in 1934 to form the Maccabees, whose motto will be the Biblical "eye for an eye." These brothers are symbolic of the two extremes of Zionism, one relying on diplomacy and negotiation, the other on armed conflict.

The other Zionists in *Exodus* fall somewhere between Barak and Akiva. Although Ari, like his father, considers armed conflict only when provoked, he is a passionate soldier. There is no doubt in the minds of the British leaders on Cyprus—or in the minds of readers—that he will carry out his threat to blow up the *Exodus* and its young passengers if the British try to board the ship. His protegé David Ben Ami is determined to rid Palestine of the British, but his zealousness is tempered by a humanity that Ari does not seem to possess.

If David's humanity is the result of his love for Ari's sister Jordana, then Jordana does not seem to share that humanity. The epitome of the woman warrior, Jordana scorns Kitty's softness, thinking that she "looked like all the soft, white, useless wives of English officers who spent their days at tea and gossip around the King David Hotel" (339). There is no time for such luxuries in the life of a soldier, and Jordana is a soldier first, a woman second. Uris seems to be criticizing the Palmach in Jordana's character. After a confrontation with Jordana, Kitty muses on the reasons behind the Jewish woman's hostility: "Too much purpose could destroy womanliness.... [Jordana] hated Kitty because she wanted to be more like Kitty and Kitty knew it" (350). While the author describes Jordana as both beautiful and desirable, he still portrays her as having missed out on the opportunity to be truly feminine.

Jordana's lack of femininity may bother Kitty, but the action in *Exodus* makes clear that if a nation is to be born and its people free, everyone must pay the price. In Uris's other Jewish novels the enemy is almost always the Nazis, but in *Exodus* the enemy is the British occupation force in Palestine. Among those forces, however, are both sympathetic and unsympathetic characters. Cecil Bradshaw and Fred Caldwell both epitomize the anti-Semitic, antagonistic British. Bradshaw plays the role of Pharaoh when the *Exodus* is being held in the harbor. Caldwell is a more sinister figure, taking part in tortures and beatings designed to extract information from Palmach soldiers, men and women, boys and girls alike. His abduction and murder by the Maccabees heightens the tensions in Palestine just prior to the United Nations vote for partition.

Not all of the British soldiers are enemies, however. Between the world wars, Major P. P. Malcolm, a fanatical Zionist, becomes the only non-Jew to lead Haganah forces. Later, Brigadier General Bruce Sutherland, whose forces liberated Bergen-Belsen, resigns from his command on Cyprus and moves to Palestine to help the Haganah. Half Jewish himself, Sutherland becomes one of the more important fighters behind the scenes.

Exodus is a novel of Israel, focusing on the rebirth of a nation that died thousands of years ago. The characters populating its pages, like the story itself, are larger than life.

THEMATIC ISSUES

A number of themes are woven throughout *Exodus*: the indomitability of the human spirit, retribution, justice, and reconciliation. By far the most prominent theme, however, is suggested by the title itself. The action in *Exodus* represents a reenactment of the Biblical exodus of the Jews from Egypt in search of the Promised Land. While the quest for a homeland is in itself a powerful theme, in this novel the Biblical overtones invest that theme with a mystical quality frequently found in Uris's work. What is being presented here is nothing less than another chapter in the long history of Jewish fulfillment of God's promise. Even General Bradshaw, commander of the British forces on Cyprus, worries over refusing to allow the *Exodus* to sail for Palestine: "Could it be that the *Exodus* was driven by mystic forces?" (188). As he ponders a response to Ari Ben Canaan's final threat of mass suicide on board the ship, Bradshaw leafs through the Book of Exodus in the Bible, recalling Pharaoh and the plagues of Egypt. With Moses's plea "Let my people go" echoing through his head, he issues the order to free the ship.

For the Jews in the novel, the Biblical overtones are not simply metaphorical; they are quite real. The settlements being established in Palestine are founded on over two thousand years of Jewish history; the names that the people and places take are old Hebrew names from the Bible. In fact, the revival of Hebrew is perhaps the most significant element in the Biblical theme of *Exodus*. Dead for almost two thousand

years, the language reemerges with the immigration of the early twentieth century. Men like Akiva and Barak embrace the ancient tongue;
and by the time the new nation is born, it has its own language. Even
Kitty recognizes the power of this history and language as she watches
young Palmach soldiers enjoying a rare holiday on Mount Tabor: "These
were the ancient Hebrews. These were the forces of Dan and Reuben
and Judah and Ephraim!" (357)

The Biblical theme is further underscored by the placement of key
scenes in conjunction with holy days. The *Exodus* sails on the second day
of Chanukah, the Festival of Lights commemorating Judah Maccabee's
victory over the Greeks. And the novel ends on the eve of Passover, at
the seder recalling the liberation of the Jews from Egypt. The rituals
associated with such celebrations lend Biblical significance to the present
action of the book.

The theme of the quest for a Jewish homeland in this novel is closely
related to a second theme: the indomitability of the human spirit. The
historical sections of *Exodus* leave no doubt about the age-old persecution
of the Jews. From the original enslavement by the Egyptians in Biblical
times, Jews have endured further slavery, brutality, and even genocide.
The novel takes place in the first few years following World War II, in
which war six million Jews were murdered by the Nazis. Despite this
heritage of persecution, Palestinian Jews and Holocaust survivors alike
heed the call to re-create their nation. The inhabitants of the Cyprus
camps are malnourished and ill, and yet they respond like freshly trained
soldiers to the Zionist call. Now Ari and his people are fighting the might
of the British Empire in its resolve to limit Jewish immigration to Palestine, as well as a heavily armed Arab army determined to drive the
Jews into the sea. Throughout this fight, the Jews have struggled against
an unforgiving land, planting forests where there has been nothing but
sand and rock for thousands of years, draining swamps and planting
vineyards, carving out self-sufficient settlements in the midst of enemy
territory. Without the spirit forged by generations of hardships, Uris
seems to be saying, the land of Israel might never have come into existence.

Minor themes reinforce the more sweeping themes of *Exodus*. Closely
linked to the success of the Jewish settlers in Palestine is their sense of
retribution. The rift between brothers Akiva and Barak occurs when Akiva embraces retaliation against British treachery. The Maccabees are
born of retribution, their motto the Biblical "eye for an eye." Their activities, such as blowing up the King David Hotel, call the world's at-

tention to Palestine. Dov Landau is a perfect candidate for the Maccabees, for his experience in the Warsaw ghetto and Auschwitz has filled him with an all-consuming desire for retribution. It is difficult for readers not to feel sympathy for the daring strikes of the Maccabees. Retribution for thousands of years of persecution fuels the zeal for building a homeland.

Retribution is thus seen as a form of justice, another theme found in *Exodus*. All of the Jewish characters, activists and negotiators alike, cry out for justice. The injustices heaped upon the Jews for thousands of years are recounted in the novel, but perhaps none are so cutting as those perpetrated by the British, who in 1917 signed the Balfour Declaration pledging a Jewish homeland in Palestine. Responsible for governing Palestine between the wars, the British are portrayed by Uris as consistently apathetic about curbing Arab violence. The ultimate betrayal comes with the White Paper of 1939. Designed to garner Arab support, the White Paper severely restricted Jewish immigration to Palestine at precisely the point when Europe had become dangerous to Jews. Such injustices cry out for righting, and Ari Ben Canaan sees the *Exodus* incident as offering the British the opportunity to finally do justice to the Jews of Palestine and the world.

While a sense of justice rules political relations in *Exodus*, humans crave reconciliation as well, particularly in personal relationships. Karen Hansen Clement personifies reconciliation, refusing to become embittered by her devastating experiences. She slowly draws Dov Landau out of despair, offering him his own avenue of reconciliation. Kitty Fremont is able to do the same for Jordana Ben Canaan, eventually convincing Jordana that she is worthy of the Jewish woman's respect. Interestingly, it is only after Kitty reconciles herself to life in Israel that she is able to achieve this reconciliation with Jordana, who symbolizes Israeli womanhood.

The truce between the brothers Barak and Akiva is achieved only after Akiva's death. Barak is adamant about his brother's exile from the family until Akiva is sentenced to death by the British. Finally breaking his fifteen-year silence, Barak pleads with Ari, "Do not let my brother Akiva hang at the end of a British rope" (421). For his part, killed in the attempted escape, Akiva finally finds "a peace that had avoided him in life" (431).

Fittingly, *Exodus* ends on a note of reconciliation. After hearing of Karen's death, Ari at last acknowledges his need for Kitty, and she her understanding of his total dedication to his homeland. As the pair enter the Ben Canaan home for the Passover seder, General Sutherland makes the most meaningful acknowledgment of his heritage when he requests, as the oldest male Jew in the group, to preside over the ceremony. His wish is granted, Dov Landau begins to read the scripture, and the reconciliation is complete. Through Karen's death, the promise of the *Exodus* has been fulfilled.

A MARXIST READING OF *EXODUS*

Marxist criticism, like psychoanalytic criticism, has its roots not in literature but in the social sciences. While Freud used a psychological model to explain human behavior, Karl Marx used an economic one. And while Freud sought to explore the individual psyche, Marx sought to explore relationships between groups. With the publication of *The Communist Manifesto* in 1848 (coauthored with Freidrich Engels) and *Das Kapital* in 1867, Karl Marx established the theory that by controlling production of goods, the *bourgeoisie*, or capitalists, effectively keep the *proletariat*, or working classes, in bondage. The economic power of the capitalists results in their determining the political and social values of the culture, its *ideology*. Through a combination of economic and political means, the capitalists control the proletariat.

Marx's theories differ from Freud's and others' in its focus on the material world. Rather than looking into the mind, as would a psychologist; the spiritual realm, as would a theologian; or the world of ideas, as would a philosopher, the Marxist looks at the actual workings of a culture in order to determine reality. The social and economic relations between people and groups are what determine identity, according to Marxist thinking. Because of this distinction, the goal of Marxism is revolution. Discontent among the working classes is a result of *alienation of labor*, meaning that workers in a capitalist society do not enjoy the fruits of their labor. Indeed, since the Industrial Revolution, workers frequently never even see the fruits of their labor. Assembly lines mean not only that workers cannot afford to own, for example, the luxury automobiles they work on, but also that they only see the piece of the product on which they are working—a windshield, perhaps. If this situation is to change, according to Marxism, workers must unite to overthrow the capitalists. Production will then be turned over to the state, which will distribute work and wealth equitably.

If such revolution is to be effective, the ideology of the capitalists must be exposed for the lie that it is. And since literature forms a part of that ideology by perpetuating its ideas, Marxists view the work of the critic as more than an academic exercise. The goal of Marxist criticism is to reveal the ideology that shapes the literature. Thus the cultural context in which literature is produced is as important as style, plot, or themes. Marxists critics such as Terry Eagleton and Ira Schor insist that literature cannot be separated from politics precisely because literature is so intricately woven into the reigning ideology of the culture.

A Marxist reading of *Exodus* is interesting because Leon Uris was an adamant opponent of the only world power based on Marxist philosophy at the time: the Soviet Union. He was also an avid supporter of American capitalist values. At the same time, the Israel that Uris portrays in his novel is in many ways a Marxist utopia, and the countries that threaten to deprive the Jews of their homeland act primarily out of economic opportunism.

While the Jews interned in the Cyprus detention camps are not technically victims of capitalism, their situation is analogous to the proletariat. Their fate is in the hands of the Allies, specifically the British, whose track record in Palestine is abysmal. Providing historical background on the settling of Palestine, Uris writes that the British readily accepted Palestinian Jewish volunteer units in World War I. As will be seen later in *Redemption*, colonial forces such as these suffered heavy casualties in battles like Gallipoli, in part because the imperialist British leaders viewed these forces as expendable. The British promise of a Jewish homeland, made after World War I, was part of the Palestinian Mandate ensuring British presence in this strategic section of the world. As Uris makes clear in this and other books, the British were not in Palestine to protect Jewish settlers but rather to protect their own economic and political interests. The balance of power following World War I gave the Middle East strategic value; the Suez Canal, controlled by Egypt, was crucial to British trade interests. A military presence in Palestine allowed the British to monitor the canal closely.

With World War II on the horizon, the British began seeking allies to protect their interests in the Middle East. Throughout the 1930s German Jews responded to the Nazi threat by pouring into Palestine. Plagued by three years of Arab attacks on the growing settlements, the British issued a White Paper in 1939 blaming the riots on Jewish immigration and prohibiting any further immigration to Palestine. Calling this "the final British betrayal" (290), Uris attributes the action to politics and economics. The British were confident of Jewish support in the impending war, but

Arab support was less certain; and to maintain their economic interests in the region, the British needed the support of Arab nations. In this way the capitalist interests of the British contributed to the deaths of hundreds of thousands of Jews who might otherwise have found refuge in Palestine.

The treachery of the capitalist British continues in the present action of the book. The value of Arab oil has become quite clear to nations beginning to rebuild after World War II. With tensions mounting in Palestine as the United Nations debates partition, the British clamp down on Palestinian Jews. Curfews, roadblocks, searches, and other indignities are heaped upon Jews—and not on Arabs—as the British seek to placate the Arab oil barons. The most devastating action taken by the British is the blockade that prevents thousands of Jews currently languishing in detention camps from finding a home. The story of the real *Exodus* illustrates the tragedy of this situation, as over four thousand refugees, denied entry to Palestine, were returned to detention camps in, of all places, Germany.

If the British represent capitalist interests in Palestine, then the Jewish settlers, like their comrades in the detention camps, are the proletariat. In fact, the formation of the retaliatory force the Maccabees can be seen as a metaphor for the revolution of the proletariat. Originally content to fight within the regulations of the Haganah, Akiva Ben Canaan breaks off to form the Maccabees only when the British, in response to Arab pressure, blockade the Palestinian coast in the early 1930s. Akiva recognizes, as his brother Barak does not, that the British are acting in their own self-interest and that they will abandon the Jews if those interests are threatened. Barak, in arguing that the Jews have done well under British rule, is succumbing to British ideology, believing that the benevolence of the British is motivated by a sense of justice rather than by an economic imperative. And even though he will not fight alongside Akiva, Barak does wonder if his brother is right: "How much pain and degradation and betrayal and suffering must a man take before fighting back?" (271).

The Jews in Palestine have developed true proletarian communities. Although there is no central government to determine the distribution of work and wealth, the kibbutzim operate according to Marxist principles. Members are assigned duties in the kibbutz based on their talents and the needs of the community. The land that has been reclaimed from the desert is planted to feed not a wealthy absentee owner but the farmers who grow the crops. The ideology of the kibbutz reflects not a governing political power but the people themselves. And when the Jews fight the Arabs, they fight for their own land and not to preserve the holdings of a wealthy landowner. In this sense, the Jews are living a Marxist dream. When that dream is threatened, the threat comes either from the capitalist British or the precapitalist, feudal Arab peasants fighting to preserve the land and wealth of a few powerful leaders.

Leon Uris may not have set out to write a Marxist tale in *Exodus*, but both the history he reflects and the story he tells extol the virtues of Marxist philosophy. For while the characters in the novel may attribute their victories over adversity to the guiding hand of their ancient God, it is equally true that their own social and economic choices have formed the foundation on which their homeland is built.

6

Mila 18
(1961)

Mila 18 is the story of the establishment, uprising, and liquidation of the Warsaw ghetto during World War II. When the Germans invaded Poland, they established Jewish ghettos in many cities, herding thousands of Jews into small, crowded areas without adequate sanitation or food, and then walled off those areas. Those inhabitants who survived malnutrition, disease, and the brutality of the Nazis waited for their eventual deportation to concentration camps.

PLOT DEVELOPMENT

The story of *Mila 18* is told from the point of view of several major characters: Gabriela Rak, the beautiful Polish Christian who chooses her country over the safety of the United States; Chris de Monti, the Italian-American journalist who tries unsuccessfully to maintain neutrality; Andrei Androfski, the Polish Jew who becomes a military hero but is shunned once the Germans take over; and several others. The story is also forwarded through the journals of Alexander Brandel, a philosopher and Zionist (a Jewish political activist intent on establishing a homeland in Palestine). The characters and journals reflect real people and events during the days of the Warsaw ghetto.

The book opens in the last days of relative peace before the start of

World War II, as the government and people of Poland desperately ignore the German threat. The military is filled with blind patriotic pride, unaware that its nineteenth-century methods will ensure defeat within moments of a German invasion. Citizens of Warsaw try to deny the inevitable—even intelligent Jews like Paul Bronski, director of the Warsaw Medical College, are convinced that their assimilation into Polish society will protect them. What they do not realize is that beneath the comfortable surface, Poland seethes with anti-Semitism, and it will take very little to inflame the Polish people into violent reactions against Jews. This attitude is personified by Dr. Franz Koenig, a German Pole who resents the Jewish Bronski's having been promoted over him at the Medical College. He, like many ethnic Germans, sees the invasion of Poland as liberation.

Interspersed throughout the early chapters of the book are historical accounts of Jewish settlements in Eastern Europe, the persecution of Jews, and the rise of Zionism. The adventure story focuses primarily on Andrei Androfski, a Polish Jew who desperately seeks acceptance from his country. Andrei makes a name for himself in the Polish Cavalry; but because he can never fully escape the barbs of anti-Semitism, he embraces Zionism.

As in Uris's other work, the adventure story is complemented by love stories. In this novel there are two: Andrei loves Gabriela Rak, a Polish Catholic working at the American Embassy. Gabriela remains in Warsaw when the German occupying force calls a truce for the evacuation of the embassy. The second affair, between Andrei's sister Deborah and journalist Chris de Monti, is complicated by Deborah's marriage to the conservative Paul Bronski. As Jews, both Deborah and Andrei are marked for eventual extermination. Their lovers, however, are Gentiles free to move among the Nazis. This freedom allows Gabriela and Chris to help the Jews in the ghetto, but it also places the two of them in danger.

The historical account of the German occupation of Poland is provided through the stories of the principal characters: Paul's position as head of the Medical College is taken from him and given to Koenig, who is also given Paul and Deborah's home when the Jews are herded into the ghetto. The terrorism of anti-Semitic gangs is fueled by Nazi propaganda that convinces Poles that the Nazis are actually saving them from the Jews. What happens to these characters mirrors what actually happened to the Jews in many Eastern European countries as the Nazis solidified their power.

The history of Jewish response to the occupation is also told through the experiences of the characters. Once Warsaw surrenders, all Jews live in fear, but their reactions vary. Andrei represents those Jews who believed that they could serve their country best by joining the free Polish forces in Russia. But Andrei learns quickly that his heroism against the Nazis means little now that the underlying anti-Semitism of the armed forces has surfaced. Paul, appropriately, represents those Jews who mistakenly believed that the key to survival lay in cooperating with the Nazis. His desire to hide his Jewishness behind an intellectual mask leads him to join the Jewish Civil Authority, an actual organization run by the Germans to keep order in the ghettos.

On the other hand, Alex Brandel refuses to serve on the Civil Authority and instead joins other Zionists who set up a front for Underground ghetto activity, the Orphans and Self-Help Society. While the diverse groups within the Society differ in philosophy, they all share a belief in resistance to German authority. The third approach to dealing with the occupation is represented by Rabbi Solomon, who, like many religious Jews during the Holocaust, looks to the Bible, concluding that suffering in silence is the lot of the Jew. Non-Jewish organizations, including the Polish Home Army and the Catholic Church, remain silent.

In order to provide a context in which to understand events in Warsaw, Uris tells of the rise of fascism and Nazism through the story of Chris de Monti, who rejects his Italian nobleman father when his father embraces fascism. Readers learn of the Italian invasion of Ethiopia and the Spanish Civil War through Chris's story. Chris's disgust with the fascists leads him to release secret reports to the free world proving the German and Italian involvement with the Spanish fascists. However, in their desire to avoid war, world leaders do not listen. Thoroughly demoralized, Chris goes to Warsaw, determined to suppress his idealism. Falling in love with Deborah Bronski ends that dream for him.

Readers learn of the establishment of the Warsaw ghetto through the lives of Emanuel Goldman, a double-agent for the Zionists working on the Civil Authority, and Paul Bronski. In many cities in Eastern Europe, the Nazis herded all the Jews into a small, walled-off section of the city to await "liquidation," or deportation to extermination camps. Goldman refuses to issue orders for the Jews to enter the ghetto, and as a result is murdered by the Nazis. His death leaves more power in the hands of Paul Bronski, who still believes in accommodating the Nazis. Andrei, meanwhile, urges armed resistance immediately, a strategy considered suicidal by other Zionists, including Alex Brandel. This disorganization in the face of Nazi terror is an accurate portrayal of what happened in many of the occupied cities: Many Jews, like Paul, refused to the end to believe the rumors of the death camps. Others, like Andrei, wanted to fight, despite being hopelessly outnumbered. And those like Alex believed that their lack of an arsenal made armed combat impossible, especially with no support from the Polish Home Army.

Relocation of Jews into the ghetto cannot be achieved without the assistance of the Gentile population and even some Jews. Polish Gentiles readily accept the Nazi claim that the Jews were their real enemies. While Uris is particularly harsh in his treatment of the Poles, he does have history on his side. As he explains through Karen's story in *Exodus*, countries like Denmark simply refused to collaborate with Nazi persecution of Jews. Not only did everyone in that country wear the yellow Star of David (required of all Jews), but they also refused to betray Jews to the Nazis, and even organized mass escapes. What happened in Poland is seen as all the more unconscionable in light of how some countries resisted the Nazis. But Uris does not reserve his disgust for the Gentile population of Warsaw. He also condemns the cooperation of unscrupulous Jews in the persecution of their own people. Max Kleperman, a notorious underworld figure, sees an opportunity to enrich himself and curry favor with the Nazis by providing the Germans with Jewish prostitutes and slave labor. He tries to maintain a positive image among the Jews by arranging release—for a high price—of family members who have been deported to prison or the camps. His ultimate betrayal of his fellow Jews takes the form of constructing the ghetto wall for the Nazis.

Alex Brandel's journal provides insight into the speculation that actually went on among Jews before the news of the "final solution" filtered its way into the ghettos. Alex reports on rumors of other ghettos and on the eventual deportation of all Jews to the island of Madagascar or to concentration camps. He also speculates about the ultimate German plan for occupied countries and the Jews, allowing readers to feel the uncertainty under which Jews in the ghetto lived. Because Alex's journal accurately chronicles life in the ghetto, emphasizing the heroism of some and the treachery of others, Rabbi Solomon calls it a Holy Book. Although he will not support the Resistance, the rabbi knows that the history of the times must be recorded and vows to protect the journal.

Through Alex's journal Uris provides a glimpse of cultural life in the ghetto: Orchestra, theater, schools, and art flourish despite below-starvation rations, disease, filth, and terror. However, when the United States finally enters the war, American aid supporting these ventures dries up. Unable to count on help from the outside, the Underground militants in the ghetto begin to arm themselves.

Uris informs readers of Nazi atrocities—and of local collaboration—through Chris de Monti's news connections. For example, on a visit to the ghetto, Chris tells Deborah that townspeople cheered during the massacre of thirty-three thousand Jewish men, women, and children outside the Ukranian town of Babi Yar. Nor are Christian religious leaders portrayed as allies in the fight to save the Jews. As Gabriela's attempt to mobilize Catholic leaders to help Jewish children reveals, many such requests were denied by bishops who were either too frightened of the Nazis or too consumed by anti-Semitism themselves to help.

The history of German attempts to liquidate the ghetto and deport its inhabitants is recounted as Paul Bronski, now a shell of a man, accepts Nazi propaganda about work camps and urges residents to volunteer for deportation. The real story of the camps is discovered when the Underground sneaks Andrei and others into Majdanek, where they witness almost twenty thousand gassing deaths in three days. A laborer describes how, after the gassings, "corpses are placed on a table and examined for gold teeth and slit open (and bled through a drainage pipe) to see if any gold or valuables had been swallowed" (355). Although these graphic first-hand reports mobilize resistance in the ghetto, when Chris smuggles the reports to the outside world, the response is apathy. The world does not want to know.

While Andrei's report unites Jewish Resistance forces, most ghetto inhabitants still cling to the hope that nothing worse will happen to them. The Germans lure unsuspecting or desperate Jews to the deportation trains with promises of food, but warnings from the Underground soon stem the tide of volunteers. Tensions come to a head when the German-organized Jewish Militia is ordered to turn over citizens for deportation. Uris describes the Militia as made up of self-loathing Jews who demonstrate the extent of their dehumanization by turning over relatives in order to protect themselves and their immediate families from deportation. After over two years of collaborating with the Nazis, the Civil Authority and the Militia are finally learning that their strategy has proved useless; the "final solution" will be carried out despite, and perhaps aided by, their cooperation.

As the Germans embark on what they have named the "Big Action" in preparation for the final liquidation of the ghetto, Andrei and other militants organize an intricate Underground army to offer all possible resistance. The first real shock to the Germans occurs on January 18, 1943, when Andrei and a few Underground soldiers kill eleven SS men who are rounding up Deborah, Rabbi Solomon, and others for deportation. The rout sends the Nazis into confusion; they have come to believe their propaganda about Jewish cowardice, and they know that the ghetto houses few fighters and fewer weapons. Nazi propagandist Horst von Epp, a rare cynic among Nazis, insists that the leaders seriously consider what they are facing in Warsaw, namely, "that one human in a thousand whose indomitable spirit cannot bow. . . . Watch out for him. . . . We have pushed him to the wall" (423).

As the Germans retreat, considering how to deal with the uprising, the Underground army mobilizes, raising a Star of David flag over the ghetto. A newly discovered bunker under 18 Mila Street becomes the headquarters for this "Jewish State." In a grimly ironic gesture, rooms in the bunker are named after death camps: Belzec, Auschwitz, Majdanek, Treblinka, Sobribor, and Chelmno. German attempts to cajole inhabitants into deportations to "honest labor" camps are foiled by the Joint Jewish Forces, who vow to shoot any volunteers. After two months of inactivity, Franz Koenig tries to bribe the Joint Jewish Forces with promises of safe passage to Switzerland or Sweden for them and their families. When even this bribe fails, the Nazis plan a massive invasion of the ghetto.

Uris invests the final fight with religious and mythical overtones as the militants celebrate Passover before making their last stand. During the seder meal, Rabbi Solomon blesses the fight, admonishing his people to remember their history: "No people upon this earth have fought for their freedom harder than we have. . . . The truest obedience to God is the opposition to tyranny!" (492). Those Jews remaining know that they will die, but Deborah's young son Stephan is smuggled out of the ghetto to tell the story, "to live for ten thousand children killed in Treblinka and a thousand destroyed writers and rabbis and doctors" (482). Even Gabriela recognizes the need for living witnesses, as she confesses to her priest that she is pregnant with Andrei's child, a Jewish child.

As Uris tells it, the final battle for the ghetto is almost anticlimactic, given the heroism that has preceded it. Nevertheless, he provides drama in the Joint Forces' decision to offer Alex Brandel the honor of firing the first shot in the final assault. In a battle that even the Jews thought would last perhaps a week, the Joint Forces hold the ghetto for over a month. With defeat imminent, Chris de Monti is smuggled out, and the youngest fighters, including Wolf Brandel and Rachael Bronski, escape to the Aryan side through the sewers. In his final entry in Alex's diary, Chris vows to return to Warsaw and exhume the diaries and extols the virtues of these fighters who held out against impossible odds for forty-two days.

CHARACTER DEVELOPMENT

Almost all of the characters in *Mila 18* are consumed by passion, and the passions of many of the characters are multiple. If the novel can be said to have a hero, he would be Andrei Androfski. Like Conor Larkin of *Trinity* and *Redemption* and Ari Ben Canaan of *Exodus*, Andrei is a larger-than-life man persecuted by an oppressor. Beneath the public accolades for Andrei's military heroism lies contempt for his Jewish heritage. When the Nazis "liberate" Poland from the Jewish curse, Andrei becomes another dirty Jew in the eyes of his fellow Poles. His militarism in the face of the Nazi onslaught sometimes clouds his judgment, but in the end Andrei is the best hope for a savior that his people have. And like Conor and Ari, Andrei's passion for the deliverance of his people is complicated by his love for a woman who does not belong in his world. Gabriela Rak's religion, ethnicity, and position place her in a world off limits to Andrei after the Nazi occupation. But as in the other novels, the couple's love transcends the differences in religion and culture.

Equally passionate, and equally doomed, is the affair between Chris de Monti and Andrei's sister Deborah. Deborah's marriage to the passionless Dr. Paul Bronski has pushed her into Chris's arms, but her guilt constantly threatens to consume her. Once the Jews are imprisoned in the ghetto, Deborah devotes her life to the care and education of the children, perhaps in part to atone for her adultery. But she and Chris cannot avoid their common destiny any more than Andrei and Gabriela can. When Chris enters the ghetto in an attempt to smuggle Deborah out, her fierce devotion to the children convinces her lover that he must work to tell the world about their plight. As with Andrei and Gabriela, Chris and Deborah's passion for each other fuels their passion to fight the Nazi aggressors.

The passions of other characters are less complex. Alexander Brandel is a passionate Zionist and leader of the ghetto's Underground. His journal of life in the ghetto is hailed by Rabbi Solomon as a sacred text; it will bear witness to the suffering of the Jews long after the inhabitants have died. The journal makes Alex an almost Biblical character. Fittingly, the son born to the Brandels during the occupation is called Moses.

Moses is welcomed into the Jewish faith by another Biblical character, Rabbi Solomon. When Alex first approaches the rabbi, asking him to help the Zionist Underground to defend the Jews, the old man answers, "We defend ourselves by living in the faith which has kept us alive all of the centuries. . . . It will bring us through this hour as it has through all the rest of our crises" (143). Rabbi Solomon remains true to his word when Nazi storm troopers invade his secret scripture class. He submits to personal humiliation but tries desperately to save the sacred texts, the Torah. When the Nazis threaten to shoot his young students one at a time unless the rabbi dances on the Torah, he obeys, but even this desecration does not alter his refusal to join the Resistance fighters. His passionate belief in God's mercy frustrates the more militant members of the ghetto community; but at the end of the novel, recognizing the fighters' bravery and acknowledging their passion, the rabbi blesses the final uprising, comparing this fight to other Biblical battles.

Other Jewish characters in the novel represent various types found in the ghetto: Ervin Rosenblum and Ana Grinspan are silent soldiers who quietly give their lives for the cause, while Wolf Brandel and Rachael Bronski are fierce young warriors determined to defend their people and destined to escape the ghetto and become living witnesses to the Holocaust. Susan Geller, deported to a death camp with a group of young children, becomes a heroic martyr when she saves the children from the horrors to come by feeding them (and herself) poisoned chocolate on the train.

Dr. Paul Bronski represents those Jews who tried to assimilate themselves into mainstream Polish society before the war. Having denied his heritage, Bronski achieves success and lives the life of a typical Pole until the specter of Nazism overtakes Poland. During the occupation and the establishment of the ghetto, he chooses conciliation in hopes of riding out the storm. The contempt for him displayed by Andrei, and later his own wife and son, indicate the author's attitude toward Paul's betrayal of his people.

The rare Jewish sympathizers in Poland are represented by Gabriela Rak and Chris de Monti. Despite their personal involvements, it is clear through Uris's characterizations that their humanity and integrity would always lead them to support their fellow humans in times of crisis. Gabriela's hatred of Nazis is so strong that she risks her life to help the

Jews. Chris's outrage at the atrocities committed by the fascists in Italy and Spain fire his soul, but the apathy of the rest of the world threatens to demoralize him. It is only when he reads an eyewitness account of the death camps that he is reenergized. At the end of the novel, it is Chris who makes the final entries in Alex Brandel's journal, and it is Chris who will retrieve and publish the account of Nazi atrocities and Jewish heroism after the war. And it is Gabriela who will live to give birth to and raise Andrei's child, as a Jew, once the war is over.

The Nazi characters in *Mila 18* also demonstrate how various types of people embraced Adolf Hitler's ideology. Dr. Franz Koenig is a mediocre man who finds in Nazi anti-Semitism an excuse for his insignificant life. When the Nazis replace Paul Bronski with Koenig, the latter becomes a big man, taking over Bronski's home as well as his job. Koenig's slow descent into degradation through the course of the novel illustrates the poisonous quality of Nazism.

Nazi Rudolph Schreiker, the Kommisar of Warsaw, is a passionate Nazi who is intent on destroying the Jews. His compatriots, Hans Frank, the Governor General of Krakow, and Odilo Globocnik, the real Nazi boss in Poland, are equally passionate in their quest to fulfill Hitler's plans. Frank and Schreiker represent the evils of Nazism in uniform. The brutality of their treatment of the Jews is matched only by the stupidity of their military strategies. Other Nazis engage in pathological behavior resulting from their brutality: ritual bathing several times a day, scratching their skin until it bleeds, drinking themselves into oblivion, or wallowing in their own brutality.

Different from the other Nazi characters is Horst von Epp, who resembles the historical character Oskar Schindler in his cynical determination to make the most of the war. In charge of Nazi propaganda, von Epp looks upon most of the Nazis with the contempt of a social better. But knowing where the power is, he plays the game. He thinks he sees a soulmate in Chris de Monti; and for a time, Chris is susceptible to von Epp's subtle bribes. But despite his understanding of the Nazi character, von Epp is unable to give up the good life that the Nazi regime has brought him. He never achieves Schindler's redemption, never acknowledges the essential inhumanity of his work.

The fickleness of circumstance is illustrated in von Epp's Jewish counterpart, Max Kleperman. Like von Epp, Kleperman believes in no religion or ideology; and like von Epp, he seizes the opportunity to make money from the war. But because Kleperman is a Jew, his opportunism eventually costs him his life.

The characters in *Mila 18* are more interesting as historical types than as individuals. Because the primary focus on the novel is the heroic resistance of the Jews in the Warsaw ghetto, it is the quest itself that constitutes the real story. In creating these characters as he has, Leon Uris shifts the reader's attention from the individuals involved to the history of the times.

THEMATIC ISSUES

Virtually the entire civilized world condemns Nazism as one of the greatest evils of history and considers European Jews during the Holocaust as innocent victims. Thus the primary theme of *Mila 18* is a rather simple one: good versus evil. The atrocities committed by the Nazis are presented graphically in this novel, and the individuals who carry out the "final solution" are portrayed as demons. In this sense, the novel has a biblical quality to it: the Jews, God's Chosen People, are subjected to another of the great trials recounted in the Old Testament. The Nazis can be seen as the descendants of the Egyptians who persecuted the ancient Jews. Indeed, Stephan Bronski's recitation during his bar mitzvah intones "that cry of anguish born of the oppressions of many Pharaohs in many ages" (321). But the evils of Nazism run far deeper than those of biblical times; this enemy comes from the depths of Hell. As Horst von Epp says when it becomes clear that the Germans will lose the war, "It will take the great philosophical and psychiatric brains a hundred years to find a standard of morals to explain this behavior" (387).

In biblical times, the Jews relied on the occasional miracle to save them from ruin. According to Uris, the Holocaust saw its share of miracles as well, the Warsaw ghetto Uprising among them. Grossly outnumbered, dangerously malnourished, and pitifully armed, a small band of ragged militant Jews hold off the great Nazi armies for forty-two days (the historical uprising lasted twenty-seven days). Even the pacifist Rabbi Solomon finally recognizes the significance of the armed struggle on the eve of the uprising, comparing this battle to those fought by the Jews of the Old Testament.

That the militants are eventually defeated does not diminish the impact of the book. For while this particular battle between good and evil may have been lost, the hope for a brighter future remains: Rachael Bronski and Wolf Brandel have escaped with others through the city's sewers to continue the fight. Gabriela Rak is pregnant with the child of militant leader Andrei Androfski, pledging to raise the child in the Jewish faith. And Chris de Monti vows to return after the war and retrieve the journals of Alex Brandel so that the world will know what happened in the ghetto. That the historical counterparts of these characters succeeded in eventually defeating the forces of evil and witnessing the atrocities committed by those forces is self-evident; the book is based on extensive historical research. Thus *Mila 18* becomes, as Rabbi Solomon suggests, a sacred text of sorts: Its central theme is the age-old theme of the Bible, with God's Chosen People emerging victorious from yet another trial.

In addition to the grand theme of the novel, other corollary themes emerge as well. The ability of the human heart to transcend the barriers of religion and culture is illustrated in the novel's two great romances. Andrei and Gabriela, Deborah and Chris—both couples fight the prejudices of their times in declaring their love for one another. This is a common theme in Uris's work. Introduced in his second novel, *The Angry Hills* (with American Mike Morrison and Greek Lisa Kyriakides), the theme of star-crossed lovers is also prominent in other novels such as *Exodus* (Israeli Ari Ben Canaan and American Kitty Fremont) and *Trinity* (Catholic Conor Larkin and Protestant Shelley MacLeod). In *Mila 18*, however, romantic love transcends more than simply cultural differences. The young militants Rachael Bronski and Wolf Brandel fall in love while living in the ghetto, demonstrating that even in a Hell on earth, human love can blossom. And the birth of Alex and Sylvia Brandel's son Moses in the ghetto indicates not only that love can blossom but that it can bear fruit as well.

Love may provide a ray of hope in the ghetto, but times of trial also reveal a darker side of human nature. Not all of the Jews in the ghetto stand firm against oppression. One of the novel's themes involves a particularly unsavory detail of the Holocaust, the cooperation of Jews in the oppression of their own people. Underworld figures like Max Kleperman and self-loathing Jews like Paul Bronski represent another truth: that there are those among the victims who will betray their brothers and sisters to the enemy. After watching Paul cater to the Nazis day after day, Deborah Bronski observes, "Each day as you degrade yourself lower and lower until you have ceased to be a human being" (323).

As the human drama plays itself out in the ghetto, the world wallows in ignorance. A recurring theme in *Mila 18* is the apathy of the outside world. The lesson Chris de Monti learned in Spain is repeated when he smuggles out accounts of the Nazi death camps: even first-hand reports of atrocities cannot spur a reluctant world to action. Uris treats this apathy as an evil equivalent to Nazi aggression, as Horst von Epp tells Chris: "I'm no more guilty than you are. . . . You, dear Chris, are all the moralists in the world who have condoned genocide by the conspiracy of silence" (387). As it is in the Bible, in *Mila 18* the guilt is shared by all of humanity—Nazis, Poles, some Jews, and the rest of the silent world.

A FEMINIST READING OF *MILA 18*

As with psychoanalytical and Marxist criticism, feminist criticism did not originate in the literary world but rather in the social sciences. Closer to Marxism than to psychoanalysis, feminist theory focuses on social relationships and openly acknowledges its political underpinnings. While there are several versions of feminist theory (as there are of psychoanalysis and Marxism), perhaps the most common version focuses on the historical oppression of women by men.

According to feminist theory, Western culture (among others) has traditionally been *patriarchal*, or male dominated. Just as Marxist theory posits that the ruling capitalist class creates the ideology of the culture, feminist theory attributes the construction of ideology to dominant males. With males defining values, beliefs, and traditions, the norm is naturally masculine; the female, then, is by definition Other. This concept of woman as Other was popularized by French writer Simone de Beauvoir in the early 1950s. Beauvoir argued that since males determine the criteria for economic, philosophical, religious, and artistic value, females become secondary, almost invisible. If women are to achieve equality, according to Beauvoir, they must redefine themselves according to their own criteria.

In practical terms, the masculine definition of femininity has focused on physical beauty, limited intellectual capacity, and emotional dependency. Women are therefore valued primarily for their physical attributes; the continued popularity of beauty contests such as the Miss America pageant is testimony to this superficial judgment of women's value. The intellectual capabilities of women are questioned in a male-dominated society; feminists would respond that traditional society does not afford women the same opportunity to become educated or to display their intellect that it affords men. Finally, feminists would argue that what appears to be emotional fragility in women is actually the result of women's having been subjugated to men in traditional roles of obedient daughters and subservient wives.

Feminist critics apply these theories to the analysis of literature, focusing either on women writers, women readers, or women characters. As is the goal of Marxist criticism, the goal of feminist criticism is political, namely, to expose existing cultural dominance of the masculine perspective and to replace it with an egalitarian view in which women are judged by their own standards rather than those established by a male-dominated society. In examining the work of women writers, in exploring the different responses of women readers, and in analyzing the portrayal of women characters in literary works, feminist critics such as Elaine Showalter and Jane Tompkins seek to end the devaluation of women in the literary realm.

An examination of *Mila 18* from a feminist perspective reveals some stereotypical portrayals of women characters; but on the whole, strong women who play major roles in the drama predominate.

The two strongest women in this novel are Deborah Bronski and Gabriela Rak. Although the two are independent women with strong personalities, they are nevertheless defined early in the novel strictly in terms of their physical attributes. Deborah is first seen as a "half-naked body . . . bathed in late afternoon shadows," with "long raven hair" that falls around her shoulders "like black silk" (4). Gabriela is described as a "classic Polish beauty with white-blond hair and sparkling eyes, but a smaller, petite version" (33). This qualification of Gabriela's "classic Polish beauty" is particularly interesting, since traditionally small stature is valued in a woman, and Polish women are generally larger than the Western ideal. In contrast, the initial views of Chris de Monti and Andrei Androfski focus on Chris's apartment, which is "solid and leathery and masculine" (3), and on Andrei's uniform, with shining leather and a "short stiletto at his side [that] glinted when the sun caught it" (17). The women occupy desirable bodies, while the men occupy commanding spaces and positions of authority.

This distinction between the descriptions of four of the main characters in the book is understandable, given its publication date of 1961. Uris's descriptions reflect the prevailing male-dominated view of the sexes at the time. What is surprising, given the culture in which the book was composed, is how Uris portrays his women characters after their initial descriptions. Both Deborah and Gabriela emerge as primary characters whose role in the drama of the Warsaw ghetto is of equal importance to that of the men. In addition, among the secondary characters who display bravery and heroism are a number of strong women, among them Susan Geller, Ana Grinspan, and Rachael Bronski.

Deborah Bronski's strength is especially significant when viewed in light of her background. Left motherless at age eleven, Deborah Androfski attributes her mother's death to the incessant demands on women in her culture. Weakened from several miscarriages and the death of another infant, Deborah's mother is still expected to accommodate her husband's sexual needs without any birth control, and to take care of the family. Jewish tradition denies her the outlet of daily prayer and companionship at the synagogue, a male privilege. Deborah's mother teaches her that sex is an evil perpetrated on women for the pleasure of men, a belief that Deborah herself adopts when Paul Bronski, her professor when they become involved, insists that she abort their first child to avoid scandal. Paul wants Deborah for his wife because of how well she will serve his purposes: "She could supply the needs of a man when he desired, and she would be good for his career" (78); he is ignorant of Deborah's guilt over the abortion.

Deborah continues to be plagued by guilt throughout her illicit affair with Chris de Monti; the guilt even follows her into the ghetto. Uris clearly portrays her as a victim first of the male-dominated Jewish culture of her time and then of the masculine arrogance of Paul Bronski. Chris, on the other hand, might be labeled a feminist for his insistence that Deborah not feel guilty about enjoying sex and for his determination that she consider her own needs and desires as well as those of her husband.

Deborah's vulnerability in her personal life does not carry over to her public responsibility once the Jews are interned in the ghetto. She becomes one of the strongest figures in the community, helping to organize a cultural life that lifts morale and offsets the negative impact of her husband's leadership in the Jewish Civil Authority. Deborah also works tirelessly with the orphans in the ghetto, helping them to maintain their spirit in the face of conditions that most adults find intolerable. At the end, knowing that she must die with the children, Deborah bravely sends Chris out of the ghetto to tell the world what has happened there.

Gabriela's role in resisting the Nazis is even more dangerous than Deborah's—and more courageous, since as a Christian with an American background, she could have evacuated Warsaw with the American Embassy staff. Instead, when the ghetto's two primary contacts with the outside are brutally raped, tortured, and murdered by the Nazis, Gabriela takes on their tasks. Gabriela's strength is particularly significant when considered in conjunction with Andrei's desperate attempts to prevent her from doing this dangerous work. Andrei does everything in his power to prevent Gabriela from taking on the job, lying both to her and to the Resistance leaders to shield her from danger. Gabriela, refusing to shirk what she sees as her duty, resists Andrei's attempts to protect her and becomes a successful agent for the Warsaw Ghetto Resistance. And she does this job without sacrificing her femininity: Her final gesture in the novel, as the ghetto is being liquidated, is the announcement that she will continue the Androfski line by giving birth to Andrei's child.

Other women in the ghetto are also portrayed as indispensable to the Resistance effort. One of the most powerful leaders of the Resistance movement, the woman who recruits Gabriela, is Ana Grinspan. With forged Aryan papers, Ana risks her life daily by traveling within Poland and Germany, carrying information and helping key people escape from concentration camps and ghettos. Another ghetto leader is Susan Geller, director of the orphanage. When it becomes inevitable that a group of children will be deported to a death camp, Susan arranges to accompany them. Calming the children by telling them that they are going on a picnic, she deprives the Nazis of their prey by feeding the children poisoned chocolate on the train. Her final act, consuming the last piece of chocolate herself, makes her a martyr to the Holocaust. Similarly strong despite her youth is Deborah Bronski's daughter, Rachael. Disgusted with her father's cooperation with the Nazis, Rachael becomes a Resistance soldier. As the ghetto falls, she leads a group of young Jews through the Warsaw sewers to safety, intent upon carrying on the fight.

All of these women defy stereotypes. Their strength, particularly in the face of male weakness, is an inspiration to others in the ghetto. They fight alongside men as equals, defying their Nazi captors with sometimes superhuman prowess. Although Uris succumbs to stereotypical descriptions of women at times, he has created in the characters of Deborah, Gabriela, Ana, Susan, and Rachael some of the strongest women characters in contemporary popular fiction.

7

Armageddon: A Novel
of Berlin
(1963)

Leon Uris's fascination with World War II continues in *Armageddon*, a novel that begins during the final days of the war and quickly moves to the escalating tensions between the Soviet Union and the Western Allies (France, England, and the United States) over control of Berlin. The story is told as most Uris stories are, through the lives of fictional characters on all sides of the conflict. In the four years following the war, Germans, Americans, and Soviets faced each other in what was to become the first great crisis of the postwar world.

PLOT DEVELOPMENT

Part one of *Armageddon*, "A Meeting at the Elbe," takes readers from the Allied plans to invade Europe to the liberation of Berlin. More than a year before the war is finally over, the Allies are devising strategies for the occupation of Germany. It is interesting for readers to realize that Allied commanders were so certain of victory that military units began designing occupation procedures six months before the D-Day invasion. Captain Sean O'Sullivan of Army intelligence is working for General A. J. Hansen, who is in charge of rebuilding German cities after the war. After being promoted to Major, Sean develops a pilot German city in Rombaden (a fictitious city). A brief history of Rombaden allows Uris to discuss the appeal of Nazism to Germans, who saw this otherwise unsavory movement as a means of achieving economic prosperity. Rombaden's merchants close their eyes to Nazi atrocities, while the ruling class collaborates with the Nazis in return for stolen artworks. Because he has lost two brothers to the Nazis, Sean's task is complicated. His hatred of Nazis extends to all Germans; thus he must struggle to treat Rombaden's inhabitants with justice.

In order to acquaint readers with the horrors of concentration camps located close to residential communities, Uris places the fictional camp Schwabenwald several miles outside Rombaden's city limits. Appalled by the atrocities uncovered when the camp is liberated, Sean orders all citizens to tour it before they are issued ration cards. Such marches actually occurred in many areas surrounding camps, and the fictional citizens of Rombaden react as did their historical counterparts: almost all insist that they never saw the trains, never saw the slave laborers marching into the factories, never heard of the medical experiments, never questioned where their Jewish neighbors were sent. Sean is appalled by the townspeople's denials.

Another German justification for embracing Nazism was that Nazis offered the only alternative to communism. Using this rationale to explain his people's compliance with the Nazis, Ludwig Von Romstein warns Sean, "You Americans will discover that we were not wrong about the Communists. They may be your allies now, but you shall learn hard lessons about them" (84). This warning is ironic, because despite Uris's disdain for German disclaimers, his novel proves Von Romstein's point.

Sean's attitude toward Germans in general is challenged when he encounters the anti-Nazi rebel Ulrich Falkenstein, recently liberated from Schwabenwald. Falkenstein confuses Sean by refusing to denounce his German heritage: "I am a German and my first duty is not to Allied victory but to the redemption of the people" (94).

Uris documents the activity in the occupied city in order to paint a clear picture of the immediate aftermath of the war. Sean tries to find jobs for liberated Schwabenwald prisoners. He must also find ways to take care of the survivors of the camps, especially the sick children, by turning churches into hospitals and working with limited supplies. During their inspection of the city, the Americans discover stolen art masterpieces in the Romstein Castle. This discovery leads Sean to the realization that one of his most trusted men, Dante Arosa, has succumbed to the charms of Marla Von Romstein and is trying to cover up the family's Nazi past.

The forces under Sean's command must also deal with rumormongers, whose false stories of atrocities fuel Allied demands for quick trials and executions of war criminals, ignoring due process. Sean risks his career by refusing to accede to popular demand, thus establishing himself as a just man despite his hatred of the Germans. As Sean begins to appreciate the complexities involved in overseeing an occupation force, so do readers.

Uris uses an epic poem from the area to speculate on the German quest to establish a master race. When Sean reads the poem, he determines that the Germans are at heart a pagan people whose anti-Semitism arises from a resentment of the Jews for having brought the notion of one God to the Western world. He sees Hitler as fashioning himself after the pagan gods, and Nazi ceremonies as resembling ancient pagan rituals.

But *Armageddon* is not a book about the Nazis. They have been defeated. As Ludwig Von Romstein has warned, the new threat is posed by the Soviet Union, and Berlin will be the first battleground. General Hansen, trying to convince Sean to go to Berlin, confirms Von Romstein's assessment. The Russians, he claims, are more dangerous than the Nazis because the communist goal is world domination. He recounts the Russian betrayal of Poland during the war and tells Sean of Stalin's purges, calling the communist leader "the supreme monster of all ages" (163). Hansen obviously speaks for Uris when he claims that the Allies were mistaken in allowing the Russians to enter Berlin first. Hansen, and apparently Uris, sees the United States as the world's only hope to thwart Russian world domination. Part one ends as Sean, acknowledging his responsibility to his country and the world, moves on to Berlin.

Part two, "The Last Days of April," takes readers back to April 1945, as Russian forces enter the city of Berlin. The perspective of Berliners, particularly those sympathetic to the Nazis, is provided through the Falkenstein family. Bruno Falkenstein, estranged brother of the Resistance fighter Ulrich, lives in his basement with his wife and two daughters after Allied bombing has all but destroyed his Berlin home. His daughter Ernestine has questioned Nazi beliefs as early as 1939. Her vain sister Hildegaard is less thoughtful. She shares her father's hatred for the Allies who have, she believes, destroyed their good life. The third Falkenstein child, Gerd, returns from an American prisoner-of-war camp full of Nazi fervor.

As the Falkensteins huddle in their basement, Russian forces enter the city and take it in a bloody street-by-street battle. Russian soldiers and their Mongol allies are portrayed as brutal beasts, beating civilians and raping women, including Herta, Ernestine, and Hildegaard Falkenstein. The population of Berlin lives in terror.

As the Russians take control of Berlin, Uris provides background information on their leaders. Through these biographical notes, readers learn of the Russian Revolution and its aftermath, of Stalin's purges, and of Soviet plans to dominate the world. Heinrich Hirsch, a firm believer in Marxism, is sent to Berlin at the war's end to organize a communist worker's paradise. Igor Karlovy, a patriotic Russian army engineer, shares Hirsch's disgust with the behavior of the occupying army. Igor goes so far as to take a young rape victim into his home to protect her. Both men work under the Russian political leader in Berlin, Commissar V. V. Azov. Azov's task is to harass the Western Allies in Berlin into withdrawal from the city, paving the way for a communist takeover.

With the stage set for conflict, Part three, "The Linden Trees Will Never Bloom Again," opens as the Allies plan to move into Russian-occupied Berlin. Just as General Hansen has predicted, the Russians use bureaucratic delays, harassment of troops, diplomatic ruses, and outright roadblocks to keep the Americans from entering the city. Once the Americans have established their headquarters, continued harassment by the Russians frustrates the Western Allies' efforts to move forward on rehabilitating the city.

Against the backdrop of political intrigue, the Falkenstein family's emergence from the cellars of Berlin offers readers the opportunity to see how Berliners deal with the hardships of life during the occupation. Ernestine is tormented by the stories she hears from the Nuremberg war-crimes trials. Hilde concentrates on survival, becoming a call girl in order to acquire food and some of the finer things that she remembers from life before the German defeat.

As the Kommandatura (the Allied commission charged with rebuilding Berlin) debates, intrigue mounts. Uris characterizes the Soviets as interested only in increasing their stronghold. He also subtly criticizes the Allies, particularly the United States, for allowing their belief in German self-determination to prevent them from putting a stop to Soviet chicanery. Unable to appreciate the extent of German demoralization, Sean O'Sullivan insists to Ulrich Falkenstein that Germans must embrace self-determination.

Sean is developing respect for the German people, however, as he witnesses a Soviet-inspired referendum designed to consolidate power. Falkenstein and Hanna Kirchner, a fellow German freedom fighter, lead a massive demonstration against the Soviets, thwarting their plans to merge all parties into what they call an anti-Fascist front. Sean carries this newfound respect to a war reparations conference in Copenhagen. The conference provides Uris with a vehicle for exploring the international implications of the emerging Berlin crisis. The Russians are revealed to be liars, even to their own representatives. They are also forced to appreciate the American commitment to rebuild Europe. Nonetheless, General Hansen warns his staff that the American people are war weary and that it will be up to the military to shake Americans out of their apathy toward Europe.

As elections in Berlin approach, the Soviets step up their campaign of coercion and terror, with little resistance from the Allies. Despite a final desperate act of shutting off electricity in the Western sectors in hopes of curbing the votes there, the free parties win by an overwhelming majority.

Uris may portray communists as despicable, but he does not underrepresent their cleverness. The elections lost, the Soviets turn to another tactic, reopening the university in the Eastern sector as a Marxist institution. Regardless, a majority of students join a Democratic Students Club, forcing the Soviets to resort to kidnapping and torture in order to discredit the club. These tactics constitute the final blow for Heinrich Hirsch, who defects and publicizes the truth about the "confessions" of the student organizers. Throughout this section of the book, Uris demonstrates how power and influence bounce back and forth between the Allies and the Soviets, much like a high-stakes international tennis match. Whenever readers become convinced that the Allies have finally won the day, the Soviets rally.

The coming of winter 1946 adds another dimension to the crisis, as unusually brutal weather takes its toll on a population already decimated by war. Refugees from Eastern Europe pour into a city unable to feed or shelter its own people. The communists take full advantage of the Berliners' desperation, increasing their harassment and terror. A full-fledged confrontation seems imminent as American military families settle in and around Berlin, establishing a visible commitment to a free Germany. For their part, the Soviets seem intent on maintaining control of their zone as a buffer against future aggression from the West.

As a conference of Allied and Soviet foreign ministers nears, the United States lays down a challenge in the form of the Truman Doctrine, stating that any attempts by the Soviet Union to expand communism in Europe will be met with force. Furious, the Soviet delegation storms out, leaving the remaining Allies to declare that Germany should be united as a republic. The line has been drawn, and plans for a Soviet blockade of Berlin begin.

At this point Uris uses a fictitious column by journalist Nelson Good-fellow Bradbury to expand upon the Soviet threat. The column, titled "A Roll Call of the Dead," chronicles Soviet expansion in Eastern Europe and labels Berlin as the pivotal point in the fight to keep Western Europe free. Clearly speaking for the author, Bradbury declares that if Berlin falls, Western Europe will fall prey to communism. The column is used in part to provide a context in which to understand the actions of American leaders in the last days before the blockade. Wavering between support of Berlin and apathy, the United States weighs it options. Finally, when Congress passes the Marshall Plan for European reconstruction, the Allies introduce new currency into Berlin to offset a Soviet plot. The Russians respond by blockading Berlin.

Part four, "The Last of the Gooney Birds," chronicles the Berlin airlift. With the U.S. government apparently still refusing to appreciate the severity of the situation, General Hansen travels to Washington to brief the National Security Council and the Joint Chiefs of Staff. Calling Berlin "our Armageddon" (460), Hansen convinces the president to lend full support to the airlift.

Uris's love for the military is evident in his descriptions of Hansen's reunion with his old pal, retired General "Crusty" Stonebreaker, famous for his work in running "the Hump" airlift in China during the war. Although not in the best of health, Stonebreaker agrees to resume active duty and oversee the Berlin airlift. He in turn convinces his former subordinate Clint Loveless to assist him. The scenes in which Stonebreaker and Loveless talk in New York reveal Uris's disdain for much of modern American materialism. Loveless is using his talents now in the business world, making money rather than helping his country keep the world free. There is no doubt in readers' minds that Loveless will eventually follow Stonebreaker to Berlin. The third member of this trio who will attempt the impossible is Scott Davidson, an ace flyer whose idiosyncratic leadership style is reminiscent of Max Shapiro from *Battle Cry*.

The Russian siege of Berlin is documented in yet another column by Nelson Bradbury, who is critical not only of the Soviet reign of terror but of Germans themselves, whose "love of freedom begins and ends with a full lunch bucket" (508). In the early days of the siege, the airlift, thought by everyone including the American military to be an impossible task, continues. Old reconditioned planes fly over Soviet-held territory to bring essential supplies to cold, half-starved Berliners. A memorial is built on the site of an airplane crash, uniting Berliners and their American occupiers in their determination to see the crisis through.

In the midst of the crisis, however, ordinary life and love go on. Sean O'Sullivan and Ernestine Falkenstein reluctantly fall in love in Berlin, while outside Berlin a reformed Hilde Falkenstein serves as nanny to Clint and Judy Loveless's children. There she and flyer Scott Davidson fall in love. Berliners become toughened under the blockade and work feverishly to build a new airfield.

But the Soviets will not give up. They offer jobs and food to Western sector Berliners who are willing to relinquish their American ration cards and currency. When this fails, they attack city government offices and instigate riots, forcing the free government to move into the Western sector. Ultimately, East and West Berlin become two cities and contact between citizens of the two sectors is forbidden. Despite every Russian effort, the airlift continues through a brutal winter.

The airlift finally succeeds in breaking the blockade in June 1949, but the price is high. Scott Davidson is killed on a flight during bad weather, and Sean O'Sullivan discovers that Ernestine's father is a war criminal. Crusty Stonebreaker suffers a heart attack. As Uris begins to tie the story up, he returns to the feelings that Sean expressed in the early pages of the novel. Ernestine insists that he must prosecute her father, and the two understand that this means an end to their hopes for a life together. Upon leaving Ernestine, Sean muses that no German and American of his generation can ever make peace. Uris seems to underscore this sentiment as he ends the book with Ernestine taking her own life, and Sean and Hilde, neither knowing who the other is, accidentally bumping into each other at the airport. Fittingly, Sean is headed back to America and civilian life and Hilde to Berlin to rejoin her family.

CHARACTER DEVELOPMENT

As in most of Uris's novels, the characters in *Armageddon* are drawn with broad strokes, the delineation between good and evil quite clear. In this novel, the Americans and the anti-Nazi Germans are almost exclusively moral and idealistic, while the Soviets and the pro-Nazi Germans are equally immoral and unscrupulous.

The protagonist of the story, Sean O'Sullivan, is the quintessential first-generation American, whose parents arrived in San Francisco from Ireland with nothing but "their hands, their backs and their hearts" (5). Sean's parents worked multiple jobs to ensure their three boys an education, and later Sean himself earned money by boxing in order to put his younger brothers through school. Those two brothers are killed in the war. Thus the O'Sullivans represent those American immigrants who not only pulled themselves out of poverty but also felt a responsibility to their adopted country. While Sean understandably hates the Germans who killed his two brothers, his ideals prevent him from taking out vengeance on his enemies.

Sean's superior, Andrew Jackson Hansen, is another representative of American immigrants, this time from Germany. He too lost a brother, in World War I. And he will oversee the occupation of Germany with honor, recognizing that it is up to the American victors to plant the seeds of freedom in German soil after the war.

Other idealistic Americans include Dante Arosa, a young, innocent intelligence officer whose innocence and compassion make him easy prey to the charms of a Nazi-sympathizing German woman. Shenandoah Blessing, the Kentucky sheriff who oversees the military police in Rombaden and Berlin, epitomizes Southern honesty and forthrightness. Clint Loveless, discharged from the army after the war, responds again to the call of duty when he leaves his lucrative New York career to help implement the Berlin airlift. He is recruited by General Hiram "Crusty" Stonebreaker, a retired career military man who cannot enjoy retirement when he knows there is a job to be done.

The military men in this novel are reminiscent of those in Uris's first novel, *Battle Cry*. They represent Americans of all walks of life, and the mix of enlistees and career men illustrates further that America's is truly a people's army. The idealism governing the behavior of these men will impress the German people to such a degree that Berliners eventually flock to the Western sector and embrace the democratic ideals espoused by these soldiers.

In contrast, the Soviets are portrayed generally as ruthless brutes intent only on subjecting the German people to Soviet will. Commissar V. V. Azov, in charge of forming the German People's Liberation Committee after the war, has risen to his present position precisely because of his brutality and lack of conscience. He prides himself on being "a man without an opinion" (254), whose greatest skill in his early career was that "he executed orders without deviation or regard for others" (254).

Azov's only humanizing feature are the ulcers that plague him when he is engaging in the most ruthless behavior, such as the torture of two German students. As with the Nazis who are tormented by various physical ailments in *Mila 18*, Azov has successfully stifled his conscience only to have it emerge in some tangible form.

The other communists are portrayed as nothing more than robots serving the Soviet Union. Marshal Alexei Popov, Captain Ivan Orlov, Rudi Wohlman, Colonel Nikolai Trepovitch—none of these characters is provided with a history or a personal life. They exist for the Party and the Soviet Union, and questions of morality, idealism, or honor never enter their thoughts. Readers cannot get a sense of them as people because they are nothing more than walking mouthpieces for Stalin.

Two members of the Soviet delegation belie this image, however. Unlike most of his comrades, Colonel Igor Karlovy is a patriotic Russian whose hatred of Germany stems from his experiences during the three-year German siege of Leningrad. There he witnessed mass starvation and freezing, and there his child was killed by a Nazi bomb. Like Karlovy, the German-born Heinrich Hirsch acts out of idealism rather than political expedience. Having escaped with his mother to the Soviet Union early in the war, Hirsch is a dedicated Marxist who sees in his adopted country the only hope for the world's working classes. As one would expect, both Karlovy and Hirsch become disillusioned by Soviet tactics in Berlin, Hirsch to the point of defection. Karlovy, to his credit, cannot defect because of his love of country.

Although the most significant characters in *Armageddon* are either Americans or Soviets, German characters also highlight the international drama. Ernestine and Ulrich Falkenstein represent those Germans who were never Nazis at heart. Ulrich's broken body bears witness to his sufferings under the Nazis, and Ernestine's torment over stories of Nazi atrocities underscores her morality. On the other hand, Ernestine's brother, Gerd, and her father, Bruno, refuse to relinquish their glorious past. Gerd believes that Germany can take advantage of the "soft" Americans and rise to great power again. Bruno blames the Allies and fate for the destruction of his way of life, never acknowledging either the evil or the failed strategies of his Fuerher.

Of all the German characters, it is perhaps Hildegaard Falkenstein that represents the country itself. While her politics are never mentioned, Hilde has enjoyed the wealth and prestige that Hitler brought to Germany; and immediately after the war, she thinks of nothing but keeping herself comfortable in desolate Berlin. As with her country, she has reached the depths of degradation by selling her body for material comforts. But, as with her country, she eventually sees the light; and when she determines to reform, she enters the home of Americans Clint and Judy Loveless and in effect becomes a part of their family. She embraces American values and ideals and forges a new life for herself. In Hilde Uris presents his image of the good German, the one who will learn from the American way. However, Hilde will still pay for her country's sins by losing her fiancé, Scott Davidson, to the Berlin airlift.

Characters like these forward the plot in *Armageddon*; but as in *Exodus*, the primary focus of this novel is a place rather than a person. Just as *Exodus* is the story of Israel, *Armageddon* is the story of Berlin. Uris sees Berlin as symbolic of the postwar order, and he considers the struggle over Berlin to be the first significant battle in the Cold War. Thus while the human characters in this novel may not be terribly memorable, the city itself will live long in readers' minds.

THEMATIC ISSUES

While several minor themes are threaded through *Armageddon*, the major theme of the book is quite clearly the emerging Soviet threat and the resulting Cold War. Uris is unequivocal in condemning Soviet treachery, in warning of the Soviet's dedication to world domination, and in criticizing American leaders' willful ignorance regarding this threat.

As he has done at greater length in several other novels, notably in *Exodus, Mila 18,* and *QB VII*, Uris concentrates briefly in *Armageddon* on Nazi atrocities in World War II. But the Holocaust is simply the background of this book; the real enemy is the Soviet Union and communism. The atrocities committed by the communists do not reach the proportions of those committed by the Nazis; the threat posed by communism is not of the same nature as that posed by Nazism. The threat of communism does not involve extermination of a people but domination of all peoples. In some ways, the communists are seen as more despicable than the Nazis, because with the exception of Heinrich Hirsch, the communists in this book have no real ideology; they simply thrive on control of entire populations.

That the leaders do not truly believe in their own propaganda is evident when events are viewed through the eyes of a sympathetic Soviet character. Igor Karlovy embarks on a tour of Germany with other Allied representatives, fully convinced that the Soviet Union was solely responsible for the defeat of Germany and that the Western Allies had preserved the industrial complexes of western Germany for a war of revenge. His faith in his leaders is shaken when he realizes that the Soviets have lied not only to the Western Allies but to their own people as well.

That the Soviets are capable of behavior every bit as brutal as the Nazis is made clear to Heinrich Hirsch when he witnesses the torture of two student leaders. He is consumed with guilt and a sense of betrayal, understanding fully that what he has witnessed is no different from what his father suffered at the hands of the Nazis. The incident represents "the final disillusion of what was once a golden idea. He still believed in Communism, but had come to detest the men who had perverted it beyond recognition" (363).

The Soviet threat pervades the book; the Soviets are seen as dangerous precisely because they have "perverted [communism] beyond recognition." Unlike the Nazis, most of whom are portrayed as believing in their ideology, the Soviets are seen as pure opportunists. Their only interest is power, their only goal world domination. And they will stop at nothing to achieve their ends.

In contrast, the Western Allies, particularly the Americans, are seen as idealistic liberators. Using Igor Karlovy's observations to verify American justice, Uris underscores the importance of such justice. Karlovy is astounded to see the welcome that Sean O'Sullivan receives when he returns to Rombaden. People flock to the square, the city band plays "God Bless America," and children shower the returning commander with flowers. Karlovy muses, "What a strange welcome for a conqueror!" (337). He compares this to the reaction of Warsaw Poles and East Germans to the Russian occupiers, where all he sees is fear and hatred. He is also perplexed by the British acceptance of miners' strikes and French toleration of student demonstrations in the Western sectors. The Western Allies are clearly dedicated to bringing democracy to the German people. Even when the Russian Trepovitch offers to extend Russian control of the university in Berlin to include the other three powers, American Neal Hazzard responds, "The school belongs to the people of Berlin" (365).

But as Uris emphasizes in the heightening tensions surrounding Berlin, American refusal to exceed its authority has a downside. Even the military leaders do not seem to appreciate the Russian threat until it is almost too late. And when General Hansen and Sean O'Sullivan do sense what is happening, their conviction that Germans must determine their own fate prevents them from taking decisive action. Conflict avoidance seems to be the order of the day for the American forces until the situation reaches crisis proportions.

Ulrich Falkenstein is brutal in his assessment of the American refusal to become overly involved in Berlin's internal matters. When Sean O'Sullivan refuses Falkenstein's request to rid the German Democratic Party of a Russian collaborator, Falkenstein explodes, warning that Soviet treachery will overcome American principles. Sean's insistence that Berliners themselves must take the initiative in internal matters clearly reflects the author's position. But it is equally clear that Falkenstein's assessment of American underestimation of the Soviet threat is correct.

The American forces in Germany come to appreciate Soviet treachery long before their political leaders do back in the States. In the latter half of the book, the conflict between leaders in Europe and those at home underscores the near blindness of the American public and its political leadership with regard to the crisis. General Hansen warns a visiting senator, "We can't leave Berlin, free. We will pay for it with ten thousand percent interest" (419). When Hansen flies to Washington to garner support for the airlift, he learns that the State Department "had treated the Berlin blockade as an accomplished Soviet victory and sought ways to get off the hook with the least loss of face" (457). Uris treats the fact that the general eventually prevails as evidence of the superior foresight of the military, the one force that he believes has come to appreciate the situation.

The Berlin crisis continues a theme that Uris first explored in *The Angry Hills*, namely, America's emergence as a world power in the latter half of the twentieth century. In the earlier novel Mike Morrison undergoes a baptism by fire as he learns that the United States can no longer ignore European problems and that this country must become a world leader. Berlin proves that point for Uris. In this novel he treats the Berlin blockade and airlift as the single most significant international event after World War II. He clearly characterizes this crisis as the first volley of the Cold War, and just as clearly sees America as the victor.

Armageddon may well be Uris's most political novel. As such, its minor themes are fewer and less significant than those in his other novels. Nonetheless, readers will encounter familiar themes, most notably the doomed love affair. Sean O'Sullivan, American soldier who lost two brothers to the Germans, falls in love with Ernestine Falkenstein, sister of a German soldier and daughter of a Nazi war criminal. The impossibility of their relationship recalls the affairs between Lisa and Mike in

The Angry Hills, Kitty and Ari in *Exodus*, Andrei and Gaby in *Mila 18*, and foreshadows the love of Conor and Shelley in *Trinity* and *Redemption*. The affair is perhaps most like Conor and Shelley's in that the pair are truly doomed. Other lovers have been able to overcome the forces armed against them, but the gulf between Americans and Germans is simply too great to span. However, even in Sean's and Ernestine's despair there is a ray of hope, for Sean does speak of hope for future generations. And given another of the book's themes, the essential decency of the American people, that hope may well be fulfilled in future generations.

A NEW HISTORICIST READING OF *ARMAGEDDON*

As discussed in Chapter 3, new historicism considers a literary work to be a part of the culture that produced it. Approaching *Armageddon* from a new historicist perspective, one first takes note of the clash of cultural values among the Allied forces, particularly between Soviets and Americans. That clash of cultures characterizes not only American and Soviet attitudes toward occupation but also the attitude of the author, an American, toward both the Soviets and the Germans. Much of the conflict in the novel arises from America's newfound responsibility for the affairs of the rest of the world.

In portraying Sean O'Sullivan's hatred of all Germans, Uris illustrates the attitude of many Americans at the end of the war, holding Germans in general responsible for the deaths of American soldiers, as well as the murder of the Jews. American isolationism prior to the war meant that soldiers as young as Sean had little experience of German culture, and those old enough to remember World War I, such as General Hansen, recalled only the militarism of the Kaiser's army. Thus Germans are characterized in both Hansen's and Sean's minds as they are for many Americans, namely, as rigidly obedient to their leaders, dismissive of individual liberties, and fanatical in their hatred of non-Aryans, particularly Jews. What the American occupying force comes to recognize in the years following the war is that while many Germans did indeed follow Hitler blindly, many others either resisted the Nazis or have come to despise their own complicity in the Third Reich.

Ulrich Falkenstein is the perfect example of the Nazi resister who still maintains his German identity. His refusal to disassociate himself from pro-Nazi Germans continually frustrates Sean, who, like many Americans at the time, equates Nazism with German patriotism. Uris himself seems to struggle with this naive tendency to oversimplify German culture, as he has Sean interpret the Legend of Rombaden epic as a true account of the German propensity to militarism and anti-Semitism. While myths and legends certainly help to articulate the values of a culture, no single legend can be said to define that culture. Sean's mistake is one that was shared by many Americans in the aftermath of the war, especially once news of the death camps emerged. Falkenstein, unlike his American liberator (and unlike many of his fellow Germans), refuses to distance himself from the atrocities, preferring instead to recognize that it was his people who did this—that even though he resisted, he must still bear some of the responsibility.

This notion of responsibility, of collective guilt, was foreign to most Americans in the postwar years. Nowhere in the book, just as nowhere in American public discourse at the time, does the occupying force question how the Allies allowed the Holocaust to occur. Questions of why the United States and other nations refused to take in Jewish refugees, of why the Allies did not bomb the areas surrounding the camps, and of why intelligence reports on the camps were not made public are not addressed by Sean, Hansen, or any of the other military officers who consistently question the complicity of the German population in the genocide. The Americans' need to distance themselves from the horror, to convince themselves that they would not be capable of such atrocities, and most of all to reassure themselves that they could not have done anything about the situation sooner is so powerful that it silences them on the issue of their own responsibility.

It is significant that Sean, the character most inclined to blame all Germans for the war and the Holocaust, is the one who does acknowledge the dangers of falling into the same trap as the Germans and rationalizing behavior that is contrary to accepted standards of humanity and justice. When Proclamation 22, the directive ordering quick trials and executions of suspected Nazis, comes down, Sean risks his career by refusing to abide by it. General Hansen rationalizes the directive by claiming that sometimes a soldier must allow his country to make a mistake, because "we believe in the ultimate right of what we are doing." Sean replies, "What if a few million Germans, or a few hundred thousand, had had the guts to stand up and refuse to commit crimes in the name of their country?" (134). The heart of the German defense at the Nuremberg trials was that the defendants were just following orders. Sean redeems himself as a soldier and a human being by distinguishing between those times when soldiers must obey and when they must deem the orders too reprehensible to follow. His decision is prophetic; in a later war, American soldiers in Viet Nam would use the Nuremberg defense to justify a massacre, and the military court would echo Sean O'Sullivan's denial of that defense.

While Sean, as the conscience of America, acknowledges that his people are as capable as Germans of complicity in crimes against humanity, neither he nor any of the other American characters can apply the same standard to the Soviets. General Hansen's attributing the stronghold of communism to the Russian willingness to accede to the demands of any dictator sounds intriguingly like Sean's initial assessment of the Germans. According to Hansen, "The Russian people . . . have tolerated a police state in one form or another from the origins of their history" (157). By blaming Soviet tyranny on an ethnic tendency toward complacency, Hansen is distancing himself from the Russians in much the same way in which Sean has tried to distance himself from the Germans. Hansen dismisses as a smoke screen the Russian desire to occupy Poland as a buffer against future Western aggression. Considered from the perspective of Americans who had not seen a battle fought on their soil since 1865, Hansen's failure to appreciate the Russian rationale is not surprising. Hansen may or may not be correct; the point is that his assessment reflects the limitations of his perspective.

Uris hints at those limitations when he tells the story of Igor Karlovy and the siege of Leningrad. For almost three years the German army surrounded Leningrad, pounding the city with shells and cutting off supply lines. Those who did not die in the bombing succumbed to starvation, disease, and cold during the long winters. The death toll of a half million, most of them civilians, was devastating. For generations Russia had been subject to attack from the West; Stalin saw his opportunity to create a buffer zone at the end of World War II by consolidating power in Poland and eastern Germany. The Americans in the novel, never having experienced an invasion by a foreign army, cannot accept the Soviet argument.

America's relative inexperience with war is the subject of discussion by many of the non-American characters in the novel. Their French allies, themselves having fought on their own soil, wonder at American restraint in the occupation of Germany. The Americans, for their part, cannot understand the brutality of the Soviets in Berlin: bloody street fighting, indiscriminate rape and beating of civilians, mass destruction of buildings and roads. Many Germans, however, do understand. The victor has earned the right to dominate the vanquished, and the American policy of fairness and mercy is perceived by Germans like Gerd Falkenstein as evidence of weakness. The Soviets make that same mistake, interpreting American resolve as weak and concluding that harassment of American forces and then a blockade of Berlin will force the Americans out of Germany. Of course, neither Gerd nor the Soviets appreciate that in American culture, ruthlessness is not synonymous with power. American authority is derived from consent rather than force, its basis philosophical rather than military. As the eventual American success in breaking the blockade indicates, such adherence to principle should not be equated with weakness.

The Berlin crisis represented the first engagement of the two powers that would dominate the world in the second half of the twentieth century. What Uris reveals in *Armageddon* is not only the strategic importance of Berlin in the new world order but also the cultural significance of that order. What the novel reveals is that the Cold War would require understanding the enemy's cultural values as well as appreciating the enemy's military capacity.

8

Topaz
(1967)

In *Topaz* Uris moves from the Berlin crisis to the Cuban Missile Crisis, presenting an espionage thriller that also involves Soviet infiltration of NATO through French sources. *Topaz* reads like a typical thriller, the story being told by a third-person omniscient narrator. Aside from one flashback to an earlier time and a few letters, the plot moves forward at breakneck speed through straight chronological narrative in a series of locales, including Washington, Paris, New York, and Cuba.

PLOT DEVELOPMENT

After a brief prologue in which presidential adviser Marsh McKittrick presents photographs of missiles in Cuba to the U.S. president, the story opens a year earlier in a deceptively peaceful scene. U.S. intelligence agent Michael Nordstrom's leisurely meal at the Tivoli Gardens in Copenhagen is interrupted by a telephone call. That call, from top Soviet KGB agent Boris Kuznetov, will set in motion a series of events that threatens NATO's very existence. The defection of the Kuznetov family is carried out with breathless precision, but the subsequent interrogation in the United States is frustrating, since Kuznetov is not only fearful but guilt ridden. Survival may have dictated defection, but he loves his country. Kuznetov clearly knows everything about the U.S. intelligence network, but he divulges very little until he suffers a heart attack. Calling for André Devereaux, a French intelligence agent, he whispers the word "Topaz." Thus ends Part I, "ININ."

The second strand of the thriller is introduced in Part II, "The Rico Parra Papers." Action shifts to New York, where André Devereaux is arranging to steal important papers from Parra, the Cuban delegate to the United Nations. In a segment taut with suspense, Uris recounts the successful acquisition of the papers, which reveal Soviet construction in Cuba. Since Americans are unwelcome in Cuba after the unsuccessful Bay of Pigs invasion, André travels to the island to determine the nature of the construction. André reluctantly agrees to withhold information about his visit from his own country because of American concerns about leaks to the Soviets within the French government. He feels much like Kuznetov, loving his country but suspicious of its leaders. This connection between André and Kuznetov underscores the complexity of international relations in the second half of the twentieth century: there are no more isolated incidents; politics have become a global concern.

André's trip to Cuba offers Uris the opportunity to describe conditions after the Castro revolution. Through the disillusioned revolutionary Juanita de Córdoba, readers see how the hope of the revolution was dashed in what Juanita calls "the rape of Cuba" (111). Juanita is not only André's contact in Cuba; she is also his lover, a fact that puts her in danger from the jealous Rico Parra. Despite Parra's public threats to her and André, Juanita sets in motion a scheme to learn about the Soviet construction. Amid much intrigue involving Russian KGB agents and Cuban secret police, Juanita's people discover evidence of offensive missiles. André leaves Cuba with documentation of the missiles only after a tense day of surveillance and near capture by Cuban intelligence forces. It is clear that he will never be able to return to Cuba, or Juanita, again.

As Part III, "Topaz," opens, readers learn that the life of an intelligence agent is fraught with complications. Returning to Washington with the Cuban evidence, André discovers that his wife has left him, weary of the unrelenting demands of espionage work. Although Uris appreciates Nicole's concern for André's health, he portrays her as selfish for wanting a normal life. Nicole's departure, however, serves another purpose for Uris, as she returns to Paris and is visited by Jacques Granville, André's friend since World War II. Granville, now a top aide to French President Pierre LaCroix, clarifies the anti-American sentiment in the French government. Granville wants to help Nicole extract André from the intelligence service out of concern about André's American sympathies.

These sympathies are sorely tested when Kuznetov finally decides to brief the Americans on what he knows of NATO. His lecture shocks André, for it points unequivocally to a Soviet agent in the highest echelons of the French government. The earlier link between André and Kuznetov is strengthened as André realizes the similarity of their positions: To remain loyal to their countries they must betray their governments. Topaz, he learns, is the code name for the organization collecting intelligence on NATO diplomats, and Columbine is the name of the top agent, whose identity Kuznetov does not know. André learns that France plans to order him to infiltrate American industrial and scientific establishments as if the countries were enemies.

Frustrated in his attempts to get Juanita out of Cuba, André turns his attention to the information presented by Kuznetov. The Russian's observations on France provide readers with the author's perspective on shifting European alliances in the decade following World War II, and particularly the role that France played in the second decade after the war. Kuznetov warns that France is NATO's weak link, arguing that President LaCroix still feels keenly France's humiliation under the Nazi occupation. Furthermore, his sense of France's inferiority to the United States leaves him vulnerable to opportunists who exploit his weakness. LaCroix, Kuznetov asserts, is Moscow's pawn. Insisting that his information points to a French pullout of NATO, Kuznetov warns that when LaCroix dies, communists will take over France. This scenario bears out Uris's interpretation of postwar geopolitics found in *Armageddon*. His belief in the Soviet threat is reinforced in this novel. And history, particularly Charles DeGaulle's bitterness over U.S. recognition of the Nazi-puppet Vichy government in France during the war, bears out his claims.

As the Topaz conspiracy comes to light, the Cuban Missile Crisis reaches its climax. The U.S. president prepares a letter that outlines Topaz and that is to be delivered to LaCroix; and as André flies to France to deliver it, American ships move in to blockade Cuba. During the flight, André recalls the Suez Crisis six years earlier, in which French suspicion of the United States and sympathy for the Soviet Union were reinforced. The chances that President LaCroix will believe and act on the U.S. president's letter about Cuba seem slim after this episode.

In France, the search for Columbine has already begun. Marcel Steinberger, the French police inspector assigned to the case, begins surveillance of NATO economist Henri Jarré, suspected of being the agent who is leaking NATO documents to the Soviets. When Columbine becomes aware that Jarré is suspected, he determines that André Devereaux is behind it and plans to undermine André's position. In true thriller fashion, readers finish Part III wondering when Jarré will be caught, what he will reveal, what will happen to André, whether or not Juanita will escape Cuba, and finally, who is the elusive Columbine.

Part IV, "Le Grand Pierre," opens with a flashback to 1940, when André Devereaux, Jacques Granville, and Robert Proust, now chief of Secret Operations in French intelligence, are working with the French Resistance, spiriting Jews out of occupied France. Fleeing to Spain, the three men eventually end up fighting for the Free French Forces under Pierre LaCroix. This interlude provides interesting background on French-American relations, revealing that although the Vichy government under Marshal Pétain collaborated with the Germans, the Americans recognized the Vichy regime, rather than the Free Forces of LaCroix, as the official French government. Critical as he may be of the French in 1962, Uris makes clear that the U.S. position during the war was untenable. This section also provides a background for the close relationship between André Devereaux, Jacques Granville, and Robert Proust. It also presents the initial meeting of André and Nicole, portraying Nicole as a spoiled rich girl who places her own comfort above the needs of her country.

But the central story of this section, indicated by its title, is the rise to power of "Le Grand Pierre" LaCroix, hero of the Free French Forces. Allied refusal to recognize his forces infuriates LaCroix, who sees himself as the legitimate representative of free France. Marshaling his fiercely loyal forces, he builds an intelligence network that keeps him informed of Allied moves and maintains a presence that will not be denied. According to Jacques Granville, "He is France" (306). This monomania, however, is precisely what worries André. His fears are realized when LaCroix accepts a bargain with the Soviet Union to consolidate his own power.

LaCroix uses his intelligence empire to assume the French presidency in a military uprising more than a decade after the war's end. André, now in Washington, still worries about the ease with which unscrupulous subordinates can manipulate "Le Grand Pierre." As his plane lands in France, André hopes that the U.S. president's letter will finally open his leader's eyes.

The climax of *Topaz* takes place in Part V, appropriately titled "Columbine." As President LaCroix is informed of American actions in the Cuban Missile Crisis, he reads the Topaz letter. André cannot prevent Colonel Gabriel Brune, whom he suspects is Columbine, from following LaCroix's orders to go to Washington to investigate the matter further, but André does arrange for Marcel Steinberger to accompany LaCroix's aide.

Colonel Brune proves himself to be untrustworthy when he returns with a report containing "proof" that the Missile Crisis is a plot by the United States and the Soviet Union to consolidate their respective spheres of power. He thinks that Topaz is part of the same plot and that André has been duped by the Americans. To his credit, President La-Croix recognizes Colonel Brune's jealousy of André and withholds judgment on him, but LaCroix's paranoia is evident as he willingly accepts the notion that the great powers are conspiring to leave France out of their dealings. The scene in which LaCroix ponders Brune's news is chilling. Revealing his delusions of grandeur, LaCroix concludes that the great powers are engaging in a game "to thwart France of her true destiny as the leader of Europe" (353).

Against the image of a strong U.S. president who calls the Soviet bluff in Cuba and wins, Pierre LaCroix is seen as a weak but dangerous fool, closing his eyes to the truth so as not to be humiliated on a world stage. And André, still reeling from the news of Juanita's death in Cuba, finally discovers the identity of Columbine. In his final confrontation with his old friend Jacques Granville, he admits that he cannot convince LaCroix of even the existence of Topaz. In a clever piece of comic relief during the suspenseful climatic scene, André tells Jacques that he has contacted an American writer with an enormous and loyal readership "despite some of the critics' complaints over his syntax" (400) to write the entire episode into a book to be titled, appropriately, *Topaz*. At the same time that this humorous self-reference eases the tension, it also causes readers to pause. Is André telling the real truth? Is the book fiction or not?

The closing pages of the book find Mike Nordstrom once again dining in an outdoor cafe, this time in Paris. His meal is again interrupted by a telephone call from a fugitive looking for asylum. And readers are certain that, despite orders to the contrary, Mike will help his friend André escape from a Columbine-controlled France. As Mike speeds off in a taxi to meet André at the Louvre Museum, the driver announces that the Soviets have backed down, and the Cuban Missile Crisis is over.

CHARACTER DEVELOPMENT

In most novels of the thriller genre, or type of literature, characters are secondary to plot. This is true of *Topaz*. Nonetheless, Uris provides some interesting distinctive features in some of his more prominent characters. For example, all of the intelligence agents share, in priority order, similar loyalties: to fellow intelligence officers (regardless of politics), to country, and to wives/families. Thus if loyalty to country conflicts with loyalty to a fellow agent, then the agent will win out. In Boris Kuznetov's words, "They cannot take from us all that is human. Someday you may need a friend" like the fellow Soviet agent who warned Kuznetov to escape (15). Loyalty to country is evident in both Boris Kuznetov and André Devereaux, who continue to be devoted to their respective countries even though they have become disillusioned with their countries' leaders. Finally, wives and families, even in happy marriages, run a not-so-close third to fellow agents and countries. In this novel, only the American agent Mike Nordstrom seems capable of reconciling his many loyalties.

All of these men are dedicated, shrewd, and accomplished, but the nature of their work means that their personal lives suffer. Boris Kuznetov must disrupt his family when he defects to the West. Because of his profession, his wife and daughter are forced to uproot themselves and live in a virtual prison for months after the defection. André Devereaux does not upset his family's daily life to the same extent; but the pressures of his job, coupled with his frequent absences from home, prompt his wife to plead with him continually to leave the intelligence service and embark on a normal life. He tries to explain to his wife why he cannot live like other men: "I can't explain . . . why I was singled out . . . but I can't . . . turn my back" (105). His response to this frustration is to engage in several affairs, most notably the emotionally charged liaison with Cuban counterrevolutionary Juanita de Córdoba. Eventually he loses both his lover and his wife.

Mike Nordstrom, less conflicted, is blessed with a more long-suffering wife who nonetheless is shortchanged in her marriage. Uris reveals the price Liz pays for Mike's profession as they discuss the failing marriage of André and Nicole Devereaux, confirming their own dedication to each other. As they plan a rare evening out, the telephone rings, summoning Mike to Kuznetov. Liz dutifully informs Mike that she'll wait for him, a response she knows by heart. For his part, Mike understands the cost to family. The implication seems to be that it is possible to reconcile an agent's life with family life, if only one tries hard enough.

Unlike the Western agents, the Cuban revolutionaries are characterized as less than flattering. Rico Parra, the least unattractive of the Cubans, is seen at Juanita de Córdoba's home, "boots propped on the rail, . . . munching a large mouthful of banana" (120). The suggestion of a gorilla is strong, even though Parra tries hard to look presentable to the respectable Juanita. Even more repulsive is Munoz, "the personal butcher of Havana and hangman of the Revolution" (127). While he is torturing Rico Parra, "Munoz's eyes rolled insanely and the sweat poured over him"; he is a raging beast (368). In general, the Cubans are portrayed as crude, offensive, and unattractive to women.

Rico Parra's hotel room in New York is strewn with trash and the remnants of meals. He and his delegation smoke foul-smelling cigars, spit on the floor, and spend much of their time ranting about Yankee imperialism. Their feelings toward women involve little more than lust and power plays. This characterization recalls those of Nazis in *Exodus* and *Mila 18* and will be echoed in descriptions of Arabs in *The Haj*. Only rarely are Uris's villains attractive; usually they are transparent, repulsive specimens of human life.

An exception to this characterization is Jacques Granville, André Devereaux's old friend from the Free French Forces who turns out to be André's greatest enemy. Instead of being offensive, Granville is "a charming silver-haired fox" (209) who has worked his way through four wives, most of them young and wealthy. When Nicole Devereaux returns to Paris after leaving André, he seduces her so effectively that she cannot refuse. It is precisely this charm that has allowed him to insinuate himself into the top ranks of the French government, and it is his penchant for the high life that has led him to work for the Soviets. Jacques Granville's charm, however, masks the worst kind of treachery, for he sells out his country, not for philosophical or political beliefs, but for money.

The leader manipulated by Granville, Pierre LaCroix, is a thinly veiled fictionalization of General Charles DeGaulle, the leader of the Free French Forces in World War II and president of France in the 1960s. LaCroix's resemblance to DeGaulle begins with his appearance and mannerisms: LaCroix, like DeGaulle, is "a giant who hovered over his countrymen," acknowledging them with "a papal-like wave of the hand" when he addresses them at the Albert Hall in London (312). And the frequent observations by his men that LaCroix is France echoes DeGaulle's familiar pronouncement, "I am France." LaCroix's strength, ego, shrewdness, and susceptibility to manipulation all reflect the characteristics of the historic French hero.

In contrast to LaCroix, the U.S. president conducts his business with quiet confidence. Never named in the novel, this president is nonetheless clearly John F. Kennedy. At one point he is seen in a rocking chair, something always associated with Kennedy. He is also described as young and vigorous, as was Kennedy. By refusing to either identify him directly as Kennedy or to give him a fictitious name, Uris surrounds his U.S. president with an aura of mystery, adding to his appeal.

Behind the scenes of the international intrigue of *Topaz* are the female characters. It is common in this genre to see females in stereotypical roles, and Uris has presented them in this way before, most notably in his first novel, *Battle Cry*. Here the stereotypical roles of the women characters seem to serve a similar purpose. In the battles of World War II there simply was no place for women. In Cold War espionage, another type of battle, women rarely played a major role either. The exception, of course, is Juanita de Córdoba, the Cuban aristocrat turned revolutionary turned counterrevolutionary. Physically, Juanita is described as "a striking woman" with "a look of total Latin femininity" (133). But she is also portrayed as strong—stronger at times than some of the men who fight with her. Responsible for an entire unit of counterrevolutionaries, she plays a dangerous game by remaining outwardly supportive of Castro. When it becomes clear that André may not escape Cuba with the evidence of the Soviet missiles, she offers herself to the repulsive Rico Parra in order to ensure her lover's safety. And when Munoz threatens her with torture, she does not shrink. Ultimately, she gives her life for the cause of freedom. In her strength, Juanita is reminiscent of Lisa Kyriakides of *The Angry Hills* and Deborah Bronski and Gabriela Rak of *Mila 18*. All of these women are both sensuous and strong.

André's wife, Nicole, is not treated so kindly. Her desire to see André live a healthy, normal life is portrayed as selfish. The most critical assessment of her behavior in the book is made by another woman, André's secretary, Brigitte Camus. When André speculates that Nicole's complaints might be justified, Brigitte replies, "No. . . . She has to be here, to stand alongside you no matter what discomfort it causes her" (201). Only when Nicole too realizes her duty is she presented as entirely sympathetic. As the drama plays itself out, she and André come together to comfort their daughter Michele, whose activist fiancé has been abducted by the French police. Nicole confesses to Michele that unlike her daughter, she has been less than a woman: "How many women make love to a man because of the joy it gives him? Yet only through that joy can a woman really know what it is to be a woman. I've never known, Michele, because to be a woman is to give" (365–366).

Espionage in the 1960s, like war in the 1940s, was very much a man's game. Thus it is not surprising that the female characters in *Topaz* are portrayed as they are. Nor is it surprising that enemies are drawn as thoroughly despicable. In the characterizations in this novel, Uris is true not only to the genre but to the times as well.

THEMATIC ISSUES

As in *Armageddon*, *Topaz* focuses on political and social themes engendered by the Cold War atmosphere of the 1950s and 1960s. The struggle between good and evil is characterized by the battle for world influence between democracy, represented by the United States, and communism, represented by the Soviet Union and Cuba. The highly charged political atmosphere complicates the lives of the characters by fostering divided loyalties and doomed love affairs, two other themes of the novel.

That democracy is a force for good and communism for evil is evident early in the book. While Mike Nordstrom, U.S. intelligence agent, is able to move about Copenhagen freely, enjoying his meal at the Tivoli Gardens restaurant, Boris Kuznetov is hovering in a telephone booth in fear of his life. It is significant that readers never hear of the crime that forces Kuznetov to defect; even he does not know what it is. In a totalitarian state, a valued agent like Kuznetov can become dispensable on the whim of one of his superiors. When this happens, his own daughter can be coerced into spying on him.

Not only is the Soviet Union dangerous, but dull as well. When American agents first see Kuznetov, they notice his "uneven haircut" and "sloppily worn" suit (12). His wife is "drab and dumpy," and their daughter has a "fine figure, but it ended right there. Severe hairdo, no make-up, flat shoes." The female agents guarding them "stuck out like a pair of sore thumbs among the lovely Danish creatures around them" (19). After living in the United States for less than a year, Kuznetov's daughter pleads to be allowed to obliterate her Russian past and become an American: "Oh, Papa, . . . I've almost died from wanting it" (50).

The communist revolution in Cuba has turned that once-lovely island into an equally dismal place: Casinos, restaurants, and hotels have been taken over by the government, colorful costumes have given way to olive-green uniforms, and commerce has come to a near standstill. The stadium and the hotels have been transformed into political prisons, and the streets are "patrolled by angry, bearded, bereted revolutionaries" (125).

Both Soviet and Cuban life pale in comparison to American life, where it is possible to give a Soviet dictator a new identity, a new appearance, and a new life. The contrast between communism and capitalism is nowhere more apparent than in the scene in which Mike Nordstrom highlights for Kuznetov just what the Americans can do for him if he cooperates. The Russian will be set up in a lucrative motel business, his daughter will be educated at the best schools, and his entire family will live in peace and prosperity.

The tension between capitalism and communism hovers over the action of the novel. But between the great powers struggling for position are lesser players who want to align themselves with those powers. Like the Irish Protestants in *Trinity* and *Redemption*, the Jewish Civil Authorities in *Mila 18*, and the Greek collaborators in *The Angry Hills*, the French and the Cubans try desperately to ride Soviet coattails to greatness. In each case, the would-be-greats bluster about their own power, but it is clear that each is in thrall to the Soviet Union. Munoz taunts the Soviet Resident in Cuba after the Missile Crisis by telling him, "We run Cuba and we warn you to start showing some spine" (371), but Cuba remains entirely dependent on the Soviet Union, both economically and militarily. And LaCroix, when warned about being manipulated by the Soviet Union, pronounces, "LaCroix is not used! . . . LaCroix uses!" (326), all the while behaving as a puppet whose strings are being pulled by the Kremlin.

Among the agents working for these countries, another theme emerges, namely, divided loyalties. Espionage work, by its very nature, places agents in constant conflict: Their loyalties to fellow agents, to country, and to family rarely complement one another. As seen above in the discussion of characters, the agents in *Topaz* struggle with divided loyalties; Mike Nordstrom is the only one capable of balancing his commitments. And even Mike, in the end, chooses to help André in defiance of direct orders from his country. But while loyalty to a fellow agent can supersede loyalty to country, there is no question in this novel, nor in Uris's other novels, that in times of trouble the needs of one's nation supersede those of one's family. Uris's heroes, from Danny Forrester in *Battle Cry* to Sean O'Sullivan in *Armageddon* to Conor Larkin in *Trinity* and *Redemption*, willingly sacrifice the happiness of their families, and at times sacrifice their own lives, for their countries.

The sacrifice demanded of these heroes does not prevent them from falling in love, however. In this novel, as in most of his other works, Uris explores the theme of impossible love. André, like Andrei Androfksi before him and Conor Larkin after him, is in love with a woman from another world. And like those other loves, André's is doomed. Forces beyond the control of the lovers will prevent them from living their lives together. Here, as in other novels, one of the lovers dies young, to be forever immortalized in the surviving lover's memory. Upon learning of Juanita's death, André proclaims, "If that beautiful woman's life meant anything to this world I have to fight on to the end" (376). Of course André does continue to fight the communists, just as Gabriela continues to fight the Nazis in *Mila 18* and Conor continues (until his own death) to fight the British in *Trinity* and *Redemption*.

In the end, André's tribute to Juanita and Mike's rescue of André are established as equally significant to the United States' victory over the Soviet Union in the Cuban Missile Crisis. The news of that victory is announced as Mike takes a taxi to the Louvre to spirit away his friend and Juanita's lover. As Boris Kuznetov tells Mike early in the novel, "They cannot take from us all that is human. Someday you may need a friend" (15).

A PSYCHOANALYTIC READING OF *TOPAZ*

Suspense thrillers, because they play upon readers' unspoken fears, lend themselves readily to psychoanalytic criticism. As discussed in Chapter 4, the psychoanalytic school of criticism focuses on the literary work as an analyst would focus on a patient's dream, namely, as the manifestation of wishes or fears that lie within the subconscious mind.

As in *The Angry Hills*, Uris's only other thriller, characters in *Topaz* represent id, ego, and superego. In this novel, the Cuban revolutionaries, Pierre LaCroix, Nicole Devereaux, and Columbine reflect the id. According to Freud, the desire for food is associated with infancy, when the id dominates the personality. Early descriptions of the Cubans involve eating and drinking, usually in rather primitive ways. Parra's room in New York is littered with empty beer bottles and dirty plates, and he is seen in Juanita's home devouring a banana. Parra and his comrades are also seen frequently smoking foul-smelling cigars, a symbol to Freud of both oral and sexual gratification. Their behavior is motivated by lust, either for sex or for torture. Juanita worries that Parra's "unhealthy desire for her" will "explode at any time" (136). For Munoz, the immediate gratification that Parra seeks in sex comes from torture. He indulges his passion to the extent that "the smell of death was a part of him" (127–128).

The sophisticated Pierre LaCroix does not appear to resemble the Cubans in any way, but his behavior also represents dominance of the id. LaCroix's identification of his own needs with those of his country indicate an infantile inability to separate the self from the outside world. Like the young child, LaCroix sees himself as the center of the universe; and since he equates himself with France, he sees France as the rightful leader of the European continent. LaCroix revels in the adulation of his people, performing for them at the Albert Hall and the Arc de Triomphe in much the same way that a toddler performs in order to be the center of attention. LaCroix's inability to recognize the reality of his situation indicates that the ego is not operative in his personality; his refusal to accommodate the needs of his NATO allies reveals a similar dysfunction of the superego.

The behavior of the Cuban revolutionaries and of Pierre LaCroix holds serious implications for the balance of power in the world. On another level, the behavior of Nicole Devereaux holds such implications for the well-being of her marriage. In the passages describing her early life with André, Nicole is characterized as selfish to the point of absurdity. A war is raging around her, her country has been invaded by enemy forces, and hundreds of thousands of her Jewish compatriots are being exterminated. In the midst of this Nicole complains to André, "I don't understand this rubbish of honor" (296), when he tells her he is going to fight with the Free French Forces. Once André and Nicole are married and André continues his work for LaCroix's intelligence unit, Nicole complains further that she and André do not spend enough time together, insisting that she does not want to hear the word "war." Her demands continue after the war when André joins French intelligence, eventually destroying their marriage. Nicole's inability to appreciate the demands of the larger society on her husband reveal an underdeveloped superego; her insistence that her own needs come first reveals an overdeveloped id.

The Cubans, LaCroix, and Nicole symbolize the dangers of unchecked id to world peace and to the life of individuals. In Jacques Granville, or Columbine, those dangers converge. Granville's sole motivation for marrying his many successive wives, for seducing Nicole, and for betraying his country is to make himself rich. His insatiable need for instant gratification has blinded him not only to the needs of other people and his country but also to any sense of morality. In Granville the essential amorality of the id is illustrated.

In contrast to these characters, Boris Kuznetov, André Devereaux, and

Mike Nordstrom illustrate integrated personalities. Kuznetov has saved his family by defecting. He resists the lure of the good life in America when refusing cooperation with his interrogators until he is certain of their trustworthiness. His love for his country prevents him from betraying it for his own enrichment. Similarly, André struggles with the conflicts between his own needs and those of his family and country. His affair with Juanita is attributed to his wife's inability to understand his dedication to intelligence work. And even in his affair with Juanita, André puts the needs of the country and the world ahead of his own desire to be with his lover. It is Mike Nordstrom, however, who represents the most fully integrated personality. Sensitive to the demands of his job on his family, understanding the conflicts plaguing Kuznetov and André, and above all dedicated to the preservation of the free world, Mike symbolizes the personality that successfully represses the urges of the id in the interests of harmony with the community. The antithesis of Columbine, Mike is a truly moral man.

It is this connection between morality and the integration of personality that gives the suspense thriller its power. Readers can be reassured in this novel that the value that their culture places on deferred gratification and on sensitivity to the needs of the community is worthwhile. Through the characters in the book, readers can play out their fantasies of indulging in the immediate gratification of their desires without consequence, for the characters will pay the price. In this sense, the novel itself functions as ego and superego, by illustrating for readers the inevitable outcome of uncontrolled id. And that outcome is terrifying in the world of *Topaz*, with the threat of nuclear war hanging over the world.

9

QB VII
(1970)

In this novel, loosely based on an incident in his own life, Uris takes on the twin issues of inmate collaborators in the Nazi death camps and the capacity for evil in ordinary, and otherwise good, citizens. Polish Catholic surgeon Adam Kelno, survivor of the fictional Jadwiga concentration camp, spends fifteen years after the war working with primitive people in Borneo. Returning to London, he discovers that he has been labeled a war criminal in a new book, *The Holocaust*, by American novelist Abe Cady. During the libel suit that he files against Cady, the horrors of concentration camp life are revived.

PLOT DEVELOPMENT

In Part 1, "The Plaintiff," Kelno's past is sketched out. Readers learn of his rehabilitation after surviving the Nazi death camps. Suspected of collaboration, he is exonerated by the Poles but later, after moving to England with his wife, Angela, he is again accused of performing experimental surgery, in particular the removal of healthy testicles and ovaries of Jewish inmates. Languishing in jail for two years, he is eventually freed when the only eyewitness that the Polish government can produce fails to identify him.

Uris uses this episode to create doubt in the reader's mind. Dr. Mark

Tesslar, a Jewish survivor of Jadwiga, insists that he was an eyewitness to Adam's experimental operations. Another survivor, himself a victim of such surgery, insists that the surgeon was Adam. But Tesslar is revealed to have a long-standing grudge against Adam, and the survivor cannot identify him. So the reader is left almost, but not quite, convinced that Adam is innocent. At this point in the story, Adam appears to be a victim, first of the Nazis and then of the Polish communists. His dream to settle down to a normal life with his wife and child humanizes him. Readers do not want him to be guilty.

Adam is established as a compassionate, driven man in subsequent chapters, when he takes his family to Borneo to work with the natives. He spends long years trying to overcome the Ulu tribe's misguided spiritual approach to illness and hygiene. His patience and persistence eventually win over the tribe, who not only live longer and healthier lives but learn a great deal about basic medicine and hygiene as well. His initial characterization of the natives as "damned savages," however, is a bit disconcerting. As the British Commissioner responds, how can anyone who has witnessed the atrocities of the "civilized" Nazis call another people savages?

This seed of doubt that Uris plants is nourished later, when Adam must perform surgery on the chief's son under primitive conditions. Adam shudders uncontrollably as the experience transports him back to Jadwiga, where he is removing another young boy's testicles. But the doubt recedes as Adam continues his work, publishing a paper that results in his knighthood. Despite the accolades that the paper receives, the reaction of his colleagues to the paper is troubling in one sense. Some scientists, while understanding the necessity of his method, are disturbed by his use of humans as experimental subjects. This reaction presents readers with a mere suggestion of the experimentation in the camps, but it is enough. The questions about Adam Kelno's past may not be pressing, but neither will they disappear.

While in Borneo, Adam occasionally succumbs to nightmares and depression. The worst episode occurs during the second year, when after several miscarriages, Angela must be sterilized. Again, Uris teases the reader. Why is it the sterilization that sends Adam into nightmares of surgery in Jadwiga? But again, the author does not dwell on the subject, and Angela is able to shake him out of the depression by reminding him of his responsibility to their son. Assisting Angela in her endeavor is missionary Ian Campbell, whose young son Terrence shows a great interest in medicine. Adam expresses his gratitude to Ian by vowing to teach Terry as much as he can and to see him through medical school when he is older. Terry will become a second son to Adam.

After fifteen successful years in the jungle, Adam is finally persuaded to return to London. He has been assured that all talk of his war experiences is past, and for a time he and Angela live a contented life in a working-class neighborhood in London. Although Adam is seen as a savior by the neighborhood people, the reader wonders why he chooses this line of work when his prominence could have earned him a lucrative practice in a prestigious area. He seems not only to be courting anonymity, but also to be atoning for some sin. The penance seems to be working until Terry returns for Christmas from Oxford with news that American author Abraham Cady has called Adam a war criminal in his new bestseller, *The Holocaust*.

Adam's reaction to this news, and to Terry's questions, makes it difficult for readers to determine his guilt. His initial reaction, recalling the concentration camp itself, evokes sympathy: "We never saw a tree or flower for four years and I don't remember the sun" (99). But then readers' suspicions are aroused once again with Adam's tirade against Jews. Calling them "cunning beyond imagination" (100), Adam claims that Jews in prewar Poland conspired to take control of the universities. The first part of the book ends with Adam, at Terry's urging, initiating a libel suit against Abe Cady.

Part Two, "The Defendants," introduces readers to Abraham Cady. The son of Polish Jews who had first settled in Palestine, Abe grows up in anti-Semitic Norfolk, Virginia. His older brother Ben, killed fighting for the Loyalists in Spain, inspires Abe to become a writer. In a long first-person narrative presented entirely in uppercase letters, Abe tells of writing a novel about Ben after quiting college because "YOU CAN'T LEARN TO WRITE FROM COLLEGE PROFESSORS" (123). After several rejections, the novel is picked up by David Shawcross, an English publisher, and becomes a best-seller.

A flyer in World War II, Abe severely burns both hands and loses one eye in a crash landing. Grounded and under medical treatment, and temporarily blind, Abe falls in love with Samantha, whose visits comfort him. In these scenes, Uris presents Abe as courageous but frightened, uncertain of his own recovery. When that hurdle is passed, Abe undertakes the dictation of a novel to Samantha, his hands still too damaged to write. The description of this process reveals Uris's fascination with the writer's craft, as Samantha becomes "the silent partner . . . to one of the unique of all human experiences." She comes to appreciate that there is nothing mystical in the process of writing, only "relentless plodding requiring a special kind of stamina" and "uncertainty, . . . drain, . . . emotional downs, . . . exhaustion" (146).

While Samantha is helping Abe with his book, she is portrayed as selfless and dedicated. When Abe and Samantha marry and move to London so that Abe can work as a war correspondent on bombing missions, Samantha asks for some dedication in return. At this point Abe reveals himself to be insensitive to Samantha's concerns, especially about being left alone and pregnant while he flies on bombing missions over Germany. For her part, Samantha suddenly appears selfish, unable to appreciate the relative insignificance of their problems in light of what the war has done to countless others. The first signs of problems not only in their marriage, but in Abe's character, appear here. Their son Ben is born while Samantha is staying with her parents and while Abe is on a bombing mission to support the D-Day invasion of Europe.

As the war comes to a close, Abe signs a deal to make a movie of his successful second novel, a war story called *The Jug*. Uris's attitude toward Hollywood is evident in his portrayal of the sleazy producer J. Milton Mandelbaums, who advises Abe that he must present ethnic groups as stereotypes and conceal his own Jewishness. The experience with Hollywood is so horrible that Abe has his name removed from the credits of the film.

To cover Abe's fortunes after the war, Uris turns again to first-person narrative. As with other narratives in the book, this section is presented in all uppercase letters. In his own voice, Abe reveals the horrors of learning that, but for one cousin, his entire extended family in Poland has been wiped out at Jadwiga. When his father dies after having finally settled in Israel, Abe vows on the old man's grave to "WRITE A BOOK TO SHAKE THE CONSCIENCE OF THE HUMAN RACE" (163). Before that can happen, however, Abe must make a success of his third book and pull himself out of debt. When the book is a critical and popular failure, Abe turns ugly.

Abe's long diatribe against Samantha after the book fails calls into question his decency. He accuses her of calling *The Partisans* her favorite of his books precisely because it has failed. He further accuses her of having an inferiority complex, of being dull, and of being incapable of acknowledging criticism or admitting her own mistakes. Her only redeeming feature, according to Abe, is her sexual prowess. Since readers do not see Samantha at this point or hear the story from her perspective, Abe's diatribe does not ring true. Instead, it reveals him to be mean-spirited. Thus, just as readers question the guilt or innocence of Adam Kelno, they now question the sincerity and character of Abe Cady.

Those questions are further emphasized when Abe, after doing a stint of writing for Hollywood against the advice of his publisher, completes his next novel. David Shawcross, always a voice of dignity and ethics, is appalled that the book is nothing more than slick pornography. David will honor his agreement to publish the work; but acting as Abe's conscience, David not only tells Abe that the book is trash but also forbids Abe to blame his writing such a book on Samantha's financial demands. Abe finally redeems himself, however, when he refuses a lucrative Hollywood deal that would prevent him from getting to work on his Holocaust book. Divorcing Samantha, Abe sets off to research the book he was born to write.

Abe's extensive travel in researching the book is reminiscent of Uris's own travels as he researched _Exodus_. While he is in Israel, Abe's now-grown children emigrate, embracing their Jewish identity. As his children immerse themselves in Israeli culture, Abe completes _The Holocaust_ and collapses from exhaustion. Returning to the United States to live off the book's earnings, Abe embarks on a new work that chronicles what he considers the downward spiral of human evolution in the twentieth century. Part Two ends when Abe receives David Shawcross's telegram informing him of Adam Kelno's lawsuit.

Part Three, "Brief to Counsel," begins with an essay on the British justice system and the Four Inns of Court, preparing the reader for the ensuing trial. Abe and David begin an exhaustive investigation to validate Abe's characterization of Adam; and despite numerous obstacles and setbacks, Abe refuses to settle the suit.

Abe and David's dedication to fighting the case is reinforced when they meet internationally acclaimed violinist Pietr Van Damm, who is willing to testify that Kelno had castrated him in Jadwiga. But Abe is so concerned for Van Damm's reputation and privacy that he refuses to allow his lawyers to use this evidence. What readers see happening to Abe in this section is a genuine transformation. Until this point, Abe has presented a rather unsavory character. The prospect of apologizing to Adam Kelno, someone whom he believes is a Nazi collaborator, transforms Abe into a champion of Jewish dignity. He and David hire Thomas Bannister, the man who tried to have Adam extradited to Poland twenty years ago, to serve as their counsel.

Once it is established that the case will continue, Uris shifts attention back to Adam Kelno, who reveals in a flashback his adolescent desire to castrate his brute of a father for defiling his mother. Adam's flashback, complete with a recollection of watching his father and mother have sex, features a segment in which he fantasizes about amputating his father's testicles with a knife. Once again, readers wonder about the truth of the charges against him. Adam's obvious anti-Semitism, coupled with this new revelation, calls into question the legitimacy of his reputation as a great humanitarian. Adam's desire for justice from Abe becomes a desire to destroy the man, prompting Terry to warn him that his attitude is beginning to resemble that of the Nazis. As this part of the book draws to a close, readers are becoming more convinced that Abe may indeed be right.

That suspicion is reinforced as Uris recounts Nazi-hunter Shimshon Aroni's successful search for witnesses to and victims of Kelno's crimes. In Europe and Israel, survivors come together to testify at Abe's trial. But he has yet to find Egon Sobotnik, the medical clerk at Jadwiga who might corroborate Abe's claims. The section ends with Dr. Mark Tesslar, who testified in the original complaint against Adam twenty years earlier, pleading with his physician to keep his terminal cancer from killing him until he can testify.

Part Four, "The Trial," introduces the age-old question, What would I have done under these circumstances? In front of Judge Anthony Gilray, Adam Kelno recounts the slave labor, beatings, degradations, and disease of concentration camp life. Readers find themselves in the position of onlookers in the courtroom, who previously "had only heard of this in abstract" but who will now witness the Holocaust drama played out "on a stage of memory and horror" (285). Even Abe, listening to Adam's description, ponders what he would have done in the same situation. His question is a legitimate one: In such circumstances, ordinary citizens may well have been coerced by the Nazis into performing acts that they would consider monstrous under normal circumstances. And if this is what happened to Adam Kelno, then Abe has indeed libeled the surgeon.

In addition to the philosophical questions raised by Adam's testimony, suspense builds as well. Adam and others make several references to the registers kept by Egon Sobotnik, which Van Damm insists will verify Adam's guilt. Adam, perhaps confident that Sobotnik will never be found, proclaims that the registers would exonerate him. Readers are left wondering if the registers will surface and, if they do, what information they will reveal.

In his testimony about the camp, Adam distinguishes between the Nationalist Underground and the Communist Underground. Both groups tried to thwart the Nazis, but Adam insists that the communists betrayed the nationalists whenever possible, citing the communist desire to take over Poland after the war as a rationale. His fixation on the communists is important, because he believes that the persecution he has endured since the war is the result of a communist-Jewish conspiracy.

Uris uses Bannister's cross-examination to illustrate the finer points of life in the concentration camps, highlighting the class system that arose among prisoners, with those assisting the Nazis enjoying privileges denied others. Bannister also makes a different distinction between the Nationalist and Communist Undergrounds, insisting that what Adam refers to as communist was actually the primary Underground, supported by prisoners of all political affiliations. The Nationalist Underground, he insists, was simply a continuation of a Polish anti-Semitic organization to which Adam belonged before the war. The cross-examination clearly has Adam unsettled, and his responses begin to swing observers'—and readers'—sympathies against him.

On the evening before the defense opens its case, Abe is afraid that he cannot face his first meeting with the survivors found by Aroni. But upon meeting them, his spirit is renewed, and readers can hear Uris speaking through Abe as he prepares them for tomorrow's proceedings, reminding them that they will speak "for six million who can no longer speak" (347).

During the defense testimony, evidence of atrocities mounts, with graphic descriptions of brutal experimental surgery. Uris takes readers through the detailed testimony of individual survivors, establishing personalities, even providing physical descriptions in order to humanize atrocities normally understood only in the abstract. He also makes this fictional testimony more credible by modeling it on actual transcripts of testimony from the Nuremberg trials, in which survivors matter-of-factly recount brutal treatment and painful medical procedures. While none of the witnesses in this trial can identify Adam Kelno, they do attest to Mark Tesslar's comforting presence. Whether they can identify Adam or not, the litany of atrocities is damning.

Interspersed with the courtroom testimony is an account of Aroni's search for the elusive Egon Sobotnik. Aroni's methods are ruthless, resulting in one woman's accusing him, rather accurately, of acting like a Nazi himself. But reading Uris's account of Aroni's manhunt in the context of the graphic trial testimony helps readers understand his methods. After all, Sobotnik's records will reveal the truth.

The case for the defense is strengthened by the testimony of a British gynecologist, whose description of the condition of female survivors appalls those present. Further testimony by other concentration camp doctors that they felt relatively safe in defying orders undermines Adam's assertion that his actions were a matter of survival. But at the last moment, the defense loses its only eyewitness to Adam's crimes when Mark Tesslar dies the night before he is to testify. Uris introduces a philosophical discussion when Van Damm insists upon testifying but Abe refuses to let him, citing the damage that the testimony would do to Van Damm's career and dignity. But, one defense lawyer argues, Abe has a responsibility to Jews around the world. Abe replies that to put Van Damm on the stand in the interests of a higher cause would be the equivalent of Adam's operating on Jews in the interests of survival. The question of which alternative is more ethical is left unanswered, emphasizing the complexities of Abe's position.

As members of the court absorb the news of Tesslar's death, Aroni arrives with Sobotnik and the Jadwiga records. This classic courtroom drama is heightened when Adam's counsel challenges the admissibility of the record. In considering the challenge, Judge Gilray ponders issues larger than Adam's responsibility. The real question, he thinks, is "What had happened at the hands of one's fellow man" (479). When Judge Gilray decides to allow the evidence, he provides Adam with time to "prepare a proper defense" (480), prompting Adam's lawyer to realize that even in the judge's mind Adam Kelno has become the real defendant. Fittingly, when Adam takes the stand again, it is his own testimony that condemns him. Bannister decimates him on the stand, and the now-broken man's final pitiful diatribe, accusing "them" of plotting against him, seals his fate. For as Bannister reminds Adam quietly, it was he, not some unknown "they," who brought the case to court. Adam's final degradation in readers' eyes occurs when he lashes out against the thoroughly disillusioned Terry, beating the young man and calling him a Jew. The jury, while it finds for the plaintiff, awards Adam only a halfpenny in damages, precisely the verdict asked for by Thomas Bannister.

Nonetheless, Abe still ponders what he would have done in Adam's situation, arguing that humans are destroying their own world and that "God is getting very impatient" (501) with humanity in general. Those sentiments may indeed be Uris's own, for he closes the novel with history repeating itself: In the six-day Arab-Israeli war that rages as the trial concludes, Abe's son, named for his brother Ben, is shot down and killed. As Abe has said repeatedly, the madness simply continues.

CHARACTER DEVELOPMENT

In most of Uris's other works, characters are either good or evil. *QB VII*, however, presents readers with more complex characters. Danny, Mac, and their fellow soldiers in the Sixth Marines of *Battle Cry* are heroes of a bloody war; Ari Ben Canaan of the Haganah in *Exodus* is one of the saviors of his country; and Sean O'Sullivan of the U.S. occupation force in *Armageddon* brings morality, ethics, and dignity to a vanquished country. But in *QB VII*, the line between heroes and villains is less clearly drawn. The two characters who face one another in the courtroom of Queen's Bench VII, Abe Cady and Adam Kelno, are neither entirely good nor entirely evil.

That their names sound similar is significant, as is the fact that both have biblical first names. That both are accomplished, driven men in their respective professions is also significant. And finally, that they are both trying, each in his own way, to exorcise the ghosts of the Holocaust, is of the greatest significance. In Abe Cady and Adam Kelno, Uris presents men who represent the ambiguities of life in a postwar, post-Holocaust world.

Adam Kelno represents those ordinary people who can be turned into monsters if given the appropriate conditions. He is first introduced as a sympathetic character, having just escaped the new communist regime in Poland. Any questions about his wartime activities at this point are dismissed by the testimonials of survivors who claim that he saved their lives. He is also portrayed as a devoted husband and father whose only hope in prison is to live in freedom with his family. In Borneo his work establishes him as a dedicated professional committed to the health of the natives. Later, in his working-class London neighborhood, he is revered by his patients and is tireless in his efforts on their behalf.

Adam's anti-Semitism is evident in his characterization of Jews as being engaged in a conspiracy against him, as well as in his diatribe when he sees Abraham Cady's book. But the world is filled with anti-Semites; would all of them be capable of committing the atrocities of which Adam is accused? That is the question that Uris leaves unanswered in this book, suggesting perhaps that it is unanswerable. No one can deny Adam's humanitarian works, both in the camp and in Borneo. Nor can anyone call him anything but a good father and husband. But as the evidence in the trial proves beyond doubt, this humanitarian, this good family man committed crimes against humanity that defy imagination. In this sense, Adam is a far more effective portrait of Nazi depravity than those found in *Exodus* and *Mila 18*, for he is the ordinary man turned into a beast.

Adam's accuser, Abe Cady, is equally complex. The son of Jewish immigrants, seasoned by petty anti-Semitism throughout his life and horrified by the knowledge of what happened to his people under the Third Reich, Abe is genuine in his dedication to telling the story of the Holocaust. He is devoted to his brother Ben, who died fighting the fascists; to his parents, who struggled to give their children a better life; and to the memory of his relatives in Poland, who died at the hands of the Nazis. He is also a dedicated writer, intent upon producing works that will endure. All of these characteristics make him an admirable character.

But Abe has another side, one that makes him more difficult to sympathize with. His ego is enormous. He considers Samantha selfish to want him with her at the birth of their first child. And although he claims his motivation for going on the bombing mission is hatred of Nazism, he admits to himself that he does it as much for the thrill as for the cause: "MY HANDS ITCH WITH JOY AS I TAKE THE CONTROLS. . . . I AM SICK AT MY OWN ECSTASY" (150–151). Later, in California, when Samantha suggests that they return to England, Abe becomes enraged with her for thinking she has "THE RIGHT TO TELL AN AUTHOR WHERE HE HAD TO WORK" (161). When Abe goes on a drinking binge and ends up penniless in a brothel, he cannot understand Samantha's anger. His long diatribes against her are not borne out by any action in which readers see her behavior, so the only conclusion possible is that his ego, his sense of himself as The Great Writer, overpowers any sense of loyalty or commitment to his wife.

But the trial changes Abe, forcing on him a self-awareness that, to his credit, he willingly accepts. He still seems blind to his personal failures, but he does begin to question his self-righteous attitude toward Adam Kelno. The first crack in Abe's armor appears when Adam's litany of horrors in Jadwiga makes Abe wonder how anyone could maintain a shred of humanity in such a place. Then, when Abe is about to meet the survivors of Jadwiga, he questions himself for "putting them on display like freaks in a side show" (345). He feels a similar ambivalence about allowing Pietr Van Damm to testify. And even after the Sobotnik registers prove that he was right about Adam Kelno, Abe still cannot stop asking himself how he would have behaved in the same situation. When he refers to the trial as "THE ONE DECENT THING I'VE DONE IN MY LIFE" (502), readers get the sense that Abe Cady has truly undergone an awakening.

Abe and Adam are such powerful figures, and the trial itself so riveting, that the other characters in the novel play only minor roles. Among them, however, are characters who help clarify some of the ambiguities in the primary characters. David Shawcross, for example, often acts as Abe's conscience. It is David who helps Abe edit his first novel into a masterpiece, David who calls Abe's *Places* trash, and David who refuses to let Abe blame his foray into pornography on Samantha. And when Abe and David meet with Van Damm, David knows that even at the risk of losing his publishing house, he must fight Adam Kelno's lawsuit.

Taken as a whole, the survivors of the camp are also voices of conscience. The dignity with which they endure their pain and the hope with which they continue to live their lives are heroic. When Van Damm is faced with the consequences of telling the world that he is a eunuch, he says quite simply, "I'm a Jew. I know my duty" (236). Daniel Dubrowski, another survivor, explains matter-of-factly why he took the place of a younger man who was scheduled to be castrated: "He was the youngest and had a chance for life. . . . It was the only human thing to do" (393). When the survivors leave London, Abe is awed by their "SPECIAL KIND OF COURAGE" and convinced that "THEY WILL ALWAYS OWN A FLEETING MOMENT IN HISTORY" (396–397). Because they speak out when they have nothing to gain but the pain of reopening old wounds, these survivors are portrayed as the true heroes of *QB VII*.

While the survivors of the surgery are seen as heroic, the doctors who refused to take part in the surgery are seen as stoic. Dr. Maria Viskova, when assigned to assist in the surgery, simply refused, contemplating suicide rather than complying with the Nazi orders. Another doctor, psychiatrist Susanne Parmentier, refused to conduct obedience experiments on Jewish prisoners. Both of these women provide a sharp contrast to Adam Kelno, who claims that if he had disobeyed orders to operate on Jews he would have been killed.

Most of the narrative in *QB VII* concerns the past; and each character's past, to some extent, either dictates or explains his or her present behavior. It is this obsession with the past that torments Abe throughout the novel. And yet at the end, even Abe's despair is tempered by the words of Thomas Bannister, who points to the significance of the young people in the novel: "If we are going to hang on to this world for a little longer it's going to be up to [Terry] and Kelno's son and your son and daughter" (502). While Terry, Stephan, Ben, and Vanessa play relatively small roles in the action of the novel, collectively they are of great significance. Implicit within the trial is the hope that the horrors it recalls will never occur again. The presence of these young people, all of whom are idealistic and moral, allows Uris to end the novel on a note of hope, a hope that the children will not follow in the footsteps of their parents.

THEMATIC ISSUES

After the trial in *QB VII* is over, Abe Cady says to Thomas Bannister, "There but for the grace of God go all of us" and asks the rhetorical question, "What the hell would I have done?" (500). In these words lies the primary theme of Uris's novel, namely, the terrifying question of what any of us would be capable of if pushed to the limit of our endurance.

Uris explores themes relating to the Holocaust in several novels, most notably in *Exodus* and *Mila 18*. In *QB VII*, however, he uncovers what is perhaps the darkest side of that episode in our history, namely, the participation of ordinary citizens in the atrocities committed against the Jews in World War II. Adam Kelno is a dedicated doctor, a devoted husband and father, and a victim of a Nazi concentration camp. His work in Borneo saves hundreds of lives and improves the health and living conditions of an entire people. His mentoring of young Terry Campbell assures the boy of admission to the best medical schools. But during World War II, Adam Kelno found himself in Hell. Suddenly none of the rules of civilization as he had known it applied anymore, and suddenly he had the opportunity to act upon his anti-Semitic beliefs in ways he could never have imagined.

As Abe Cady listens to Adam's account of life in Jadwiga, he continually returns to the question, What would I have done? And for Abe, the question is a legitimate one. He has assumed that because he is a writer, the rules of marital fidelity do not apply to him. Nor does he see anything wrong with assuming that his wife will sacrifice her life to his career. In short, he sees himself as belonging to a class apart from other men. If he can justify his treatment of Samantha by calling her shallow and claiming that he has achieved success despite her dragging him down, then he can understand the superiority that people like Adam Kelno feel because they are Aryan.

Even Judge Gilray is affected by the larger implications of the trial, recognizing that in all of us there is an inability to understand those whom we perceive as different. And when we focus on the differences, when the Jew or the Black or the woman becomes Other, then we are capable of behaving toward that person in ways we would not otherwise dream of. Adam Kelno, family man, respected doctor, steps over that line. Whether or not Abe Cady would do so, whether or not Uris would do so, whether or not any reader would do so, is a question that cannot be answered.

Pondering this question throughout the novel leads Uris to an even more sweeping theme, namely, the possibility that humanity has dug its own grave. The action takes place in London in 1967, when the rebellion of youth was in full swing. Upon returning to London from Borneo, Angela Kelno is appalled at what she considers "THE DISMANTLING OF HUNDREDS OF YEARS OF CIVILIZATION AND TRADITIONS" (93–94). Angela tends to blame the young people for the condition of the civilized world, but Abe believes differently. When Ben tells Abe that he and his sister consider their father a hero, Abe responds cynically, "Accept the gift of my generation to your generation. Concentration camps and gas chambers and the rape of human dignity" (345). Earlier in the novel, Abe comments at length on the condition of the human race, what he calls "MAN'S INEVITABLE DRIVE TOWARD SELF-EXTINCTION" (193).

Thomas Bannister, however, does not see things in the same way that Angela and Abe do. When Abe warns that "God is getting very impatient" (502), Bannister disagrees, offering that even if this civilization destroys itself, eventually another will arise that "will last for eternity because people will treat each other the way they ought to" (502).

That the novel ends with the news of young Ben Cady's death can be interpreted in two ways. It may confirm Abe's contention that humans never learn from their mistakes. Abe's brother Ben died a hero, but in a lost cause, the Spanish Civil War. A possible implication is that the younger Ben's cause is also hopeless. But it is also possible that there is hope in this latest death, that heroism is still alive in the younger generation. Bannister insists that the hope of humanity lies in the young people; the sacrifice of Ben Cady may justify that hope.

Interpreting young Ben's death as a hopeful sign is consistent with a final theme in *QB VII*, namely, the strength of the human spirit. The parade of survivors who testify for Abe Cady in the trial all share a common trait: They have survived in the fullest sense of the word. They may describe themselves as "vegetables," they may look weak, and they may be unable to reproduce, but they go on living. And they travel thousands of miles to bear witness to an unspeakable atrocity in the hope that they can prevent it from ever happening again. As Abe tells them before they begin their testimony, they are speaking "for six million who can no longer speak" (347). That they do speak, and with such simple eloquence, bears witness to their own strength. Despite the horrors it chronicles, despite the monstrosity of Adam Kelno's crime, *QB VII* ultimately is a tribute to the indomitable human spirit.

A FEMINIST READING OF *QB VII*

While some feminist criticism focuses on the portrayal of female characters in a literary work (see Chapter 6), another approach analyzes the work's portrayal of a male-dominated society. In *QB VII* Leon Uris demonstrates the destructiveness of masculine aggressiveness and dominance as played out not only in the Holocaust but in the personal life of Abraham Cady as well.

Feminist critics such as Judith Fetterley and Carolyn Heilbrun explore texts written by men in order to uncover the ideology created by dominant males in a patriarchal society. In this version of feminist criticism, works are examined to determine the extent to which women's voices are silenced by the dominant male power structure. As discussed in Chapter 6, this patriarchal society is based on male definitions of values, beliefs, and traditions. According to novelist and scholar Virginia Woolf, such masculine-oriented definitions often keep women from making significant achievements by assigning females supporting roles in male endeavors. Furthermore, those women who defy the odds and do succeed in their own right are often not recognized because of the intrinsic value placed on male achievement. Female achievement, by contrast, is devalued.

This failure to acknowledge female voices, according to feminist critics, results in the perception of women as inferior to men. Thus when women do not achieve at the level that men do, the cause is often determined to be women's inferiority rather than men's refusal to afford women the means and opportunity for success. And when women do achieve, they are often seen, not as models to emulate, but rather as dissatisfied creatures seeking to belittle men. Feminist critics examine the behavior of male and female characters in literary works in order to expose the underlying cultural assumptions at work in the portrayal of men as strong and aggressive and women as weak and subservient. This branch of feminist criticism also focuses on male aggressiveness as a behavior designed specifically to reinforce male dominance. Seen from this perspective, one interpretation of Nazi anti-Semitism might focus on masculine aggression. The Nazi philosophy celebrated war, the strength of the Aryan (especially the male), and rule by force rather than by consent. The scapegoating of the Jews can also be seen in this perspective as resulting from a masculine expression of power. Adam Kelno attributes his father's alcoholism to his father's despair over constantly being under the control of Jewish moneylenders. This kind of perceived assault upon manhood was used by the Nazis as a rationale for persecution of the Jews. Historically, every action that the Nazis took against the Jews, men or women, was a demonstration of power over the Jews.

Adam Kelno's description of life in the Jadwiga concentration camp reinforces this image of masculine domination. Order is maintained in the camp through intimidation and beating. Hierarchies emerge among prisoners based on how easily individuals or groups can adapt to the Nazi methods. And survival is a matter of your exerting as much power as possible over those beneath you.

It is significant that the experiments being conducted by Kelno and his associates in the camp involve reproduction. Historically, Nazis used human subjects for experiments on various diseases, on the body's response to extreme cold, on the physical attributes of dwarves, on bone regrowth, and on a host of other conditions. By choosing the experiments on sterilization, Uris focuses on the male desire to control reproduction. Long considered the female's domain, reproduction is seen by the Nazis as the most significant function of the body over which they must assert control. If the master race is to be realized, then reproduction cannot be left to nature. More significantly, control over reproduction must be firmly in the hands of the men who rule the Third Reich.

Adam Kelno, although not a Nazi, nevertheless carries out the masculine-dominant role of the Nazis when he operates on Jewish inmates at Jadwiga. He controls not only the reproductive capacity of women but also of men who in his view have compromised his own manhood. There is even a suggestion, in his flashback to his father's sexual dominance over his mother, that Adam is re-creating his desire to castrate his father and possess his mother through these operations.

If the exercise of masculine aggression is seen as symbolic in Adam Kelno's story, the exercise of masculine dominance is more literal in Abe Cady's story. As a writer, Abe represents those male writers who dominate the literary canon, leaving little or no room for female writers. Abe even uses a female, his wife, as a writing tool when he does not have the use of his hands. But when Samantha's needs begin to interfere with his own, Adam's response is arrogant fury. Having spent his entire marriage asking Samantha to accommodate herself to his work, Abe then berates his wife for being dull and stagnant. This assessment of Samantha's intellectual capacity is consistent with a male-dominated society's judgment of women: After denying women the opportunity to educate themselves, men accuse women of being unintelligent.

While on one level Abe seems oblivious to the contradictions in his character, on another he seems to recognize the mess that the male-dominated power structure has made of the world. The book he intends to write when the lawsuit is filed is to focus on "MAN THE PREDATOR, THE PLUNDERER, THE DESTROYER" (192). And the lawsuit he fights is one that seeks to justify his exposure of the most outrageous demonstration of masculine aggression in history: the Holocaust.

Those who support Abe in fighting the suit, those who demonstrate true heroism in the trial, are, significantly, women and eunuchs. Dr. Maria Viskova refuses to obey Nazi orders to conduct experimental operations, choosing instead to take her own life rather than exercise such destructive power over the lives of others. Psychiatrist Susanne Parmentier similarly refuses to conduct obedience experiments on Jewish prisoners. And renowned violinist Pietr Van Damm is willing to jeopardize his career by publicly testifying that he was castrated by Adam Kelno. Among the other survivors of Jadwiga are a number of other women and castrated men who demonstrate through their dignity a heroism that is incomprehensible even to Abe.

It is through witnessing the selflessness of these survivors that Abe Cady becomes humanized. His character becomes noticeably less aggressive, perceptibly more compassionate, as the trial progresses. He demonstrates his final recognition of the destructiveness of masculine aggression when it becomes clear that Van Damm must testify or the case will be lost. Initially determined to fight to the end regardless of the outcome, Abe refuses to do so if the price is the sacrifice of Van

Damm's dignity. Whether or not admitting to having been castrated constitutes a loss of dignity is not the question. The real point is that Abe relinquishes his aggressive stance in the interests of protecting another human being. The real hope, then, of the novel is that men like Abe will work to dismantle a social system built upon force and aggression and rebuild it in the image of the true heroes of the novel.

10

Trinity
(1976)

and *Redemption*
(1995)

Written almost twenty years apart, both *Trinity* and *Redemption* chronicle the bitter relationship between the Irish people and their colonizers, the British. Both novels focus on two families, the Irish Catholic Larkins and the British-Irish Protestant Hubbles. As he did in *Exodus*, Uris treats the story of Irish resistance to British rule as a heroic battle of epic proportions.

TRINITY

Trinity recounts the story of Conor Larkin, a hero of the Irish Republican cause. Covering a time period from 1885 to 1915, Uris reveals in this novel not only Conor's maturation as a young man (he is twelve when the story opens), but also his evolving dedication to the cause of Irish freedom from England. From the death of Conor's grandfather until Conor's own demise, the young man develops a fierce hatred for the British and their occupation of Ireland. Upon his grandfather's death, Conor hears the story of the Great Famine, the myriad betrayals of the Irish by the British, and the brave uprisings of great Irish heroes like Wolfe Tone and his own great grandfather Ronan Larkin. In contrast, the actions of the British aristocracy are characterized by the merger of two great forces in the north of Ireland: the land-holding Hubble family and the industrialist Weed family. Between them these two families represent the oppression of the Irish by their powerful neighbors. In the course of the story, Uris explores the beginnings of the partially successful Irish drive for freedom from British rule.

Plot Development

Part One of *Trinity*, "Ballyutogue," begins with the first-person narrative of eleven-year-old Seamus O'Neill. Seamus, blessed with youthful innocence and Irish wit, is an entirely sympathetic character whose view of Ireland, and of his friend Conor Larkin, is essentially the author's. Conor's grandfather, the legendary Kilty Larkin, has died. During Kilty's wake, Uris provides readers with a history of the Great Famine and the Uprising of 1867. These stories are told by shanachie (storyteller) Daddo Friel, who rode with Kilty on some of the raids against British landowners before the famine. The history of British oppression of and brutality against the Irish provides the backdrop for the undeclared war that Conor and his fellow patriots will eventually fight later in the novel. And the wake provides an opportunity for politics to be discussed, as candidate for Parliament Kevin O'Garvey comes to pay his respects. To many at the wake, O'Garvey and a Liberal government in England represent the best hope for Irish home rule in history.

In these early pages, Uris informs readers of the political structure of Ireland, particularly the northern counties. Under British rule for centuries, the Irish are generally a docile people, held in check by the Roman Catholic Church, which in Uris's eyes operates in league with the British in return for control over the people's spiritual lives. In the north, the British have imported Scottish Presbyterians to work in their mills, and they keep the Scots in line by pointing to the threat posed by the Irish natives. In this way, according to Uris, the British are able to employ a cheap labor force and ensure that the Irish peasants live at not much more than subsistence levels. Daddo's story reveals the cunning and bravery of men like Kilty Larkin and his father Ronan, both of whom suffered torture at the hands of the British. Daddo implies, and Kevin O'Garvey's run for office suggests, that the time has come for a renewed uprising against the British colonizers. The man to lead this new uprising is the legendary Charles Stewart Parnell, the historical figure who actually did spearhead the drive for Irish independence toward the end of the nineteenth century.

The early pages of the book also provide a glimpse of Seamus's and Conor's boyhood days in Ballyutogue, where their shared fascination with Irish history leads them inevitably into Republican activities. Readers see as well the powerful bond between young Conor and his father Tomas, whose spirit, according to Daddo, was crushed by the Great Famine. Tomas's conviction that there is nothing to be gained by rebellion will clash mightily with Conor's growing radicalism.

Daddo Friel first tells his story to Conor during Kilty's wake; but later, when Conor is ordered to watch over his father as the man sleeps off a colossal drunk, the ghost of the young Daddo appears to the boy and recounts an extensive history of Ireland, British rule, and the troubles in the north. It is through the ghost of the young Daddo that Conor learns of his own heroic ancestry and of the treachery of the aristocratic British landowners in the area, the Hubbles, who flee to England during the worst of the famine. And it is through Daddo's ghost that Conor hears of whole families evicted from their cottages, dying by the roadside, their mouths stained green from eating grass. Finally, Daddo tells Conor of how Tomas, charged with keeping the farm going while his father traveled to England to find work, witnessed the starvation deaths of his mother, his brothers, and his sisters. Part One ends with Conor's pledge on his grandfather's grave that he will make the family proud.

Part Two, "The Orange Card," opens with talk of the upcoming parliamentary elections. With Catholics voting in this election, and with the Irish Land League Party putting up candidate Kevin O'Garvey, the British overlords are becoming worried not only about the Catholics but also about the working-class Protestants who are listening to O'Garvey's charges of corruption in high places. Change is in the air among the ruling classes as well. Industrialist Frederick Weed, owner of the Belfast Iron Works, forges an alliance with Roger Hubble, heir to the Hubble landholdings near Derry, through the marriage of Hubble to Weed's daughter Caroline.

The election is to take place not long after the summer marching season, in which Ulster Protestants parade to commemorate past victories over Catholics. The Protestant organization known as the Orange Order is named for King William of Orange, who defeated the Catholics hundreds of years earlier. The greatest parades take place on Apprentice Boys Day in honor of thirteen apprentice boys who held the gates of Derry against a Catholic army, eventually dying for the Protestant cause. Readers see the fervor of the marches and the church services commemorating the apprentice boys through the wondering eyes of Conor and

Seamus, who sneak away from a political meeting that their fathers are attending in order to see the enemy's celebration. The boys are chilled to hear the fanatical, hate-filled words of Revered Oliver Cromwell MacIvor, a fiery preacher intent on extending his influence into the political realm. As MacIvor drives his flock into an anti-Catholic frenzy, the residents of the Catholic ghetto called Bogside prepare for an attack by the Protestant mob. The description of the attack calls to mind the pogroms against Jews in *Exodus* and *Mila 18*, with those in power pitting an oppressed but loyal group (in this case, the Protestant working class) against another oppressed group (the Catholics). Conor and Seamus, at twelve years of age, lose their innocence as they look in their fathers' eyes and realize that "this was our legacy, the tarnishing of dreams, the finality of what was real in Ireland" (177).

The riot incited by MacIvor is so bloody that even Roger Hubble is shocked, in part by the deliberate shedding of blood and in part because he fears the power of MacIvor. Frederick Weed, who brought MacIvor to Derry, insists that the preacher is under his control, but Hubble is not so sure, wondering aloud about what would happen if MacIvor were to turn his hatred against the British overlords. His warning to Weed that they may eventually become ensnared in their own trap will reveal itself to be prophetic.

In the aftermath of the riot, the Catholics in Bogside hold a rally for their candidate, arguing that the political climate in England is ripe for passage of a bill allowing home rule for Ireland. The intensity of the meeting is enhanced when a surprise speaker takes the podium, none other than the legendary Republican leader Charles Stewart Parnell. When Conor and Seamus are invited to a private meeting with the great man, Conor's fate is sealed. His father knows now that bringing the boy to Derry to reveal to him the futility of fighting has backfired and that the boy will be forever wed to the cause.

As the election nears, Seamus recounts British bribes and threats designed to keep the Catholics from voting. When those attempts fail and the Land League Party of Kevin O'Garvey wins eighty-six seats in the British House of Commons, Weed and Hubble go to work to destroy any hope of home rule. Uris takes this opportunity to re-create Conservative Lord Randolph Churchill's trip to Ireland in the hope of bringing down the Liberal government of Gladstone. Weed and Hubble make use of Churchill's political ambitions to strengthen their Union Preservation Party and to whip up Protestant fears of a free, unified Ireland. Part Two ends on a somber note as Churchill's playing of the "Orange card," the threat of a free, Catholic Ireland, defeats not only the Home Rule Bill but also the Liberal government.

Uris returns to domestic matters in Part Three, "The Booley House," as Conor's mother, Finola, nearly dies in giving birth to his youngest brother, Dary. The characterization of the Roman Catholic Church as yet another oppressive force is emphasized in these scenes as Finola wails that the child's premature birth and poor health are God's punishment for Tomas's rejection of the Church. For his part, Tomas's defiance of the Church results from the excommunication of his father for engaging in Republican, or Fenian, political activity. This condemnation of the Church for being a willing party to the oppression of the Irish people will recur throughout the novel.

The birth of Dary Larkin is presented in stark contrast to that of Jeremy Hubble. Village doctor Cruikshank and midwife Mairead O'Neill, Seamus's mother, attend both births. But while Dary is born into poverty and oppression, Jeremy Hubble is born into wealth and privilege. His parents, Caroline and Roger Hubble, will see to it that he inherits the Weed-Hubble legacy intact.

The complex world of allegiances and fears that Conor and Seamus grow up in is nowhere more evident than in this section, when the British establish a new National School in Ballyutogue. Seamus, being the youngest in his family, is allowed to attend, but Conor is not. Conor's father not only sees schooling as unnecessary for his son, who will inherit the farm, but he also objects to Irish Catholic children learning nothing but English history, literature, and religion. Nor is the priest of the parish, Father Lynch, comfortable with a challenge to his sole authority as teacher of the Catholic children. And the Protestant leadership is concerned about the idea of Catholics attending the school and about the liberal curriculum presented by the teacher, Mr. Andrew Ingram. Regardless, Seamus goes to school and returns each afternoon to teach Conor all that he has learned.

Conor's education continues in two venues: one, the local blacksmith shop where he apprentices; the other, the schoolhouse itself, where Mr. Ingram discusses books with Conor after school and work hours. Contrary to Tomas's fear, Ingram is well-versed in Irish history and culture and imparts his knowledge to both boys. This section of the novel takes its name from the Booley House where Conor and Seamus spend their fourteenth summer as shepherds. They load their cart with Ingram's books and immerse themselves in the history of Irish Republicanism. When Ingram visits, he and Conor discuss the farm, the Larkin inheritance. Although Conor's younger brother Liam is a born farmer, Tomas insists that the farm be passed on to Conor. Ingram ties the dilemma to Ireland's history: "People leaving Ireland is the tragedy of Irish life. . . . Passing the land is the only way [Tomas] knows of closing the circle of his life" (257).

The idyllic life of the Booley House is only an interlude for Conor and Seamus, who are growing into manhood amid the turmoil of a new fight for freedom. Their reaction to the discrediting and finally the death of Parnell echoes that felt by the Irish people: "We were croppies again, standing out in the cold and freezing with our noses pressed hungrily against the window . . . waiting . . . waiting . . . waiting . . ." (264).

At the end of Part Three, Ballyutogue is experiencing what countless Irish villages have experienced for generations under British rule: the exodus of young men. Seamus goes off to college, Liam seeks his fortune in New Zealand, and an embittered Conor leaves for Derry. As countless other young Irish men have learned before them, these three will discover that once they have left Ballyutogue, they can never call it home again.

Part Four of the novel is titled "Bogside," after the Catholic ghetto in Derry. In the first three parts of the book, readers see how poor life is in the rural villages. In Part Four, Uris turns his attention to life in the city. The Catholic Conor is denied work as a blacksmith despite unmatched skill at the forge. And Kevin O'Garvey, in London with the House of Commons, is forced to make a pact with the devil. In an attempt to keep the Select Committee on Industrial Relations from inspecting Roger Hubble's shirt factory in Derry, where conditions for poor Catholic workers are appallingly dangerous, Hubble's representative offers O'Garvey financing for small businesses in Bogside. Torn in conscience, and convinced that Hubble would sidestep any new safety regulations suggested by the Committee, O'Garvey succumbs. This commentary on the unscrupulous business dealings of the British overlords in Ireland is as scathing as any Uris has made on Nazis or communists. The British industrialists will stop at nothing to maintain both their profits and the loyalty of Irish Protestants. And that means keeping Irish Catholics in poverty and despair.

The weight of that despair is lifted temporarily as the funding promised to O'Garvey materializes. Conor opens a forge and, despite setbacks, establishes a thriving business. He also begins playing football in the Gaelic Athletic Association and attending underground Fenian meetings.

Conor lives the good life until he undercuts Federick Weed's inflated bid on work for the Derry school district. Weed retaliates by having Conor's forge destroyed by fire. Conor's first battle with the powerful British industrialists appears to have been lost until Kevin O'Garvey threatens to expose the deal to divert attention from the shirt factory unless Hubble's people rebuild the forge.

Conor may have won a round, but Uris makes it clear that whether the battleground is political, economic, or domestic, the hard life in Ireland at the turn of the century will take its toll. At the midpoint of the book, a despondent Tomas dies, leaving Conor with the responsibility not only of standing up to the British but of caring for his family as well. With the death of Tomas and the departure of young Dary for the seminary, the only two left in the old house are Conor's mother, Finola, and his sister, Brigid. Uris describes the pair as typical of what the hard life of Northern Ireland can do to a woman, as they silently go about their duties, knowing neither love nor hate.

The web in which Conor finds himself entangled expands in this part of the book to include the Hubbles. When Conor accepts a commission from Caroline Hubble to restore an antique wrought-iron screen at the Manor, he develops an affection for her and her young son Jeremy. This experience leaves him feeling cursed: He wants to hate the Hubbles but cannot, and he wants to change Ireland but feels helpless to do so.

Conor's despair deepens when the Witherspoon & McNab shirt factory burns, killing over a hundred workers and burning a hundred more, most of them women and children. An intricate coverup is guaranteed success when Kevin O'Garvey, the only person aware of the deal to keep the Select Committee from inspecting the factory, mysteriously disappears. The fire and its aftermath leave Conor thoroughly demoralized, and Part Four ends as did Part Three, with a leave-taking. As the twentieth century begins, Conor leaves Derry and any semblance of a normal life that he has ever known.

When Part Five, "Dusty Bluebells," opens, Seamus O'Neill has returned to continue his story. He has become a journalist, and Uris uses Seamus's profession to report on the evils of the British Empire, particularly the Boer War in South Africa. Seamus's reports on conditions in British concentration camps set up to hold Boer men, women, and children recall those in earlier novels on both the Nazi death camps and the European refugee camps after World War II. The relevance to the Irish question is clear: "I believe a seed was planted in the Transvaal and the fruits of the matured tree would spread discontent throughout [the British] imperial scheme. . . . I know somehow that Ireland and the Irish people would be among the first" to challenge Britain's age-old rule (414).

While Seamus has been honing his skills as a writer and a crusader, Conor has been wandering the world trying to rid his soul of Ireland. Uris portrays Conor as an unwilling conscience of his nation, frustrated by the apparent stranglehold that Britain has over his people. When Seamus writes to Conor that the spirit of revolution is resurfacing in Dublin, Conor returns, offering a dissertation on the apathy of the Irish people. His tirade clearly echoes the author's own frustration with the compliance of colonized peoples in their own oppression. On his return, Conor pledges that he will never leave Ireland again; and as the second half of the novel begins, Conor the rebel emerges.

Conor has returned to an Ireland ripe for revolution. The Sinn Fein (Ourselves Alone) Party is in its infancy, working toward a political agreement for home rule. But it is in the person of Long Dan Sweeney, veteran of countless raids and uprisings and inmate of countless British prisons over a twenty-year period, that Uris presents the essence of the Irish revolutionary. Single-minded in ways that other revolutionaries like Andrei Androfski of *Mila 18* and Ari Ben Canaan of *Exodus* are not, Sweeney has foresworn any personal life. Like Ari's Uncle Akiva Ben Canaan, Sweeney has dedicated his life solely to the revolution. Sweeney warns his small band of revolutionaries that the press will paint them as cowards and terrorists. But so long as they remain willing to be martyred, the British can be broken.

Conor is assigned to work in Belfast, "the mongoloid child of British imperialism" (436). Seamus compares this city to Derry, where the imperialists maintain their power and wealth by keeping poor Protestants and Catholics at each other's throats. Uris will call up this image again in *The Haj*, as he accuses Arab leaders of blaming the poverty of their people on the poor Jews in Palestine.

Conor's infiltration of the Weed Works in Belfast goes almost too smoothly at first. Exploiting his friendship with Jeremy Hubble, Conor joins Frederick Weed's Belfast Boilermakers rugby team, thus acquiring a job in the locomotive shop of Weed's Iron Works. Conor plans to find a way to use the shop to smuggle arms into Ireland.

Conor concludes that Frederick Weed's personal train is the ideal vehicle to move the arms to Ireland from England, where the Boilermakers will be on tour. The personal price one must pay for devotion to a revolution becomes clear during the tour. Conor has been asked to chaperone young Jeremy Hubble and is bothered by his affection for this child of his enemy. He is also tormented by thoughts of what his activities will mean to him and his new love, Shelley MacLeod. As is the love between Andrei and Gaby in *Mila 18*, Conor's affair with Shelley is all-consuming and makes Conor wish he were an ordinary man rather than a revolutionary. His torment reaches its height when he runs from a meeting with his fellow rebels, the meeting at which the final plans for gun smuggling were to be made. The reader's sympathy is with Conor here, even though he is jeopardizing the cause. As with Conor, readers search for a way out, a way to avoid Conor's having to become the hero of the revolution.

Having decided that he will leave the Brotherhood and take Shelley to Australia, Conor finally feels at peace. But what Daddo Friel and Charles Stewart Parnell have seen in the young man is still alive. Uris suggests that Conor's dedication to rebellion is a sacred calling: first by having the ghost of Daddo Friel immerse Conor in the history of his people, and then by having the legendary Parnell recognize a special kinship with the boy. Now it is the ghost of Kevin O'Garvey who visits Conor, in a dream. But it is not O'Garvey's ghost who convinces Conor to fight on; it is Shelley, telling him that it is his fate to be a rebel, that he cannot run from his calling, that the dream of a free Ireland will pursue them wherever they run. Part Five ends with Shelley's leaving Conor but promising that she will come to him if he ever needs her again.

Part Six, "Sixmilecross," is named for the spot where the Brotherhood's gun-running operation meets its end. At first, however, the Brotherhood's successes are heartening. Arms are pouring into Ireland, and the Liberals are returned to power in England. The Home Rule Bill is resurrected. In Ulster, the stranglehold of the British overlords is being weakened by O. C. MacIvor, who seizes the opportunity to break from Weed's grasp and form his own Loyalist Party. Roger Hubble's prediction about the danger posed by MacIvor has come true. The preacher has previously organized an elite group of his most self-righteous followers called the Knights of Christ, designed exclusively to foment unrest and unleash riots. A Knights riot at the Weed Works results in Conor's being beaten almost to death, at which point Shelley, true to her word, returns to nurse him back to health.

A more politically significant result of the riot is Weed and Hubble's decision that MacIvor's populist movement has gone too far. In true imperialist fashion, the British overlords close down the Weed Works, locking workers out, and blow up MacIvor's Presbyterian seminary. As with the Nazis in *Exodus* and *Mila 18* and the communists in *Armageddon* and *Topaz*, the British crush opposition ruthlessly in order to maintain their power.

The unrest among the Protestant population and their British masters does not slow Conor's plans to make one last run—this time with a thousand guns—before shutting down the operation. The run is to terminate at Sixmilecross. And terminate it does, when a train filled with British soldiers instead of smuggled guns pulls up to the crossing. Although the raid devastates the Brotherhood, it does arouse the sympathy of the Irish people, and it forces the British to acknowledge the existence of the seret army. The publicity allows the Brotherhood attorney, Robert Emmet McAloon, to make a deal with the British attorney general: short sentences for the suspects in return for public silence from the Brotherhood. But the Brotherhood is divided on this strategy. While Long Dan Sweeney acknowledges that the deal is a sensible one, fellow veteran of British prisons Brendan Sean Barrett wants to capitalize on the publicity, warning that the British will never honor the deal. Readers of *Exodus* will share Barrett's concerns, aware of British betrayal of the Jews in Palestine. Conor too disdains the arrangement, but for other reasons. He tells Seamus, "I'm Conor Larkin. I'm an Irishman and I've had enough" (605).

Barrett's warning is prophetic, as the British arraign Conor and his fellow prisoners in a secret session. The only Irish witnesses are Seamus and Atty Fitzpatrick, a noted actress and member of the Brotherhood, but both are bound to silence. Conor's address to the court provides Uris with the opportunity to expose the British occupation of Ireland as illegal under English Common Law, which prohibits a person from taking a neighbor's land by force. Conor's refusal to recognize the legitimacy of the British court is riveting, causing Seamus to rethink his pledge of secrecy. Conor's final words to the judge before being removed from the room leave his friends, and the reader, mesmerized: "You are a stranger in my land, mister. In the end, your fake legality will be exposed and you'll crawl out of Ireland, reviled" (613).

The British compound their treachery by passing the Detention and Emergency Powers Act, giving the attorney general absolute discretion in determining special crimes that are to be tried outside normal judicial rules. And since the British conclude that Conor's tirade has breached the agreement with McAloon, the Sixmilecross defendants will be tried under the new law. That law, as described by Uris, features precisely the provisions actually used by the British in Northern Ireland throughout this century.

As Atty and Seamus publicize Conor's speech, Republican sympathies throughout Ireland begin to mount. In prison, Conor defies his captors, singing his way through a brutal lashing. It is only the news of the murder and mutilation of Shelley MacLeod at the hands of fanatical disciples of O. C. MacIvor that breaks him. He goes through a dark night of the soul, but with the help of his brother, now Father Dary Larkin, he escapes from prison at the end of Part Six.

Part Seven takes its title, "A Terrible Beauty," from a poem by William Butler Yeats commemorating the 1916 uprising against the British. In this section Uris recounts the slow growth of the Irish Republican Brotherhood at the end of the first decade of the twentieth century. Still devastated by the death of Shelley, Conor is sent to America to raise money for the cause. He is called home when the Brotherhood begins planning an organized campaign against the British. He must also face Atty Fitzpatrick, with whom he has shared his greatest sorrow and with whom he is probably in love, despite his mourning Shelley.

As he prepares to take on his new assignment, Conor tells Seamus, "Nothing ever happens here in the future. It's always the past happening over and over again" (664). Comparing Ireland and England to a pair of comets hurtling toward each other, he wonders if they will finally crash into one another. The reader can only surmise that the explosion is imminent.

Conor has become one of the most respected voices in the Brotherhood, and for that reason Long Dan sends Atty to him to ask that he become Long Dan's successor. Conor's reason for refusing is chilling. He does not believe that the Brotherhood can beat the British: "All we can hope for is a glorious defeat" that will lead to "more glorious defeats" (674). He sees the Brotherhood in much the same light as Andrei in *Mila 18* saw the Warsaw ghetto Underground, namely, as more of a symbolic force than a practical military option. Nonetheless, the power of the symbol is strong, and the force must fight on, knowing that it cannot win.

The climax of the novel approaches as political intrigue in the British Parliament results in secret plans for separating Ulster from the rest of Ireland if a Home Rule Bill is passed. Uris uses a series of news dispatches written by Seamus O'Neill to trace the fate of the Home Rule Bill and the Liberal Party in Parliament and to describe the massive rallies organized by Weed and Hubble to arouse the people in the north. Including actual historical accounts such as Winston Churchill's aborted visit to Ulster to support the bill, the news stories lend both credence and immediacy to the mounting crisis.

As tensions mount, Frederick Weed organizes the Ulster Volunteer Force (UVF), a private army designed to protect business interests in the province if fighting breaks out. Although the force is clearly illegal, the British are helpless to stop it. When the Liberal government orders British troops into Ulster to counter the UVF, all officers of the British division resign in protest. The government backs down, rescinding the order. Liberal Whip Alan Birmingham, speaking prophetically, warns Churchill, his party's leader, that failure to act now will result in Britain's becoming hopelessly entangled in Ireland. Of course, any reader aware of current events understands how accurate Birmingham's prediction is.

In the south, the Irish form their own force to counter the UVF, the Irish Home Army. And having refused to act against the private army of the north, Britain cannot act on this new threat to peace. However, when World War I breaks out in 1914, England accepts the UVF as a force to fight the Germans, while refusing, out of legitimate fear, to recognize the Irish Home Army. But the war with Germany is not the primary concern of the Brotherhood, who plan to blow up the UVF's largest arms cache at Lettershambo Castle in Ballyutogue.

It is fitting that Conor Larkin's last battle occurs in the place where his earliest battles with his father were fought. And it is fitting that in this, his final battle, he must detonate the dynamite while his friend Seamus remains in the castle. As he has known all along, the fight for independence calls for the greatest sacrifices. After the successful demolition of the castle, Long Dan and Conor make a final suicide stand against the encroaching British forces, having had, in Dan's words, "our . . . fill of terrible beauties" (747). Against the "terrible beauty" of the exploding castle, Long Dan Sweeney and Conor Larkin give their lives to the cause of a free, united Ireland—a cause that each knows is all but futile. In an epilogue, Uris writes of the public outcry at the funerals of Dan and Conor and of the Easter Rising of 1916 that eventually led to the formation of the Irish Republic. But repeating Conor's words, Uris ends the book by focusing on the troubles that continue to this day because, "You see, in Ireland there is no future, only the past happening over and over" (751).

Character Development

Most of the major characters in *Trinity* are mythical in stature, larger than life. In this regard, the characters resemble those in Uris's other books dealing with classic struggles against tyranny, *Exodus* and *Mila 18*. In *Trinity*, the hero is Conor Larkin, a man who closely resembles Andrei Androfski of *Mila 18* in his combination of revolutionary zeal and passion for life. But Conor also resembles *Exodus*'s Ari Ben Canaan in his characterization as standing head and shoulders above the other actors in the drama.

Conor comes to the revolution from a long line of legendary characters. His great grandfather, Ronan Larkin, fought in the uprising of 1798 with the great Irish patriot Theobald Wolfe Tone and suffered the torture at the hands of the British. Ronan's son Kilty continues the tradition, breaking the tithe, or mandatory contribution to the Anglican Church, and striking fear in the hearts of the English landlords with his carefully orchestrated terrorist raids. A hero of the Fenian rising of 1867, Kilty too felt the lash of the British master. Kilty's son Tomas, the only other member of the family to survive the Great Famine in 1845, has no taste for revolutionary activities; nonetheless, he is a great man in Ballyutogue. When the Catholics are first granted the vote in 1885, it is Tomas, Conor's father, who defies a Protestant mob to cast the first Catholic vote in an election that sees eighty-six members of the Irish Party join the Republican hero Charles Stewart Parnell in Parliament. When the ghost of shanachie Daddo Friel tells Conor the story of the Larkin family during Kilty's wake, it appears to be the boy's fate that he too will become a hero of the revolution.

Conor's stature is enhanced by the hero-worship of his friend, Seamus O'Neill, who narrates much of the story. It is Seamus who, at age twelve, first intimates that Conor is destined for greatness. When Conor meets Parnell after the bloody Apprentice Boys Day riot, Parnell instantly recognizes in Conor a combination of the poet and the revolutionary, the essential characteristics of the true Irish hero. Conor first mixes the two at a meeting of the Gaelic League, an Irish nationalist organization, in Derry. At the end of his extemporaneous lecture on the hero Wolfe Tone, his audience is moved to tears.

Conor's poetic nature leads him to wander the world to escape the troubles that plague his land and his soul. His journey represents those of many mythic heroes who must find themselves before they take up the mantle of leadership. As Conor tells Seamus, "I tried, Seamus, I tried, but the world was not large enough to dim the vision of Ireland or purge the curse of it from my soul" (427).

When he returns to Ireland, heeding the call of the Brotherhood, Conor's poetic nature gives way to that of a ruthless revolutionary. His dedication to the cause allows him to use Caroline and Jeremy Hubble, for whom he has a genuine affection, in order to set up his gun-running scheme. His conscience does not prevent him from recognizing that the cause must come before all else. At no time is he more fully aware of the price of heroism than when he parts with Shelley MacLeod, the great love of his life. He cannot have her and pursue his calling, so he reluctantly gives her up.

The superhuman strength that comes of such sacrifice is evident when a haggard, beaten, and half-starved Conor stands up to a British court and delivers a rousing speech on the illegality of the British occupation of Ireland. His strength also serves him during a particularly brutal flogging, when instead of crying out he sings a rebel song, then refuses a stretcher and walks back to his cell. When Conor finally dies in the raid on Lettershambo Castle, the adulation of his people assures him a place in Irish history.

Conor's mythic stature allows him to have an second great love in his life, Atty Fitzpatrick. Like Conor, both Atty and Shelley are larger-than-life characters as well. Shelley fiercely guards her independence in a society with rigid rules of conduct, especially for females. Conor calls her "an awesome woman" (459), and she is, a Protestant Ulsterwoman standing up bravely to the condemnation of her people for her relationship with the Catholic Fenian Conor. Atty Fitzpatrick is equally awesome. One of the great actresses in Ireland, and independently wealthy, she nevertheless devotes her life to the Brotherhood. Atty is the only woman on the Supreme Council of the Brotherhood, an "Irish Joan of Arc" (549), in Seamus's words. Her identification with her country is so strong that Seamus also compares her to "Mother Ireland herself" (550). Both women are the equal of Conor Larkin, and he knows it.

Other members of the Brotherhood also cast large shadows, in particular Long Dan Sweeney and Brendan Sean Barrett. Both have spent much of their lives in British prisons, and both have steadfastly refused to be broken. Barrett endures indignities and torture at the hands of the British and simply keeps smiling, eventually going on a hunger strike that breaks their hold on him. Long Dan, imprisoned for twenty years at age sixteen, tells Conor of being brought out to his own scaffold every night before his scheduled execution and hung feet first by a sadistic warder. Years later, after having been released from prison, Dan meets up with the warder by chance—and breaks the man's neck with his bare hands. Long Dan Sweeney and Brendan Sean Barrett are the revolution for men like Conor.

That Ireland produces good men can be seen in other, lesser characters such as Father Pat McShane, a revolutionary priest who cares for the poor in Derry. It is Father Pat who convinces Conor that one can be a good Catholic and a good revolutionary at the same time. Conor's brother Dary, also a priest, lives his religion by supporting Irish independence. It is Dary who orchestrates Conor's escape from prison. And Seamus O'Neill, Conor's lifelong friend and occasional narrator of the story, uses his education and his writing talent to further the cause of his people.

Among the Protestants there are admirable characters as well. Andrew Ingram, the teacher first in Ballyutogue and later in Derry, refuses to segregate the Catholic children in his school and insists upon teaching his students Irish as well as English history. It is Ingram who first tells Conor that he is fated to fight for Irish freedom. Once Conor engages in that fight, he meets Robin MacLeod, Shelley's brother and captain of the Boilermakers, who loves Conor like a brother and refuses to allow sectarian differences to interfere with their friendship. It is Robin who warns Conor of the impending anti-Catholic riot at the Weed Works.

But Ireland also produces the sour, narrow priest Father Lynch, whose suspicion of anything that might bring light, joy, or hope into his parishioners' lives makes him a despicable character. Father Lynch's satisfaction when Finola Larkin confesses to enjoying sex with her husband leads him to order her to live a celibate life. He is motivated as much by hatred of Finola's husband Tomas, who defies Church rule, as by piety. Father Lynch's Protestant counterpart, the Reverend Oliver Cromwell MacIvor, makes the Catholic priest's petty attempts at controlling his flock seem pathetic by comparison. MacIvor's goal is to spread hatred of Catholics throughout Ulster and to control the mob himself. He is evil incarnate; there is nothing redeeming about him. Similarly, Roger Hubble is a conniving, ruthless aristocrat who uses MacIvor and everyone in his employ to maintain his power in Ulster. His father-in-law, Frederick Weed, considers his adopted country simply another conquest in his industrial empire. Blind to the dangerous conditions under which his employees work, dismissive of reports about the pollution that his factories pour into Belfast's air and water, and single-minded in his quest to control Ulster politically as well as economically, Weed is the essence of the unscrupulous industrialist.

Since the novel is set during the thirty years surrounding the turn of the twentieth century, women do not play a significant role either in business or politics. The exceptions, of course, are the great women: Shelley MacLeod, Atty Fitzpatrick, and Caroline Hubble. Shelley's personal sense of independence and Atty's devotion to the cause are matched by Caroline's determination to transform Ulster, and Derry in particular, into a civilized community. As beautiful and striking as Shelley and Atty, Caroline Weed Hubble is also portrayed as a headstrong woman intent on living life on her own terms. She meets her match in Roger Hubble, but she makes use of their union to introduce Derry to the arts and to beautify Hubble Manor. Caroline is particularly interesting because, unlike many other characters in the novel, she is complex. While she is clearly and unashamedly a member of the oppressor class, she nevertheless respects Conor's artistic talent as well as his dedication to a free Ireland, and she defends her son Jeremy's devotion to an Irish Catholic girl, flying in the face of aristocratic tradition.

Other women in the novel fill more stereotypical roles. Seamus's mother Mairead is an accomplished midwife, proud but aware of her place in society. The once-fiesty Finola Larkin, Conor's mother, is ultimately beaten down by the Church's teachings on the sinfulness of sex. After confessing to Father Lynch and receiving her penance, Finola transforms her home into a place devoid of love and laughter. Deprived of her one great love because of his poverty, Finola's daughter, Brigid, becomes the essence of the hard, cold spinster for whom warmth and love are but distant memories. In contrast, two other female characters, the young Fenian Maud Tully and Jeremy's love Molly O'Rafferty, are portrayed as strong, independent women. Maud gives her life to save her young niece in the shirt factory fire, and Molly maintains her dignity when Jeremy is coerced by his father into abandoning her. Interestingly, both young women are pregnant when they make their brave stands.

Because *Trinity* is a historical novel, Uris introduces historical figures into the story, sometimes allowing them to interact with his fictional characters. Parnell, for example, is a close friend of the fictional member of Parliament Kevin O'Garvey. He also encounters Conor and Sean when the two are young boys. Randolph Churchill, the vehement Conservative who fought to maintain a British Ulster, is seen in the company of the Hubbles and Frederick Weed. And Winston Churchill, the famed Liberal, argues with his fellow Liberal Alan Birmingham over how to respond to the formation of the Ulster Volunteer Force by Frederick Weed.

The characters in *Trinity* resemble those in an earlier novel, *Exodus*. The heroes in each work are of mythical stature, and the demands of the cause overshadow any personal concerns, even those of love and family. Perhaps the most significant similarity, however, is in the personification of the land itself. Just as Israel figures prominently in *Exodus*, so too does Ireland in *Trinity*. All of the action, all of the motivation, all of the relationships in the novel can be traced directly to the land and its power over the people. That power is sometimes devastating, as seen in the Great Famine, and often all-consuming, as seen in Long Dan Sweeney's lonely life. But like the power of Israel, the power of Ireland will not be denied. After Lettershambo Castle and the Easter Rising, the sacrifices that Ireland demands of her people continue until this day.

Thematic Issues

The title of this novel itself identifies the primary theme of the book. The various trinities within the narrative involve politics, nationalism, religion, and personal relationships. The primary trinity of the book, of course, is that comprising the Northern Irish Protestants, the Irish Catholics, and their English masters. The tension among the members of this trinity is what makes up the tragedy of Northern Irish life.

In the Western world, particularly within the Catholic religion, the concept of trinity is a holy one. The three components of the Holy Trinity are God the Father, God the Son, and God the Holy Spirit. Among them, these three Gods in One are responsible for all that is good in the world. Thus, Uris's use of the term "trinity" in this political context is ironic, because the British-Protestant-Catholic trinity is anything but holy and good. The British, at the pinnacle of the trinity, manipulate the Protestants, descended from Scottish Presbyterians imported for labor in Ulster's factories and farms, by drumming into them the threat posed by Irish Catholics. With their attention focused on the Catholics, the Protestants do not recognize that their true oppressors are the British industrialists and aristocrats who keep them one step ahead of poverty. The Catholics, of course, after centuries of oppressive laws, are all but helpless within this trinity. The strength of the British is illustrated when Oliver Cromwell MacIvor seeks to wrest power from the gentry and control the Protestant working class himself. In Uris's terms, MacIvor creates his own "unholy trinity" consisting of the Universal Presbyterian Church, the militant Knights of Christ, and the political Loyalist Party (557). After a few successful riots, MacIvor's organizations are crushed when Frederick Weed locks workers out of his factory and bombs the Presbyterian Seminary. Weed is successful because of his own trinity: politicians, industrialists, and aristocrats, all of whom have a vested interest in maintaining the status quo.

Other trinities exist within the larger context of this political trinity. Among them are the landowners, the industrialists, and the Irish population—a trinity unique to the latter days of the nineteenth century. Landowners have traditionally kept the population in line by exacting rents and controlling crops. But a combination of misuse of the land itself and the industrial revolution disrupts the social order. The merger of the Weed (industrial) and Hubble (landed) interests allows control of the population to remain in the hands of the wealthy.

An additional trinity designed to maintain British control of Ireland includes British politicians, the Roman Catholic Church, and the Irish population. In return for control over the spiritual life of the population and for generous financial contributions to church buildings, the Catholic bishops strive to maintain the status quo, excommunicating men like Ronan and Kilty Larkin for Republican activity and keeping the population focused on the hereafter rather than on the earthly conditions in which they live their lives. The Presbyterian Church is used to keep the Protestant population in line in much the same way. By maintaining a close connection between the patriotic Orange Order and the Protestant Church, the British masters are able to equate loyalty to the crown with religious purity.

The theme of trinity extends itself to personal relationships as well. The first such trinity that emerges consists of Tomas, Conor, and Liam Larkin—the three men of the Larkin family. The struggle among these men all but destroys the family, with Liam going off to New Zealand, Conor retreating to Derry, and Tomas destroying his health through his grief over the loss of his sons. On the Protestant side, Roger Hubble, Frederick Weed, and Caroline Weed Hubble constitute a formidable trinity when they join forces to consolidate power in Ulster. But the human sensibilities that lead Caroline to sympathize with her son's love for a Catholic girl eventually destroy her marriage. Symbolically, her emerging tolerance for Catholics represents the sensibility that will ultimately undermine the British-Protestant-Catholic trinity. A more productive trinity comprises Conor, Seamus, and Andrew Ingram. This trinity nurtures the artistic and political sensibilities of the two boys and provides them with an anchor throughout their lives.

The most significant of the personal trinities involves Conor, Shelley MacLeod, and Atty Fitzpatrick. The three together represent the fate of Ireland. Conor's love for Shelley is doomed from the start because she is Protestant and closely tied, through her brother Robin, to Frederick Weed. Conor's love for Atty is equally doomed because of the Brotherhood, which remains the primary loyalty for both her and Conor. This trinity, which should represent the hope of Ireland, instead represents Ireland's tragedy.

The various trinities in the novel are often related to class issues. Uris condemns the gentry and the aristocrats for keeping both Protestant and Catholic laborers in or near poverty. The corruption of the Catholic and Protestant Churches contributes to this oppression. The volatile social conditions created by an unscrupulous ruling class lead to personal turmoil for both working-class people and aristocrats. The demands of aristocracy, for example, force a weak Jeremy Hubble to abandon Molly O'Rafferty and their unborn child. And enslavement to the land compels Tomas Larkin to exile one son and alienate another. The love between Conor and Shelley is doomed because of the enmity between Protestants and Catholics, an enmity kept alive by the ruling class. Similarly, Conor and Atty are doomed because the commitment of each to fighting the oppressor keeps them from living normal lives. The social situation created by the British continually insinuates itself into the lives of the Irish people. By robbing a people of their right to self-determination, the British prove themselves to be the creators of the unholiest of trinities.

REDEMPTION

Redemption fleshes out the stories of the main characters of the earlier novel, in particular the Larkins, the Hubbles, Shelley MacLeod, and Atty Fitzpatrick. In addition, the story of Liam Larkin and his oldest son Rory illustrates the words spoken by Conor and echoed by Uris at the end of *Trinity*: "It's always the past happening over and over again" (664). Perhaps a third of *Redemption*'s plot covers the same ground as *Trinity*, with the remainder exploring further the issues raised by the earlier novel.

Plot Development

Part One of *Redemption*, "Footsteps," begins with the first entry into a private journal by the young Winston Churchill, establishing one of the methods Uris will use to provide readers with his interpretation of the historical framework of the book. The bulk of the section, however, tells the story of Liam Larkin's settling in New Zealand. Ending with the grieving of Liam's family over Conor's death in the Lettershambo Castle raid, the first part of the book establishes the troubled relationship between Liam and Rory, in which Liam re-creates Conor's relationship with Tomas, his father.

Rory's struggle with his father reaches a climax with the news of Conor's death, as the two, both of whom loved Conor dearly, are nonetheless unable to comfort one another. World War I has begun, and in his grief Rory announces to his lover, Georgia Norman, his decision to run off and join the British Army. Unlike Danny Forrester in *Battle Cry*, who joins his country's army out of a sense of patriotism, Rory joins the army of a country his beloved Uncle Conor died fighting against. Still, his decision is not surprising, since it is clear from the beginning of the story that Rory will eventually follow in Conor's footsteps. The questions are simply when and how he will leave New Zealand. The Great War provides him with his opportunity.

Part Two, "The Visit," returns to an earlier time, taking up the story of Atty Fitzpatrick's youth. Witnessing the death of young peasant children from cholera, Atty's rage at the social system that allows such destitution is kindled when she is a mere seven years old. Her blossoming into young womanhood and her fixation on a man seven years older hint at the passion that will be seen later when she and Conor fall in love.

Shifting from Atty's youth to Conor's, Uris introduces a scene that conflicts with its counterpart in *Trinity*. Rather than have Conor first visit Hubble Manor and view the great screen as an adult owner of his own forge, Uris has him accompany blacksmith Josiah Lambe to the Manor when Conor is a boy of twelve. The boy becomes enthralled with the screen and with Lady Caroline Hubble. Although the scene is at odds with the earlier novel, it does serve three purposes. First, juxtaposed with the story of Atty's youthful love, it forges a bond between the two before they ever meet. Both are capable of passionate attachments, in each case to people considerably older. Second, since Caroline Hubble will play an even more prominent role in *Redemption* than in *Trinity*, the scene establishes her relationship with Conor and his Republican sympathies.

The third purpose of the conflicting scene is made clear as Winston Churchill recalls in his secret files that he accompanied his father, Randolph, to Ulster and Hubble Manor at age twelve. He too becomes enthralled with Lady Caroline, whose path will cross his as well as Conor's in years to come. The contradictory scene thus establishes Caroline's central role not only in the personal life of Conor Larkin and Winston Churchill but in Ireland's struggle for freedom as well.

In order to reacquaint readers of *Trinity* with the stories of Atty and Conor, Kevin O'Garvey and Andrew Ingram, Uris summarizes in this section some of the significant events in Conor's life and the life of Ireland. Readers are provided a glimpse of the relationship between Atty and her husband Desmond as well, suggesting that the passion in their marriage had more to do with the cause than with their love for each other. The story of Kevin O'Garvey's deal to keep the Select Committee from investigating conditions in the shirt factory is retold as well, but with an added twist: Andrew Ingram discovers the deal, which also includes money for him to found a college in Derry. Andrew leaves Derry in disgust, hoping to redeem himself for his inactivity by returning to work in anonymity in Scotland. Uris allows Conor to remain ignorant of the deal for a longer period, one in which his dedication to the cause is tested by his equally fierce dedication to his art and to Caroline Hubble. The restoration of the great screen at Hubble Manor becomes in this book a metaphor for the seduction of talented Irish people from their true calling, with both the screen and the woman distracting Conor. But Conor, struggling to the last, resists a very real seduction by Caroline in a scene that will later underscore her refusal to dismiss the cause of the Irish as her fellow aristocrats do. Her secret visit to Conor after the factory fire, a scene in which both she and Conor express their guilt over whatever complicity they may have had in the deal, establishes her as a woman with a conscience.

In *Trinity* Uris mentions that Conor's wandering after the factory fire takes him to his brother Liam in New Zealand. In *Redemption* this visit is fleshed out, and the two threads of the novel—the past that Conor builds and the future that Rory will fashion—are intertwined. Rory becomes enthralled with his uncle, causing Liam to fear that the boy will yearn for the kind of life that his great-grandfather Kilty lived. The old struggle between Conor and Tomas is played out again as Liam tries desperately to offset the impact that Conor has had on Rory. Sensing the tension, Conor leaves New Zealand, but not before handing Rory a list of books on liberty, the same books that set Conor's mind wandering a generation earlier.

Part Three, "Dweller on the Threshold," opens with an interesting plot device, a letter to Rory in which Conor gossips about the family and his friends in Ireland. But between the lines Conor recounts the significant events of his life: the rebirth of revolution in the form of Long Dan Sweeney and the Irish Republican Brotherhood and the imminent gun-running scheme. These words do not find their way into the letter; they are for readers' eyes only. Nonetheless, Uris's presentation of subsequent letters indicates that Rory is well aware of something between the lines; and while his own letters are filled with news about Ballyutogue Station, they silently cry out with the desire to join Conor in the fight.

Conor's letters remind readers too of his affection for Jeremy Hubble and of his love for Shelley MacLeod, and their painful parting when it becomes clear to Shelley that Conor must fulfill his destiny. A lengthy conversation between Seamus and Long Dan Sweeney elaborates upon the depth of the love between Conor and Shelley and establishes the fact that Conor's meeting with the now-widowed Atty Fitzpatrick is orchestrated by Seamus and Dan to help bring Conor back into the Brotherhood in soul as well as in body. The meeting, as readers of *Trinity* know, results in a powerful attraction, but one that Conor, still grieving over the loss of Shelley, resists.

The plot in this section is also forwarded through more of Winston Churchill's secret files, in which his defection from his father's Conservative Party to the Liberals is recounted, as is his association with Frederick Weed and Caroline Hubble.

Several chapters are devoted to a summary of Brigid Larkin's life after losing her only love, Myles McCracken; to Dary Larkin's ordination; to the rise of Oliver Cromwell MacIvor; and to Shelley's return to Conor after he is beaten. The story of the Sixmilecross raid, its impact on the Brotherhood, and Conor's capture is recounted in a series of news releases. In a previously untold story, readers learn of Shelley's hiding out with Atty after the disaster, during which time the two become as close as sisters. Also untold in *Trinity* is Jeremy Hubble's reaction to Conor's arrest. Alternately loving the Conor who was like an older brother and hating the Conor who betrayed him, Jeremy is tormented by the demonstrations in Dublin occasioned by Conor's imprisonment.

Jeremy's doomed love affair with Molly O'Rafferty takes on a new twist in this book as well. Caroline and her father both see Roger's manipulation of his son Jeremy as the work of an evil man. Together they plan to undo Roger and consolidate their hold on the Weed industrial empire. The scandal to bring him down is the cover-up of the shirt factory fire. It is here that readers learn for certain the nature of Kevin O'Garvey's disappearance: Frederick Weed and Roger Hubble ordered his assassination. This section of the book ends with Caroline Hubble alternately gloating over her newfound power over Roger and mourning the loss of Conor Larkin.

Following Part Three is an interlude titled "The Missing Years," ostensibly compiled by Atty Fitzpatrick from notes written by Seamus O'Neill. The section comprises a summary, in Seamus's voice, of Conor's trial and imprisonment, of Shelley's death and Conor's mourning, of Conor's voyage to America, and of Conor and Atty's coming together in their mutual grief over Shelley. Seamus also reminds readers of the independent power Conor exercises after his return, as well as Long Dan Sweeney's desire to hand the reins of the Brotherhood over to Conor. The interlude ends with Conor revealing to Seamus his plans for the Lettershambo raid and his understanding that the fight for freedom will be long and costly.

Part Four, "That Wild Colonial Boy," returns to Rory's tale immediately following news of Conor's death. Not much more than a boy, Rory feels himself a man as he takes emotional leave of Georgia, promising to return for her. As he sets off for war, his thoughts are torn between memories of Georgia and the legend of his Uncle Conor.

The action shifts quickly to the Hubbles, where Caroline and her father are plotting to blackmail Roger Hubble into giving over his ownership in the Weed empire. During an interchange after their son Christopher's wedding, Caroline and Roger review their lives together, and it becomes clear that Caroline has become quite sympathetic to the Republican cause. As she takes leave of her husband for the last time, it is clear to the reader that the Caroline Hubble of *Redemption* is a far deeper character than the Caroline of *Trinity*.

Moving to London to oversee her father's industrial empire in England, Caroline takes up Liberal causes. She becomes an unofficial advisor to Winston Churchill, who is pressured into becoming Lord of the Admiralty, a position that takes on added significance as war looms. The unethical maneuverings of Frederick and Roger to keep Ulster British, explained in detail in *Trinity*, are summarized here. But Uris goes into far greater detail than in the earlier book in describing Caroline's plans to move Weed Ship & Iron forward with new technologies. Her insistence that the war will keep the factories running, and that postwar production should include airplanes, puts her far ahead of other industrialists in her forward thinking.

Throughout *Redemption* Uris takes readers behind the scenes played out in *Trinity*. In this section, that look behind the curtain involves the resignation of the officers ordered to occupy Ulster to counteract the Weed-Hubble private army. Included with those officers are both Jeremy and Christopher Hubble, led by commanding officer Major Llewellyn Brodhead. The resignations, part of a plot to bring down the Liberal government, cause Churchill great consternation. It is through consultation with Caroline Hubble that Churchill negotiates the compromise that allows the government to survive. Part of that compromise includes the tabling of the Irish Home Rule Bill in exchange for British recognition of the Irish Home Army, the Catholic force. But the Lettershambo Castle raid, occurring two months after the start of the Great War, makes clear that Ireland will continue to fight for its freedom, for "England's war and Ireland's struggle for freedom had nothing to do with each other" (388).

When the action shifts again to New Zealand, a confrontation between Liam, searching for Rory, and Georgia results in Liam's recognizing Georgia's strength and passion. Georgia encourages Liam to communicate with his son, to redeem his sins against Rory. Rory himself is next seen on a troop train, where he befriends another runaway, sixteen-year-old aristocrat Chester Goodwood. The camaraderie of the men and boys marching off to war is reminiscent of Uris's first novel, *Battle Cry*. As in the earlier novel, the men in the Seventh Light Horse Battalion represent an odd assortment, including Rory, Chester, and their leader Johnny Tarbox, who once worked as a hand at Ballyutogue Station. They will be led by General Brodhead, Major Chris Hubble, and First Lieutenant Jeremy Hubble. With the formation of the joint Australian–New Zealand Expeditionary Force (Anzacs), Rory and Jeremy, Conor's two spiritual sons, finally meet. As in *Battle Cry*, the lives these soldiers think they have left behind will haunt them as they form themselves into a fighting unit. In particular, Rory is tormented by dreams of Liam, and Jeremy is finally compelled to reconcile with Caroline.

The actual planning of the war is covered in Churchill's secret files, where he writes late in 1914 of British hopes to crush the Ottoman Empire by first securing the Turkish-held Gallipoli Peninsula, gateway to Constantinople. The excitement conveyed in Churchill's plans, however, gives way to serious doubt as the seasoned officer Brodhead expresses grave concerns over a plan that he sees as politically rather than militarily inspired. The orders to take Gallipoli are further complicated by the placement of British officers at the head of the Anzac troops. The clash between the class-conscious British, personified in Chris Hubble, and the wholly democratic Anzacs, personified in Johnny Tarbox, makes for a difficult mix. Bridging the gap is Jeremy Hubble, who is capable of mingling with officers and enlisted men alike.

While the Seventh is in Cairo awaiting training, the men engage in drinking, fighting, and gambling, much like the soldiers in *Battle Cry*. The Jewish Palestinian Zion Mule Corps joins the Seventh, creating a force of many colors, religions, cultures, and nationalities. But as Uris illustrated in his first novel, civilian distinctions do not mean much in a fighting force. Those who are able to contribute to the comfort of the brigade while in Cairo become the most valuable comrades. Jeremy is able to arrange for luxury accommodations for his friends, including Rory, Chester, Johnny, and Mordechai "Modi" Pearlman of the Mule Corps. The brotherhood shared among these men about to go off to war is humorously memorialized when they all have mules tattooed on their buttocks in a scene that recalls some of the lighter passages of *Battle Cry*. Even Chris, the unrelenting commanding officer, is humanized when he becomes hopelessly drunk after receiving a "Dear John" letter from his wife and requires Jeremy and the others to extricate him from a compromising situation. His loss is added to that of Rory, who hears from Georgia that she is reconciling with her husband, and of Jeremy, who hears from his mother that his child was stillborn and Molly has retreated into a convent. As always in wartime, the pain shared by the men will help forge them into a fighting force as their appointment with their destiny nears. Part Four ends as the storm clouds gather over Gallipoli.

Part Four is followed by a second interlude, "Gallipoli," told by Rory Larkin. His narrative of the seemingly endless battle is as powerful as the battle narratives of Uris's first novel. Rory focuses on details that civilians never think about, such as the blistering heat, the inability to bathe, and the foul rations. The boredom soldiers feel when not in battle is almost as powerful as the fear when engaged with the enemy. The primary purpose of this narrative, however, is to chronicle the folly of the British leaders. London insists that the soldiers fight on, even after it is clear that the generals have grossly miscalculated the situation. Christopher Hubble's men are landed on the wrong beach under merciless fire from the Turks. Chris is reprimanded by General Godley for an initiative that saves the entire brigade, simply because in the chaos of the first battle Chris did not clear his orders with a superior officer. Godley, looking for glory, orders a charge on a meaningless hill, resulting in the decimation of an entire New Zealand force. Because the British high command cannot bear the thought of losing face, the forces on Gallipoli suffer tens of thousands of casualties in a three-month-long battle for nothing.

If Gallipoli illustrates the ineptitude and corruption of the high command, it also reveals the nobility of the common soldier. Johnny Tarbox is killed leading his men to shore, Chester Goodwood proves invaluable to the survival of the troops, and countless other soldiers sacrifice their own lives to save others. In one particularly moving episode after a devastating battle, a truce is called so that both sides can bury their thousands of dead in a mass grave. On a personal level, Rory tells Jeremy of his relationship to Conor and the two reminisce about their common hero. Rory also encounters Calvin Norman, Georgia's former husband, and overcomes his desire to kill the man who had been abusive to the woman he loves. Finally discovering that Georgia has lied about still being married, he writes to her seeking reconciliation.

Before the British government finally acknowledges defeat, Jeremy and Chris are killed by friendly fire, Chester Goodwood and several other comrades of Rory's are killed, and the government of Winston Churchill is brought down. As Rory tries to overcome despair and Churchill agonizes over his responsibility for the deaths not only of Caroline's two sons but of tens of thousands of other men, the interlude closes.

The section that follows is a prelude titled "A Retrospective on the Easter Rising of 1916," written by Atty's son Theobald Fitzpatrick. Theo, named for the Irish hero Theobald Wolfe Tone, has taken over his father's Republican activities. In this prelude Theo offers yet another glimpse behind the scenes of the action in *Trinity*: Atty Fitzpatrick, consumed with grief over Conor's death, retires from active duty in the Brotherhood. Because of the deaths of Long Dan, Conor, and Seamus, the Brotherhood has new leadership. Theo also comments on the dangerous attraction developing between Father Dary Larkin and Theo's sister Rachael.

But the primary focus of Theo's narrative is the intrigue that leads to the Easter Rising of 1916. As Ireland jockeys for a place at the peace table once the Great War is over, the Brotherhood, now under the leadership of Padraic Pearse (an actual historic character), takes command of the Irish Home Army and launches a doomed war of independence.

Through a series of sometimes comic, sometimes tragic blunders, the rising is contained within two days, but not before Pearse reads the Irish Declaration of Independence from the captured Post Office in Dublin. As Theo recalls, however, the rising does not enjoy the support of the Irish people, the Americans, or the rest of the world. Taking place during the Great War, it is seen as a stab in the back of Britain and the Allies. Ireland is placed under martial law, with General Brodhead sent in to restore order. But the British overstep themselves when they sentence to death without benefit of trial ninety-six men captured in the rising. The swiftness of the executions of now-famous men begins to turn public opinion against the colonizer. The prelude ends with Theo contemplating the impact of the British action.

Part Five, "Sir Roger Casement Is in the Tower of London," finally brings the stories of the Hubbles and the Larkins together. Returning from battle wounded and weary, Rory finds his way to Dublin, where Brodhead has set up headquarters. The disdain in which Uris holds the British high command is evident in Brodhead's purpose: Broadhead wants Rory to support him in an inquiry into the Gallipoli disaster, helping cover up official blunders. He also wants Rory to work with him in taming Ireland. Taking advantage of being in Ireland, Rory meets Caroline Hubble and visits Sixmilecross in a pilgrimage to his uncle's memory. The Larkin family is reunited as Dary brings Rory to Ballyutogue and reads to Rory a letter of reconciliation from Liam. At Conor's grave, Rory dedicates himself to the revolution, telling Conor, "I think I know why I am here in Ireland. I'm in a position to strike a blow" (742). The message he asks of Conor takes the form of Dary's introducing him to the Brotherhood.

The fates of all of the surviving major characters are hurtling toward one another at breakneck speed in this last section of the book. Father Dary and Atty's daughter Rachael have fallen in love, and Dary has embraced the Brotherhood. Atty is tormented by the resemblance between Rory and Conor, and her response to the much younger man is as much sensual as it is political. Caroline Hubble discovers Rory's identity and conspires with him to eliminate Brodhead, who she knows is responsible for her sons' deaths. Brodhead himself makes the job easier by executing a "Brotherhood lad" and brutally leveling his village, reigniting Irish Republican sentiments.

That sentiment is fueled further by the public treason trial of Sir Roger Casement, long a thorn in the Empire's side and guilty by admission of dealing with the Germans to help arm the Easter Rising. Casement's final statement, referring to the Irish cause as "the noblest cause men ever strove for, ever lived for, ever died for" (798), is haunting.

When Rory and Caroline kill General Brodhead, Rory is injured and must be spirited out of Ireland. This plot device allows Caroline to meet a final time with Winston Churchill, where she confesses to killing Brodhead and convinces Churchill to spirit Rory out of England and back to New Zealand. In the final chapter of the book, Liam narrates a summary of British response to the 1918 Irish demand for home rule and ends on a peaceful note, with Liam overseeing his vast acres and thinking proudly of his family. Unlike *Trinity*, *Redemption* ends on a hopeful note, with Rory, Georgia, and their two children, Rory and Liam, riding to meet Liam beneath a New Zealand sky.

Character Development

Although Rory Larkin is the primary character in *Redemption*, he is one of only a few new characters in the novel. Most of the other major characters appeared first in *Trinity*. Of those characters, Seamus O'Neill, Conor Larkin, and Shelley MacLeod are essentially the same as in the earlier book, while others develop further in the years after the Lettershambo Castle raid.

Rory Larkin is almost a mirror-image of his Uncle Conor. Engaged in the same battle with his father that Conor engaged in with Tomas, Rory rebels against Liam's insistence that he remain on the land and longs to follow in Conor's footsteps. Rory becomes enthralled with Conor during the latter's stay in New Zealand and, despite his father's disapproval, embarks on reading Republican books just as Conor did twenty years earlier. Rory's courage and skill emerge in the battle of Gallipoli, as does his moral fortitude when he is faced with Georgia's abusive husband, Calvin Norman. Resisting the urge to kill the man, Rory finds within himself a capacity for forgiveness and human compassion that he never knew existed. By the time Rory is ready to carry on Conor's work, he has earned his position in the Irish Republican Brotherhood.

Given the theme of redemption in the novel, it is not surprising that a number of other characters also mature during the course of the narrative. Perhaps the most pronounced maturation occurs in Lady Caroline Hubble. Slightly sympathetic in *Trinity*, Caroline becomes a true friend to Conor and Rory in *Redemption*, as well as a strong supporter of the Republican cause. As Caroline finds herself drawn to Conor, she cannot help but question the beliefs that make her his enemy. At the same time, Caroline becomes increasingly disenchanted with her husband and his unscrupulous exploitation of Ireland and its people. She also questions her own complicity in his schemes. Visiting Conor after the shirt factory fire, she confesses her sin of omission: "I never went above the first floor of that wretched place. There was conspiracy on the wind and I made it a point not to find out" (190). It takes years for her to redeem herself entirely, but when Rory finds her toward the end of the war, Caroline has been seasoned by tragedy. The loss first of Conor and then of her two sons causes her to rethink her purpose in life, and she achieves both personal and political redemption when she assassinates General Brodhead.

Caroline's sons also mature: Jeremy by gradually discovering his responsibility for other men in his unit and Chris by becoming humanized when his wife leaves him. The last that readers see of Jeremy in *Trinity* is when he reveals his weakness and cowardice in the face of his father's blackmail. Decimated by the loss of Molly and the contempt of his mother, Jeremy embarks on a life of drinking and debauchery. It is only when the bloody fields of Gallipoli call upon him to be a leader of men that he reclaims his dignity. As Rory tells Caroline after Jeremy's death, her son "transformed himself into a most splendid human being" (727). Similarly, Chris recognizes his kinship with other men when his wife leaves him. Again, as Rory tells Caroline, Chris "found out something the hard way about the loyalty and love men can give each other" (728).

While loss seems the common denominator in the maturation process of these characters, it is almost always connection with another human being that is the catalyst. Caroline, for example, matures as a result of her relationship with Conor. Both Jeremy and Chris mature in the company of fellow soldiers who depend on them. Liam Larkin also matures in the novel, also suffering loss and also spurred by a connection to another person. It is Georgia Norman's decency and obvious love for his son that convinces Liam to reconcile with Rory.

While the major characters in *Trinity* are fleshed out in *Redemption*, the later novel includes many of the representative characters of the earlier one. Long Dan Sweeney, the single-minded revolutionary, for example, reappears in *Redemption*, as does Roger Hubble, the unscrupulous aristocrat. Other representative characters in the later novel include General Brodhead, who stands for all that is wrong in the imperial forces of Great Britain. Brodhead's incompetence in battle, coupled with his desperate maneuvers to cover up his complicity in the Gallipoli disaster, represents all that is wrong with colonial forces. His brutality in Ireland reinforces that image. By contrast, Winston Churchill follows his conscience and abandons the Conservative Party; and when he learns of the disaster at Gallipoli, he takes full responsibility for it. His honorable behavior offers some hope for the future of England.

A particularly interesting feature of both *Trinity* and *Redemption* is the strength of the female characters. Almost all of the major women exhibit a strength not found in many other Uris novels. Shelley MacLeod nobly sends Conor away when she realizes what his destiny is. Atty Fitzpatrick dedicates her life to Irish freedom as a sixteen-year-old girl and loses both a husband and a lover to the cause. Caroline Hubble acknowledges her complicity in the exploitation of Ireland and changes her ways. Georgia Norman lies to Rory about being married in order not to tie him down. And Molly O'Rafferty refuses to be bought by the aristocracy. While characters such as Atty and Caroline are larger than life, the other women are portrayed as normal people who respond nobly when called upon.

The new characters in *Redemption*, as well as those who carry over from *Trinity*, all share one thing in common: the pull of Ireland. Although the later novel is set in several other locales, Ireland is always present. Even Rory, who never sets foot on Irish soil until he is over twenty-one, has always known that he must come to his true homeland. Thus *Redemption*, like *Trinity*, has as its major character not a person but a place that haunts everyone.

Thematic Issues

Just as the title of *Trinity* announces its primary theme, so too does the title of *Redemption*. Many of the characters have committed sins against their country, their loved ones, or themselves, and thus must be redeemed. The relationship at the core of the novel, that between Liam and his son Rory, is a reenactment of the relationship between Tomas and his sons in *Trinity*. Unlike Tomas, who finds redemption only on his deathbed, Liam is able to redeem himself and live to enjoy both his son and his grandchildren.

Liam's sins against Rory reflect those of his father against Conor both literally and symbolically. Literally, both men want to keep their sons on the land and prevent them from becoming martyrs to a hopeless cause. Symbolically, the desire involves continuing the Larkin line and maintaining solid roots. Liam is first offered the opportunity to redeem himself when Conor dies and Rory reaches out to him for comfort. All that Liam can say is "I need to be alone, boy" (24). After Rory runs away, Liam is offered his second opportunity for redemption when he finally finds Georgia Norman. Telling Liam that "God . . . gave us the ultimate human power, the power of redemption" (393), Georgia urges the man to reconcile with his son. Liam follows Georgia's advice and writes a letter in which he begs his son's forgiveness, assuring him that the land will be waiting when he returns. Liam's reward is to enjoy his reunited family for the rest of his life.

For his part, Rory's redemption involves forgiving his father and coming to terms with his Irish heritage. Rory is tormented by dreams of Liam after he joins the military. In a late-night conversation with Johnny Tarbox, Rory's attitude toward his father softens as he wonders if he too isn't partly to blame for their battles. His redemption comes in the form of forgiving both himself and his father and returning to Ballyutogue Station after the war. Rory's second redemption is a more personal one, the result of the pull of Mother Ireland. Ever since Conor's visit to New Zealand, Rory has been filled with the desire to fight for the Republican cause. His pilgrimage to Ballyutogue and his prayers over Conor's grave provide him with the strength to continue Conor's mission. The assassination of General Brodhead redeems Rory in his own mind. After he has proved himself a true son of Ireland, he can return to the peaceful life of New Zealand.

Conor himself is in need of redemption as well. Although in *Trinity* Conor must pull himself away from his dream of a peaceful life with Shelley, it is in *Redemption* that readers see the earlier crisis that threatens to turn him from his destiny. The lure of his art and his love for Caroline Hubble both act as a powerful force to draw Conor away from the struggle for freedom. Conor indulges himself in his art for three years as he restores the great screen, and during that time he conducts a silent, spiritual love affair with Caroline. It is only when Caroline presses him to consummate their love that Conor realizes that he is "on a one-way path to hell" (170), later confessing to Maud Tully that the lure of creating a great work of art and of loving a woman like Caroline kept him from his duty to Ireland. Conor's redemption is the hardest of all, costing him first his freedom and then his life.

Having spent her life in self-indulgence, Caroline Hubble comes to her redemption later than Conor does. But after the shirt factory fire, Caroline visits Conor, at last accepting her responsibility for the disaster:

"Part of the reason it burned down was that I am the Countess of Foyle ... and allowed it to happen" (189). Begging Conor's forgiveness as the symbolic forgiveness of the Irish people, Caroline begins her journey to redemption at this moment. She continues to redeem herself when she defends Molly O'Rafferty, when she reconciles with her son Jeremy after dismissing him for his weakness, and finally when she avenges her sons' deaths and the rape of Ireland by assassinating General Brodhead.

Jeremy's redemption is more personal. Although his reconciliation with his mother represents a redemption of sorts, it is the sins against himself that must be redeemed if he is to be a man. Jeremy redeems himself by becoming a leader of men and a comrade during the disastrous battle of Gallipoli. His newfound dignity costs him his life, but memory of him lives on in Rory and his mother.

Despite the loss of so many young lives, Uris does not present war itself as evil. In fact, the men in the Seventh form ties every bit as close as those of the Sixth Marines in *Battle Cry*. War brings out the nobility in these men, with Jeremy Hubble finally emerging from his self-pity, Chris recognizing his kinship with colonials, Chester Goodwood finding strength, and Rory finding compassion for the man who abused his great love, Georgia. A sense of kinship with fellow soldiers even extends itself beyond enemy lines. During the truce called in order to bury thousands of dead soldiers after a particularly brutal battle, the Anzac troops find themselves sharing stories, cigarettes, and even home addresses with their Turkish counterparts as together they dig a mass grave to inter the bodies from both sides.

Trinity and *Redemption* represent a departure of sorts for Leon Uris. All of his other works relate to World War II, more often than not with a focus on the Holocaust. In these two novels Uris seems to have found another people who, like the Jews, have suffered brutally at the hands of tyrants. In this sense, despite the surface differences between these novels and his others, both *Trinity* and *Redemption* represent an expansion of the themes that the author has explored in his fiction for more than forty years.

A Marxist Reading of *Trinity* and *Redemption*

As does *Exodus*, both *Trinity* and *Redemption* tell the story of a people betrayed by British imperialism. From the Marxist perspective described in Chapter 5, the evils perpetrated on the Irish and the colonial troops at Gallipoli are motivated not by political, religious, or philosophical beliefs but rather by economics. The colonials suffer in order for the British industrialists to maintain their wealth and power. In the case of the British during the nineteenth and early twentieth centuries, capitalism and colonialism were two sides of the same coin.

Forty years before *Trinity* opens, the Irish population was decimated by the Great Potato Famine. While the crop failure resulted from a plant disease, the loss of life can be attributed directly to the British capitalists. Refusing to send aid to Ireland and continuing to export food and livestock from the island to England, British greed sent thousands of Irish men, women, and children to their deaths and many more to sea in overcrowded vessels. And even before the famine, Kilty Larkin's story reveals an age-old fight against landowners who exact high rents and offer no services. When the renter improves the land or the property at his own expense, the owner raises the rent because the property has become more valuable. Kilty's raids against such practices may be small in scale, but they are nevertheless classic revolutions of the proletariat.

In the present time of *Trinity* the evils of colonization are demonstrated not only in the primary story of Ireland but also through references that Conor makes to his travels and through Seamus's news reports from South Africa. Upon returning to Ireland, Conor tells Seamus, "I saw Bogside [Derry's Catholic ghetto] after Bogside of the colonizer's creation" (426). And Seamus, reporting on British concentration camps in the Transvaal, senses that the news of these atrocities will undermine British imperialism: "Something was going to happen in the twentieth century to overturn the age-old order" (414).

But before that something does happen, the colonization of Ireland results in corruption of otherwise honorable men, as witnessed in Kevin O'Garvey's deal to keep investigators out of the shirt factory. The resulting fire, killing over a hundred workers, is directly attributable to the arrogance and greed of the colonizer. Similarly, the deplorable conditions of the Catholic slums in Derry and Belfast reflect a political and economic structure in which the native masses pay with their lives to support the wealth of the foreign few. When Conor makes his great speech to the British court, he captures the essential evil of empire, referring to Britain's destruction of "an ancient civilization by laws repugnant to every concept of God and democracy" (611). Conor's conclusion, "All you're really in it for is the money" (613), is echoed later by Liberal Party Whip Alan Birmingham, who tells Roger Hubble, "Your entire parasitic band are in it for the pound sterling" (681).

Both Conor and Birmingham are referring to the construction of an ideology to support the capitalist agenda. In Ulster that ideology consists of a fanatical hatred of Catholics and an equally fanatical determination to remain a part of England. That determination has nothing to do with patriotism, however. It is simply necessary to remain part of England in order to maintain the most attractive business climate for the owners of factories and land.

The British capitalists in *Trinity* and *Redemption* are represented by the Weeds and the Hubbles. Frederick Weed, who has built his industrial empire with the sweat of overworked, underpaid laborers, seeks to consolidate his power by joining ranks with the equally unscrupulous landowner Roger Hubble. The history of the Hubble landholdings around Derry reek with the evils of capitalism. In order to maintain the family's wealth, the Hubbles keep the poor Protestants in fear of the even poorer Catholics, thereby diverting the attention of either to the real threat, the Hubbles themselves. Weed has done the same in Belfast, pitting his Protestant factory workers against the Catholics. Since most of the Protestants in Northern Ireland are descended from poor Scots imported for cheap labor, Weed and Hubble are able to appeal to their loyalty to England in the constant struggle against Irish Republicanism.

The Weeds and Hubbles have another ally in their campaign to keep the working classes oppressed, an ally commonly used by the capitalist class to maintain its power. Both the Protestant and the Catholic Churches support the status quo, the Protestants by preaching against the heathen Catholic and the Catholic by preaching subservience to God's will. It is in the Presbyterian church in Derry that Oliver Cromwell MacIvor preaches the sermon that results in a riot against Catholic Bogside on Apprentice Boys Day. And it is from the pulpit that MacIvor incites the riot at the Weed Iron Works that nearly costs Conor his life. For their part, the Catholic bishops excommunicate men like Tomas's grandfather Ronan for rebelling against his oppressors, urging the population to suffer their poverty in silence in hopes of salvation after death. Such collaboration between the churches and the capitalists is common, according to Marxist theory. When Karl Marx called religion "the opiate of the people," he was referring to the use of religion to keep the oppressed classes from examining their plight and fomenting revolution.

In *Redemption* the evils of capitalist colonization and empire are explored in the attitude of the British officers toward the colonial troops. Chris Hubble illustrates this attitude before his own redemption when he refuses to acknowledge Johnny Tarbox's equality, despite the man's superior knowledge of cavalry troops. When Jeremy is friendly toward the Anzacs, Chris warns him that "we must never loosen the leash on them" because "privilege is our birthright" (448–450). Uris also implies that the disaster at Gallipoli is the epitome of imperialism, with the privileged classes in England using colonial soldiers to preserve the wealth of the empire. Jeremy informs Rory as the troops languish on Gallipoli that he intends to fight colonialism when he returns to Ireland. "Empire is wrong," he reasons; "no one has the right to send men to places like this when the final objective is greed" (628).

Rory is able to make good on his promise when he finally reaches Ireland. In helping Caroline Hubble to assassinate General Brodhead, the British commander in Ireland, Rory strikes a blow for the Irish working classes. The eventual granting of home rule to Ireland can be attributed in part to such actions. By the end of *Redemption*, Kilty Larkin's dream of breaking the stranglehold of the British landowner and factory owner on the Irish working person's throat is realized—except in his own province, Ulster. The strength of the capitalist ideology throughout Northern Ireland is such that the price of independence for the rest of Ireland is the continued oppression of the north at the hands of the British.

11

The Haj
(1984)

Twenty-six years after publishing the story of the founding of Israel in *Exodus*, Leon Uris returns to Palestine to present the tale from the Arab perspective in *The Haj*. Despite the point of view, however, *The Haj* paints a portrait of Arabs that is no more flattering than that of *Exodus*. The only difference between the two characterizations of Arabs is that in the later novel, the painting is a self-portrait. Told largely through the words of Ishmael, son of Haj Ibrahim of Tabah, *The Haj* explores the history of Jewish settlement in Palestine and the eventual displacement of Palestinian Arabs as a result of Jewish statehood.

PLOT DEVELOPMENT

After a prelude in which Ibrahim takes on the role of muktar, or leader, of Tabah in his midtwenties, the story opens in the voice of Ibrahim's son Ishmael, who informs readers that while he will tell much of the story, other voices will be heard as well. It is through this device that Uris is able to communicate history and other incidents to which Ishmael is not privy. Part One, "The Valley of Ayalon," provides an overview of Arab life, which Ishmael describes as being poor, treacherous, and brutal. While Tabah is a poor village, it has a rich history and is strategically located on the road to Jerusalem.

Having learned to read and count, Ishmael places himself in his father's favor by informing Ibrahim that his brother, Farouk, and older son, Kamal, are cheating him on rent collections. This family intrigue is presented by Ishmael as typical of Arab relationships. Also presented as typical is Ishmael's humiliation when his fifty-year-old father takes a second, sixteen-year-old wife. The glimpse of Arab life seen in these early chapters is an unsavory one.

When Palestinian Jew Gideon Asch informs Ibrahim in 1925 that Jews are settling nearby, Uris provides a brief explanation of the history of Palestine, emphasizing the strategic importance of the Suez Canal, over which both British and Turks want control, and the complicating factor of Jewish settlement in the area. Intrigue among Arabs increases with the Jewish settlements, resulting in the 1929 massacres organized by Jerusalem's Mufti Heusseini. Heusseini's control over the illiterate masses of Palestinian peasants recalls the British control over Northern Irish Protestants in *Trinity*.

As Gideon and Ibrahim become friends, they debate the prospects for survival of the increasing number of Jewish settlements. Through their conversations Uris comments on the failure of Arabs to cultivate their land, while Jews make the desert bloom. Also obvious from the discussions is the author's interpretation of Arab treachery as an accommodation to hard desert life. Ibrahim, now using the title Haj after his pilgrimage to Mecca, informs Gideon that the only way to survive in Palestine is through cunning, not mercy.

During the 1930s Ibrahim's words take on added significance, as the Nazis promise Heusseini power in exchange for anti-Jewish riots. Heusseini, pressuring villages into sending "volunteers" to fight the British and the Jews, enjoys several successes before being routed by a combined British-Jewish force, at which point he turns on his Arab brothers. Some wealthier Arabs find it profitable to do business with the Jews, while others consider it their sacred duty to eliminate the infidels. Palestinian Jewish soldiers join the British armed forces, but Britain must be careful of its treatment of Arabs because of its need for their oil. The complex interrelationships between local and international politics is illustrated in Uris's description of the years preceding World War II.

Ibrahim and Tabah survive the war comfortably, and nine-year-old Ishmael is sent to school in the city of Ramle, where he learns to hate Jews. Ishmael is confused, however, when he sees his teacher laughing and joking with the Jews. Uris characterizes this behavior as typical of the Arab attitude toward the Jews—profess hatred but take advantage of Jewish goodwill. Ibrahim also follows this code, forbidding Ishmael to associate with Jews even though Ibrahim's closest friend is Gideon Asch.

Through Ishmael's narrative of school life, Uris also characterizes Arab village life as backward and Islam as a religion built on hate and fanaticism, encouraging a fatalistic acceptance of earthly life in hopes of a better life hereafter. He explores the lot of Islamic women as Ramiza, Ibrahim's young bride, recounts in graphically chilling detail the female circumcision of young Bedouin girls. When Ramiza bears a son, Ibrahim's experienced first wife is not allowed to help the teenage mother, who neglects the infant. Ibrahim refuses to allow the only available doctor, a Jew from Shemesh, to minister to the dying baby. The vision of Arab fanaticism regarding both women and Jews is frighteningly clear as the first part of the book concludes with Ibrahim screaming obscenities at the departing doctor and at his friend Gideon.

Part Two, "The Scattering," covers the period immediately following the war and preceding the founding of Israel. The story of the birth of the Israeli terrorist force Irgun (called the Maccabees in *Exodus*), as well as the United Nations vote to partition Palestine and the violent reaction of the Arabs, is told here from the Arab perspective, with Ibrahim and his fellow villagers uneasily contemplating the upcoming fighting. Confused over the Arab press's conflicting propaganda regarding the Holocaust, Ibrahim begins consulting Jewish newspapers to sort out the truth. He is also wary of talk of brotherhood among men who have been cheating each other for generations. Convinced that the Jordanians, Egyptians, and Syrians will carve up Palestine for themselves, Ibrahim is nevertheless unable to refuse powerful Effendi Fazwi Kabir's orders to evacuate Tabah so that the newly formed Arab army of liberation may take advantage of its strategic location. After taking advice from a German prostitute during his visit with Kabir, Ibrahim asks himself why, if he can learn from a woman, can he not also learn from a Jew. He longs to renew his friendship with Gideon, all but destroyed by Ibrahim's behavior on the night of his baby's death.

Uris makes it clear at this point that he believes the real betrayal of Palestinian Arabs was not at the hands of the British, the United Nations, or the Jews, but at the hands of other, more powerful Arabs. He cites the flight of the felahin, or professional class, from Palestine as evidence of the lack of solidarity that the privileged feel with the peasants, who are left to the devices of the leaders who are plotting to divide Palestine among themselves. The Effendi betrays Ibrahim by making a secret deal

with his brother Farouk, promising the man Ibrahim's riches if he succeeds in convincing his brother to evacuate the village.

Not only does Uris portray Arabs here as treacherous, but as incom-
petent, cowardly soldiers as well. Although Israel's David Ben Gurion
fears the worst, realizing that the Jewish army is hopelessly understaffed,
underarmed, and underfinanced, the Arabs are unable to come up with
a single significant victory early in the war. The villagers of Tabah join
hordes of refugees fleeing Palestine for a cause that few of them understand or support. Ibrahim realizes his brother's betrayal when he tries
to obtain financing for passage to Gaza, finding his bank accounts wiped
out. He is further betrayed, although unknowingly, when his wives and
daughter-in-law are brutally raped by Ibrahim's supposed ally, Liberation Army leader Kaukji, in retaliation for a humiliating defeat at Ibrahim's hands ten years earlier. Ironically, it is Gideon Asch, the enemy,
who finally arranges the escape of Ibrahim and his family from Kaukji's
soldiers.

Part Three, "Qumran," opens with the Arab attack on Israel as soon
as it declares statehood. Uris's condemnation of Arabs intensifies as
Ibrahim and his family find themselves homeless and penniless in a sea
of refugees within Arab territory. As the radio reports false victories
against the Jews, Ibrahim discovers that the influx of refugees has killed
traditional Arab hospitality. Those Arabs who still have homes struggle
desperately to ward off the refugees. Ibrahim's family, representative of
all Palestinian refugees, receives a chilly welcome from other Arabs and
survives only by submitting to the extortion of those more fortunate.

In the city of Nablus, where the family has sought shelter, Ishmael's
skill at forgery, similar to that of Dov Landau in *Exodus*, turns the family's fortunes around for a short time. By forging a letter from a fictitious
British officer, Ishmael is able to introduce his father to Mayor Clovis
Bakshir. The ensuing conversation between Ibrahim and Bakshir further
reveals the author's attitude toward Arab handling of the Palestinian
refugee situation. Ibrahim reminds Bakshir that Arab leaders have been
planning this military action for months, ordering the abandonment of
villages for army use without making any provision for refugees. Ibrahim concludes that the Jews have treated him far better than his own
leaders have.

Bakshir's side of the conversation offers Uris's commentary on the
inability of Arabs to govern themselves: Arabs want government to take
care of them, but they refuse to pay the necessary taxes. And Palestinians
have always allowed others to rule them, never taking the initiative in

governing themselves. It is inevitable that Palestine will belong to people other than Palestinians, whether they be Jews, Egyptians, Syrians, or Jordanians. Bakshir is casting his lot with Jordan.

Uris explains the complicated situation in the Middle East by focusing on the choice forced upon Ibrahim. Jordan's King Abdullah, filled with visions of ruling a great Arab nation, welcomes the Palestinian refugees, but not out of humanitarianism. His idea is to swell his country's population in order to increase his stature among Arab leaders. Although he is willing to live in peace with a Jewish state, fear of assassination prevents him from signing a peace treaty with Israel. But with a huge population to boost his status, he may be able to wait out the war. Thus Ibrahim finds himself a pawn in a larger game of Arab-against-Arab intrigue. That the Palestinian refugees were, and still remain, pawns has been one of the accepted interpretations of Middle East history since the founding of Israel. Uris makes it clear here that he not only subscribes to this view but also considers Arab leaders wholly responsible for the plight of the refugees.

Convinced that he has been offered a fool's bargain, Ibrahim takes advantage of the mayor's largesse and secretly loads a stolen army truck with supplies, fleeing to the caves of Qumran until he can lead his people back to Tabah. The family is assisted by a sixteen-year-old truck mechanic named Sabri Salama, a fellow refugee. The Arab tradition of mistrust rears its head again, as Ishmael, despite his affection for and gratitude to Sabri, nevertheless fears his friend's usefulness to the family.

This mistrust is what distinguishes Uris's Arab characters from others. Their ingenuity makes Ibrahim and his family admirable, but the undercurrent of mistrust subverts readers' admiration for them. In his other books, Uris presents people who are forced to live under dangerous conditions: the soldiers in *Battle Cry* and *Redemption*, the fugitives in *The Angry Hills*, the Holocaust victims in *Mila 18* and *QB VII*, and the Jewish settlers in *Exodus*, among others. But except for the Nazi-sympathizing Berliners in *Armageddon*, no other group under duress is portrayed so unsympathetically as the Arabs in *The Haj*. Everyone jockeys for power as secret alliances between family members flourish throughout exile in the cave.

The coming of autumn brings bad weather and bad news to the cave dwellers. Sandstorms, rains, and floods make living in the cave all but impossible, and news of the Arab failure to defeat the Jews leads to the unraveling of alliances. As a variety of secret deals and treachery among Arab leaders comes to light, the holy cause of eliminating the Jews seems doomed. With all of the intrigue swirling around him, Haj Ibrahim maintains his watch outside the cave and dreams of returning to Tabah. Part Three ends with the image of helpless Palestinian refugees amid the battles and negotiations that will determine their fate.

Readers' sympathy for the refugees is diminished considerably as Part Four, "Jericho," opens with a detailed description of the Palestinian refugee camp to which the family has traveled. Ishmael, disgusted with his people, talks of overcrowded, filthy, unsanitary camps in which the people refuse to help themselves: "We did not plant a tree. . . . We did not open a school. . . . We did not even collect and remove our own garbage." Instead, says Ishmael, "We rotted and complained. We blamed the Jews" (330). Ibrahim confirms Ishmael's assessment of his people when he determines that his only hope of returning to Tabah is to find Gideon Asch and negotiate with the Jews.

As Ishmael tries desperately to help his father discover how to contact Jews from Jericho, the boy has a mystical vision in which Jesus appears to him, acknowledging that rather than being the Son of God, as Christians believe, he is in truth a prophet of Islam. The vision allows Ishmael to concoct a plan to contact the Jews. He and his sister Nada had discovered a cache of ancient artifacts while exploring the caves at Qumran, and now he proposes that his father negotiate with archaeologist Nuri Mudhil, who sells artifacts to Jewish museums.

The negotiations with Mudhil not only result in contact with Gideon, but they achieve two other purposes as well. First, Ishmael becomes enthralled with Mudhil's knowledge of antiquity and longs to work with him. Second, Mudhil's story of his pathetic childhood and his pronouncements on the Arab people allow Uris to further characterize Arabs as evil. Crippled from birth because his parents were first cousins, Mudhil was forced by his parents to beg and was later beaten by his father when he accepted the kind help of a Jewish man. The man, an archaeologist, eventually bought Mudhil from his parents and trained the boy. The significance of this story, from incestuous marriages to abusive parents to magnanimous Jewish saviors, underscores the author's attitude toward Arabs.

Mudhil encourages Ibrahim to become a delegate to the conferences on the fate of Palestinians, warning that Abdullah and other Arab leaders are interested only in their own enrichment. His words are confirmed by the first conference, a sham designed to justify Jordan's land acquisitions. Tensions mount within the camps, now controlled by Abdullah's forces, as the Palestinian youth form military gangs. Ishmael's brother Jamil is among them.

Ibrahim forges an unusual alliance with the Bedouin Sheik Taji and the Christian Arab Charles Maan, both of whom agree that Abdullah is not to be trusted and that the best hope for Palestinians lies in negotiations with Israel. Intrigue in the Arab world being what it is, Abdullah's chief of police, Colonel Zyad, threatens Ibrahim through his sons, causing the Haj to spirit Ishmael out of Jordan to safety. The intrigue becomes more complex when the three allies attend a conference in Zurich on Palestinian unity, taking advantage of press coverage to publicize Abdullah's holding a number of Palestinian boys, including Jamil, hostage.

Ibrahim's long stay in Zurich provides Uris with the opportunity to further explore his character. The Haj's strength of purpose becomes clear when his enemies are able to isolate him from his allies, forcing him to stand alone for Palestinian autonomy. But his ultimate despair is equally clear when he meets with Gideon Asch one final time, admitting that his cause is hopeless. Ibrahim derives some satisfaction from saving his own life by assassinating the Effendi Kabir, but the section ends with the brutal torture and death of his son Jamil at the hands of Zyad. The official story is that Jamil, a Palestinian martyr, died fighting the Jews. Thus Ibrahim and his family are honored by their people, but the Haj knows that both he and they have been beaten.

Part Five, "Nada," is essentially the story of a beaten man, a beaten people. Ibrahim, devastated by the assassination of his friend Charles Maan, no longer has the stamina to lead. When Abdullah is assassinated, a massacre of Palestinians ensues; Ibrahim does nothing, and Ishmael expresses disgust with his father. The condition of the refugee camps is so terrible that the United Nations sends one of its most respected administrators, Per Olsen, to initiate the Jericho Plan to build schools, clinics, farms, industry, and sanitation facilities. But soon tribal jealousies, corruption, unwillingness to work, pilfering of supplies, and general apathy kill the project. Ibrahim's commentary echoes the author's sentiments as he bids farewell to Olsen: "[The project] required teamwork. Teamwork requires trust. There is no trust among us" (467).

As Ibrahim's world begins its final unraveling, Uris recounts the further degeneration of the Palestinian people. Ibrahim becomes a parasitic bureaucrat and renews his hatred of Jews by listening to Egyptian President Nasser's anti-Israeli propaganda. The threat posed by Egypt is illustrated in letters from Sabri, who has joined the fedayeen, or holy warriors. Ishmael, concerned about Nada's fedayeen activities, tries to think of a way to save her from the hopeless life of a Muslim woman. When Ibrahim sends her away to be a nanny for a United Nations family, she enjoys a sexual liberation that will eventually seal her fate.

The fate of the Palestinians is no more hopeful, as Egypt's Soviet-supported attempt to seize the Suez Canal results in another war with Israel and more Arab losses. Another blow is dealt when Jordan seals its border, abandoning the refugees.

The final disaster that befalls Ibrahim is, fittingly, of his own making. When Nada refuses an arranged marriage and announces that she is not a virgin, Ibrahim reverts to tradition and kills her with his own hands. A grief-stricken and enraged Ishmael avenges her death by telling Ibrahim of the rape of Hagar, Ramiza, and Fatima years ago. Ibrahim dies of a heart attack and is buried with great ceremony, leaving Ishmael the new muktar.

The final word on Arab culture is spoken by Mudhil when Ishmael asks him why it had to end this way. Mudhil responds, "You were born into a culture which has no place for . . . love to express itself. We are accursed among all living creatures" (522). Mudhil predicts that the Islamic world will eventually destroy itself in madness, a prediction borne out symbolically by Ishmael. Overcome with grief, Ishmael goes mad and returns to the caves of Qumran, searching in vain for his lost sister as he hears the voices of his people pleading with him to save them.

CHARACTER DEVELOPMENT

With one exception, the characters in The Haj are even more starkly drawn than in Uris's other novels, representing either entirely good or entirely evil. The title character, Haj Ibrahim, fluctuates between the two poles in his struggle to come to terms with the upheaval presented by the Jewish settlement of Palestine and the founding of Israel. Ibrahim's struggle results from the conflict between his traditions and the new world order. Because The Haj is Uris's interpretation of Islam and Arab culture, the portrayal of Ibrahim and other characters focuses on their response to that culture's traditions.

The sympathetic characters in the novel all despise the brutality, fatalism, and anti-Semitism of Islam. Ishmael first begins questioning the tenets of his faith as a child. His father's treatment of his mother when he takes a new, young wife is something that the young boy cannot understand. Ishmael learns early a central truth of Arab culture: No one can be trusted. Because he is a thoughtful child, this revelation causes him to question that culture. His questions go deeper when he attends school in Ramle and listens to his teacher rage against the Jews, only to see the man befriending them at the kibbutz.

When Ishmael and his family become refugees, the boy questions his culture further. Witnessing fellow Arabs who close their doors to the exiles, he wonders at the fickleness of Arab hospitality. And observing the people in the refugee camps who refuse to help themselves, he is disgusted with their lack of initiative. Ishmael sees through the false bravado of Arab soldiers and learns to manipulate his father by appealing to Ibrahim's vanity. He sympathizes with the fate of women, particularly the brilliant, energetic Nada, whose spirit will be crushed by Islamic restrictions. It is Nada who utters the words that distinguish Ishmael from other Arabs, including their father: "You are a better man than Father because . . . because you cannot kill what you love" (447).

Perhaps because he is a better man than other Arabs, Ishmael neither dies a hero's death nor lives happily ever after, as many other Uris heroes do. Fighting his very culture, a force far stronger than the mightiest army, Ishmael has no choice but to retreat into madness. There is nothing redeeming in his heritage; thus he has nothing to cling to when Nada is killed.

Nada herself rejects Islam and Arab culture entirely. From childhood Nada defies convention, begging Ramiza to tell her about sex and female circumcision, climbing the sheer cliffs of Qumran, learning to read, and joining the fedayeen. Having seen what her culture does to its people, Nada exhibits a fierce independence when she leaves home. Embarking on an affair with her employer, she remains detached from the relationship, maintaining a control unheard of in her male-dominated culture. Like her brother, however, Nada must pay dearly for flouting Islamic taboos. When she defiantly announces to her father that she is no longer a virgin, she knows what is in store for her. "So avenge the shame your daughter, the whore, has brought upon you" she taunts (518).

The only entirely sympathetic Muslim character is Dr. Nuri Mudhil, the archaeologist who helps Ibrahim find Gideon Asch and who takes Ishmael under his wing. Interestingly, it is Mudhil who offers the most damning assessment of Arab culture, telling Ibrahim that his people live in "hate, despair, and darkness. . . . The Jews are our bridge out of darkness" (353). Mudhil's profession also endears him to readers. He alone among Arabs has a reverence for the past; he tells Ibrahim that the Jews have done more than the Arabs (who simply sell artifacts for profit) to preserve Islamic relics. Mudhil's ability to revere his culture's artifacts while condemning its morals and ethics makes him a more complex character than he originally appears to be.

Charles Maan, a Christian Arab, is among the nobler characters in the novel. He works tirelessly to return Palestinian Arabs to their homes, and he refuses to engage in self-indulgent hatred of Jews. Maan stands up to the power-hungry Abdullah, arguing incessantly for Palestinian self-determination. And like Mudhil, Maan is a realist regarding the commitment of other Arab nations to the Palestinians. Echoing Mudhil, he warns Ibrahim at their final meeting that the only hope for Palestinian Arabs lies with the Jews. Maan's defiance of Arab culture results in his brutal assassination by Arab leaders.

Gideon Asch is the only prominent Jewish character in *The Haj*. Since the novel reveres Jews and reviles Arabs, it is not surprising that Gideon is a sympathetic character. A true child of Israel, Gideon's courage is illustrated in his service in the British Army, when the Iraqis sever his hand. When he returns to Shemesh, he simply goes on as he has before. Gideon is also shrewd, announcing his presence in Tabah as soon as the settlers arrive to build Shemesh Kibbutz and easily overcoming a night attack by Ibrahim's men. Once the kibbutz is established, instead of using the curses, threats, and treachery common to Arabs, Gideon uses the law. When a young man from Tabah assaults a pregnant Shemesh woman, Ibrahim waits for the inevitable attack from the Jews. It does not come. Instead, Gideon exercises the kibbutz's legal water rights, shutting off the supply to Tabah. His only condition for turning it back on is peace, allowing Ibrahim to save face and deal with the attacker in his own way.

Gideon's frustration with the rigidity of Islamic culture is evident when Ibrahim's baby is dying. He responds to Ibrahim's rejection of the Jewish doctor with genuinely righteous rage. Begging Ibrahim to relent, Gideon is interested only in the life of the child. His humanitarianism reveals itself again when he helps Ibrahim's family escape from enemies intent on destroying them. His frustration with Arab culture is articulated in his final meeting with Ibrahim, when he asks, "What kind of perverse society, religion, culture . . . is it . . . that knows only hatred, that breeds only hatred, that exists for hatred?" (424). Although Ibrahim is too mired in his traditions to understand it, Gideon Asch is the conscience not only of the Jews in Palestine, but of the Arabs as well.

The evil characters in *The Haj* are less interesting than the good characters, primarily because they are interchangeable. The least of the evil ones is Ibrahim's envious brother Farouk, whose only crime is cheating his brother out of his rents and then his village. That Farouk's sins against his brother are seen as minor is an indication of the depth of Uris's condemnation of Arab culture. The other Arab characters—Mufti Heusseini of Jerusalem, General Kaukji of the Arab forces, Colonel Zyad of the Jordanian police, Effendi Kabir of Damascus, King Abdullah of Jordan—are alike in their brutality, their unscrupulousness, and their penchant for betraying fellow Arabs. Theft, rape, mutilation, and torture are the stock-in-trade of these creatures. Together they are responsible for the homelessness and statelessness of hundreds of thousands of Palestinian refugees. Because readers see more of Kabir than of the other characters, his characterization is most memorable. In Zurich he is described as an impotent, obese, perpetually intoxicated man who oversees a house full of prostitutes and guests engaged in every sexual perversion imaginable, including torture. Kabir's depravity illustrates the corruption and depravity of the Arab leaders who have sold their fellow Palestinian to enrich and empower themselves.

The only strong voice of morality among Arab leaders belongs to Haj Ibrahim. His dedication to Palestinian self-determination, his willingness to risk his life for his people, and his understanding of the need for peace with the Jews sets him apart from other Arabs in the novel. Ibrahim tries desperately to spur his people to rebel against their masters. But the same culture that prevents him from allowing a Jewish doctor to treat his dying child prevents his people from emerging from their lethargy and fighting for themselves.

The difference between the Haj and his people is that he struggles with tradition. Occasionally he wins, as when he establishes a peaceful coexistence with the Jews of Shemesh Kibbutz and when he finally recognizes Gideon Asch as a friend. When his people are exiled, Ibrahim's only goal is "to return to Tabah and reunite my people there. . . . I will not return to Tabah alone" (353). His struggle to find a way to resettle Palestine contrasts starkly with the fatalism that keeps his people in squalid refugee camps. He has been taught to simply accept the will of Allah, but he cannot abandon his people.

While Ibrahim is successful in overcoming the fatalism of his faith when it comes to saving his people, he is defeated by that faith within his own family. His baby dies because he refuses treatment by a Jewish doctor, the family's safety is compromised in Qumran because he will not allow Nada to guard the cave, and Jamil dies because Ibrahim places his hope in the younger Ishmael. Ibrahim's final defeat destroys his daughter, his favorite son, and himself. When he retreats into tradition and kills Nada for shaming the family, he sets in motion the events that lead to his own shame and death and that condemn Ishmael to madness. In the end, it is neither the Jews nor his Arab enemies that destroy the Haj; it is himself and his adherence to his culture. Uris's ultimate condemnation of Arab culture is evident in the final pages of the novel, when Ibrahim destroys not only himself but the hope of Islam, Ishmael.

THEMATIC ISSUES

One primary theme weaves its way throughout *The Haj*, and all subthemes are drawn from it: the destructive power of Islamic and Arabic tradition. This tradition consists of fatalism; subjugation of women; mistrust of everyone, even family members; and hatred, particularly of Jews.

During one of their early discussions, Haj Ibrahim rejects Gideon Asch's plans to improve life in Tabah. Life must go on as it always has, claims Ibrahim, even if that means poor sanitation, hunger, and disease. He explains, "Islam . . . provides us with the means to survive the harshness of this life and prepare us for a better life hereafter" (55). This belief follows the Palestinian refugees into exile and contributes to their misery in the camps. Ishmael says of the Jericho camp, "The lack of desire to do anything about our own plight made Aqbat Jabar a camp of the living dead" (329). Even the Bedouin, who consider themselves the only free Arabs, are lulled by the same apathy. Ishmael, hiding among them, states that the Bedouin have taught him "a passive acceptance of the unmercifulness of life. Everything was predestined by fate, and there was little one could do but accept the bitterness of earth and look forward to the relief of the trip to paradise" (439). As a result of this fatalism, villages such as Tabah remain desolate while kibbutzim such as Shemesh bloom in the desert.

Although a certain degree of fatalism may be understandable in the refugee camps, Uris reveals in other novels that the human spirit can make a community out of the most hellish places. In *Mila 18* the Jews transform the Warsaw ghetto into a place of culture and learning, despite deplorable living conditions. The ghetto prisoners achieve this level of civilization by developing structures to govern themselves. The same type of organization is seen in the refugee camps in *Exodus*, where the inmates run the camps with precious few resources. Children are taught, food is distributed, and illnesses are treated in the camps—all of which contributes to morale. Even the peasants of Northern Ireland are able to maintain their pride and culture in the face of a poverty forced on them by the British. According to Uris, no such initiatives exist among Palestinian Arabs. When Haj Ibrahim, their only enlightened leader, works with the United Nations to develop the Jericho Plan, he is defeated by corruption, theft, and apathy. And because he has not simply submitted to the will of Allah, he is denounced as a Zionist spy.

Fatalism is only one of the self-destructive forces of Arab culture as portrayed in *The Haj*. Another force that contributes to the culture's backwardness is its attitude toward and treatment of women. Uris demonstrates the appalling situation of women in many ways. Ibrahim threatens to abandon his first wife, Hagar, when she does not produce a male child. Even after she bears him four healthy sons, he sends her away and marries a sixteen-year-old Bedouin girl. The brutality of their wedding night emphasizes the culture's total disregard for a woman's well-being, even one as young as Ramiza. On the morning after the wedding her bloody nightgown is displayed, demonstrating her virginity and her husband's potency. Later, when Ramiza has not recovered fully from childbirth, Ibrahim exercises his rights to her body, causing her excessive pain and bleeding. She has no right to refuse him.

When the family is hiding in the caves at Qumran, Uris illustrates the more insidious aspects of Muslim treatment of women. It becomes clear that Nada is better able than some of the males to guard the cave. When Ishmael proposes to his father that Nada be assigned night guard duty, Ibrahim not only refuses but also orders Ishmael to stop teaching Nada to read. He warns his son that women are subject to men, and Nada's happiness is something to be defined by her father, and later her husband. This rigid adherence to a tradition that does not take into account Nada's intelligence and independent spirit forces her to express her independence defiantly in several sexual affairs. When she confronts her father with this news, she signs her own death warrant.

If the Arab culture as portrayed by Uris in *The Haj* treats its women poorly, it does little better in treating its men, primarily because of the essential lack of trust among men. Early in the book readers learn that Ibrahim's brother Farouk and son Kamal are cheating him of rents. Ishmael dutifully reports the theft to his father, but even he holds back enough information to skim money for his mother off the rents. Later, when he sneaks into the kibbutz to help teach the children Arabic, Ishmael's best friend betrays him to Ibrahim in hopes of currying favor with the Haj. Ishmael learns a lesson from the episode: ''Never trust anyone, especially your best friend" (112). That lesson will serve him well in Arab life, for as his father has discovered years earlier, even his fellow Arabs are not above betraying him to the Jews. It is the Effendi Kabir who sells Tabah's water rights to Shemesh Kibbutz, and it is the Effendi, in concert with the Mufti of Jerusalem, who orders Ibrahim and his people to evacuate Tabah. After the evacuation, Kabir gives control of the village to Ibrahim's brother Farouk.

The mistrust among their own people also causes Ishmael and Ibrahim to suspect Sabri, whose mechanical expertise saves them when they flee to Qumran. Although Sabri proves at every juncture that he is trustworthy, both Ishmael and Ibrahim remain suspicious. Ibrahim warns his son, "The best traitors are the ones like Sabri who can gain your trust" (305).

The basic failure to trust results in the worst treachery, particularly when refugees begin pouring into Arab cities. Farmers and landowners extort money from the exiles, only to put them out once they are no longer able to pay. Ibrahim finds himself in more danger from Kaukji than from the Jews; in fact, he contacts Gideon Asch to spirit him out of Nablus when Kaukji's soldiers close in. As the war against Israel continues, Ibrahim realizes that Arab leaders have a vested interest in the refugees. Not only do the leaders want to use the exiles as pawns in their campaign for world sympathy, but they also plan to divide Palestine among themselves once the Jews are driven out. There is no sense of responsibility for people who are homeless on the orders of their leaders. The treachery of the Arab leaders reaches its zenith during the Zurich conference, when Ibrahim must kill Kabir in order to avoid being assassinated himself. In asking for nothing more than fair treatment for his people, Ibrahim has made himself the enemy of his people's unscrupulous leaders. His fate bears out his own prophecy from before the war: *"The common enemy is ourselves"* (173).

Of all the subthemes in Uris's exploration of Arab culture, the most deadly is hatred, especially of the Jews. That hatred manifests itself early, when Gideon Asch first visits Tabah. Announcing the development of the new kibbutz, he asks Ibrahim if they can coexist peacefully. Ibrahim's response is a night raid on the kibbutz. The litany of hatred continues throughout the novel. Ishmael learns hatred from his teacher, who preaches hatred of the Jews daily. Ibrahim beats Ishmael for visiting the kibbutz. Nuri Mudhil's father beats him for entering a Jewish hospital. Ibrahim allows his child to die rather than be treated by a Jewish doctor. Arab leaders incite riots by spreading tales of Jewish brutality. And the goal of the true Muslim, according to those leaders, is to destroy every Jew in Palestine.

According to Uris, it is this hatred that is responsible for the self-destruction of the Palestinian people and for the disintegration of Ibrahim's family. Focusing hatred upon the Jews allows the Palestinians to deny their own responsibility for their plight and diverts attention from the treachery of their leaders. That failure to accept reality, implies Uris, is the primary reason that Palestine is still in turmoil today.

But in this novel the real tragedy is visited upon Ibrahim and his family. The Haj's desire for vengeance is so great that it overpowers his love for his daughter. Similarly, Ishmael's desire for vengeance against his father blinds him to the fact that Ibrahim is a slave to tradition. Uris's assessment of the destructive forces of Arab culture is given voice by Nuri Mudhil, himself a Muslim. As Mudhil tells the grieving Ishmael at the end of the novel, "Hate is our overpowering legacy and we have regenerated ourselves by hatred from . . . generation to generation" (522). The conclusion of *The Haj* leaves readers with little hope that this legacy has died.

A NEW HISTORICIST READING OF *THE HAJ*

In 1979 the world was shocked when the Iranian revolution toppled the government of Shah Reza Pahlavi and established an Islamic state. The subsequent hostage situation in which employees of the American Embassy in Tehran were held for over a year focused the world's attention on a culture that the West knew little about. When *The Haj* appeared in 1984, much of the population of the United States had concluded that Islam was a fanatical religion founded on hatred and repression; that conclusion was reinforced nightly by television images of enraged Iranian mobs burning American flags, singing the praises of the Ayatollah Ruholla Khoumeini, and chanting anti-American slogans. Leon Uris's book did nothing to alter that image. A new historicist reading of the book, as discussed in Chapters 3 and 7, reveals that it reflects precisely the image of Islam prevalent in much of the Western world in the aftermath of the Iranian revolution. Such a reading also reveals that the behavior of the Muslims in the novel reflects their response to a world that is suddenly falling apart after generations of remaining precisely the same.

The characterization of Arabs in *The Haj* is an accurate reflection of the

Western view of Islam and Palestinians in the 1980s. The West, particularly the United States, had supported Israel since its founding. The
determination and skill demonstrated by the Israelis in several wars had
earned the small country the respect of its allies. At the same time, the
increasing terrorist activities of the Palestinian Liberation Organization,
including bombings, hijackings, and the highly publicized attack on Israeli athletes at the 1972 Munich Olympics, had turned world opinion
against the Palestinian cause. Several oil crises during the 1970s, insti-
gated by the largely Arab membership of OPEC (Organization of Petro-
leum Exporting Countries), had increased American mistrust of the Arab
world. Finally, the apparently fanatical anti-Western behavior of the Iranian revolutionaries had solidified public opinion in the United States
that the so-called Islamic Revolution in the Middle East was the product
of a culture built upon hatred and fanaticism.

    The Haj reflects these sentiments precisely, focusing particularly on the
apparent treachery of the Arab world. When Haj Ibrahim cannot even
trust his own brother and son, when professional Arabs abandon their
poorer brothers and sisters at the first sign of trouble, and when Arab
leaders send Palestinians into exile without providing for their well-
being, it seems that the only conclusion a reader might come to is that
the fault lies within the culture itself. The only difference between public
opinion of the Arab world and Uris's presentation is that Uris has Arabs
themselves making the judgments. Ibrahim tells Per Olsen that his Jericho Plan is doomed to failure because Arabs are incapable of cooperation. Ishmael condemns his fellow refugees for languishing in camps
without attempting to improve their living conditions. And Professor
Mudhil tells Ishmael, "We are accursed among all living creatures" (522).
By placing these damning words in the mouths of Arabs, Uris reinforces
prevailing Western attitudes toward the Islamic world. If enlightened
Arabs themselves condemn their culture, then how can Westerners
argue?

    The difficulty experienced by Westerners in trying to understand Is-
lamic culture stems from the vastly different value systems underlying
each culture. Westerners, for example, consider virtuous any attempt to
better one's living conditions on earth. Islamic culture, on the other hand,
emphasizes the acceptance of living conditions as the will of Allah. Some
relief from poverty or disease can be expected from fellow Muslims in
more fortunate circumstances, since the Prophet Mohammed admonishes
every Muslim to help the poor. But the idea of attaching moral value to

increasing one's wealth or stature is not consistent with Islamic culture as it is with Western culture. Thus for Uris, or the American public, to conclude that Arabs are lazy and shiftless is to judge them by a standard that is foreign to their culture.

The basic difference between Western and Islamic values as demonstrated in *The Haj* lies in the value placed on self-determination. The Jewish settlers are praised in the novel for their ingenuity in transforming the desert into fruitful land. Those in the kibbutzim also govern themselves according to democratic standards. And when the new state of Israel is established, its government is fashioned after the British parliamentary model. Seen through the eyes of a culture that values self-determination, the Jews are necessarily considered admirable. In contrast, the Arabs, who take the land as it is, who allow their leaders to determine their fate, and who depend on their leaders to tell them who is a friend and who is an enemy, appear in Western eyes to be parasitic. What is missing from this assessment is questioning the assumption that self-determination is inherently good.

What Americans responding to news of the Islamic Revolution did, and what Uris does in his novel, is to accept the underlying assumptions governing Western culture without question. The same is true of the Arab characters in the novel. Just as Uris neglects to question the value of industriousness, most of the Arabs refuse to question the value of their fatalism. Haj Ibrahim repeatedly tells Gideon that it is useless to expect Arabs to embrace progress. "Islam . . . provides us with the means to survive the harshness of this life and prepare us for a better life hereafter" (55), he says. "You are pushing us into a world we do not know. We must have something we understand" (56). But in offering this argument, Ibrahim is ignoring the central question Gideon asks him: "Could it be, Haj Ibrahim, you use Islam as an excuse for your failures, an excuse to quietly accept tyranny?" Gideon warns him, "Islam cannot hide from the world any longer" (56). The events surrounding World War II and the partition of Palestine certainly suggest that Gideon is correct. Even if the Arabs do not alter their basic beliefs, they cannot ignore the intrusion of the outside world into their once-closed society. In refusing to question the assumptions underlying their cultural values, the Arabs in the novel condemn themselves to a life of tension, instability, and violence.

When considering a novel such as *The Haj*, the new historicist looks not only at the cultural assumptions governing the behavior of characters in the novel, but the assumptions governing the author and readers as well. In this novel all three fail to challenge those assumptions. The resulting clash of cultures resonates throughout the novel, making it an intriguing study of the collision between two vastly different worlds.

12

Mitla Pass
(1988)

Mitla Pass resembles *QB VII*, in that its main character is a novelist whose career mirrors that of Leon Uris. Like Uris and Abraham Cady, Gideon Zadok's first book chronicles his experiences in World War II. He endures the criticism of editors and critics, spends time writing Hollywood screenplays, and eventually feels compelled to write a book about Israel. And like Abe Cady, Gideon is a less-than-sympathetic character. *Mitla Pass* appears to be an honest self-portrait of a man well aware of the strengths and the failings of dedicated writers. As in other novels, Uris relates part of the story through an omniscient narrator, with the remainder alternating among first-person narratives of Gideon; his wife, Valerie; and several other characters, both major and minor.

PLOT DEVELOPMENT

Named for a disastrous battle in the 1956 Sinai War between Israel and Egypt, *Mitla Pass* begins with the historical decision by Israeli Prime Minister David Ben Gurion to attack Egypt in anticipation of an Egyptian attack on Israel. In Part One, "Geronimo!," the principal characters in the drama are introduced. In addition to Ben Gurion, whose role is primarily to verify the historical accuracy of the novel, readers are introduced to Gideon, his lover Natasha, and his wife Val, as well as several other secondary characters. The tension between Val and Gideon becomes evident when on the night before the troop movement to Mitla Pass, Gideon sends Val and his daughters out of the country and meets with Natasha, perhaps for the last time. Uris then shifts to an evening three weeks earlier as Val waits for Gideon to return from a previous raid, recalling their first meeting, their courtship, and the early years of their marriage. Through a third-person narrator and then Val's own voice, Uris presents the competing demands of family and writing as the primary reason for the storminess of the Zadoks' marriage. The secondary reason, which emerges a bit later in the book, is Gideon's penchant for other women.

Gideon's wild side is established in Val's reverie, as is the fact that his first book, *Of Men in Battle*, was a struggle to write and to get published. Gideon's dedication to writing is matched in the early years of the marriage by his devotion to Val and their daughters, Roxie and Penny. When Penny is seriously injured in an automobile accident, Gideon offers God his career for her life. He eventually gets both, but the writing career does not resume without additional struggle. Uris may well be reflecting his own attitude when Gideon's editor, failing to understand the writer's style, butchers his book. Gideon and Uris also share a similar attitude toward Hollywood, namely, that it is a Hell filled with scheming devils.

Throughout this section Uris uses several interesting techniques to forward the story. Letters from Gideon's father, Nathan, reproduced in full, are characterized by a whining, accusatory tone. Gideon's struggles as a writer and a human being can apparently be traced at least in part to his troubled relationship with his father.

Another technique involves Gideon's presenting a confrontation between himself and Val as a screenplay and then as straightforward narrative. The topic of the confrontation will be familiar to readers of *QB VII*: Val wants Gideon to take a studio's offer of steady work for high pay, while Gideon feels that his writing will suffer if he stays in Hollywood. Like Samantha in the earlier novel, Val is portrayed as grasping and more interested in security and money than in her husband's talent. When Gideon capitulates, writing his new novel from Hollywood, it becomes clear that he has compromised his writer's soul. According to Gideon, the book fails because "I was writing about people who were suffering, but I never felt their pain and the readers saw right through me" (86). Gideon is clearly speaking for Uris here. The author's own extensive research on all of his novels, including field experience, reflects his belief that authors must experience what they write about. Gideon learns that lesson, as well as another, namely, that he must face his fear of loneliness if he is ever going to succeed as a writer. After renewing himself by spending months alone on a tiny, sparsely inhabited island in the Caribbean, he announces to Val that he is going to Israel to write his great work.

Part One ends as Gideon lies under the stars just hours before the planned attack on Mitla Pass, recalling a rare moment of warmth with his father. Part Two, "Shtetl Boy," opens in 1906, when Gideon's father is a boy. Nathan lives with his family in a *shtetl*, a town open to Jews in the Pale of Settlement in Russia. Uris uses the boy's travels in search of work to illustrate the harsh treatment accorded Jews in Russia, as Nathan endures countless taunts and several beatings. His experiences recall those of the Rabinsky brothers in *Exodus*; but unlike the Rabinskys, Nathan reveals a petulant streak. Although he too embraces Zionism, he is never quite able to meet the challenges confronting him. Caught in a battle in World War I, it is his knowledge of languages and not his cunning or bravery that saves him. When Nathan finally reaches Palestine, he finds himself unsuited to kibbutz life and leaves for America in 1921. Nathan's tendency to blame anyone or anything but himself for his failures is reflected in his letters to his son.

The history of Gideon's family continues in Part Three, "America! America!" In a morphine-induced reverie, the wounded Gideon lies on the ground outside Mitla Pass and recalls finding his mother in bed with another man. The narrative then shifts immediately to 1887 Ireland, where readers meet Moses Baliban, Gideon's maternal grandfather. Moses is portrayed as even less sympathetic than Nathan. Emigrating from Ireland to the Baltimore area, the widower Moses establishes himself as a tailor and seeks a mother for his two sons. His marriage to Hannah Diamond reveals him to be a mean, stingy man, a tyrant in his home. Hannah's characterization is equally unsympathetic, as she leaves Moses and teaches her daughters to disdain men, especially Jewish men. The only man who deserves their attention, according to Hannah, is Moses's son Lazar, a virtual prisoner in a house full of women.

Uris's portrayal of Jewish immigrants to America contrasts starkly with his treatment of those who settled Israel in *Exodus*. With the exception of Lazar, the members of Moses's family are selfish, whining characters who elicit no sympathy from readers. Particularly unsympathetic is Hannah's daughter Leah, Gideon's mother. Having left her husband, Leah and her daughter Molly appear on Hannah's doorstep at the end of Part Three, telling tales of physical abuse.

Part Four, "Arise, Ye Prisoners of Starvation," opens in October 1956, with Ben Gurion contemplating the progress of the war. On the battlefield, Gideon recalls his Uncle Lazar, who was wounded at Belleau Wood in World War I, and his Great-uncle Matti, Nathan's brother, who settled in Palestine. As the soldiers wait for their orders, Shlomo, Gideon's aide in Israel, recounts Gideon's volatile, passionate affair with the concentration camp survivor Natasha. Natasha's attraction to Gideon becomes more understandable when readers hear of her hatred of her father; Gideon too has a troubled relationship with his own father. But the secret that torments Natasha is her sense of guilt over her father's death at Auschwitz, inadvertently caused by a message from her. Tormented by dreams in which he reaches out to her from the fog, Natasha engages in a series of destructive affairs—until she meets her match in Gideon.

As Gideon and Shlomo while away the hours on watch over Mitla Pass, the two talk about women and marriage, offering Uris the opportunity to provide another flashback into Gideon's early life. Gideon tells Shlomo that there are only two women in the world whom he has ever fully trusted, his half-sister Molly and his sixth-grade teacher, Miss Abigail Winters. The scene at Mitla Pass is immediately followed by Molly's story, told in her own voice.

Readers learn from Molly that Gideon's parents met when Nathan, a communist union organizer, orchestrated a strike at the factory in which Leah worked. After Leah and Nathan married and Gideon was born, the family moved from place to place as the Communist Party dictated. Uris's portrayal of communists is consistent here with the portrayal in *Armageddon*: While the ideology may be sound, the Communist Party is populated by bullies and thugs. Gideon's parents are clearly more commited to communism than to their family, and Molly becomes a mother to little Gideon. What Leah does instill in Gideon is a love of literature.

That literary inclination is fostered by Miss Abigail Winters, Gideon's sixth-grade teacher. Returning to third-person narration, Uris describes Gideon's birth as a writer under Miss Abigail's tutelage. The teacher also introduces Gideon to the joys of flying and to the fact that not all communists are like his parents and their comrades. Dedicated to her beliefs, Miss Abigail fights in the Spanish Civil War, urging Gideon in her letters to cling to his ideals. Abigail is to Gideon what Ben Cady is to Abe in *QB VII*: Both Abigail and Ben are avid fliers, and both communicate their dedication to the cause of freedom. Both also die for that cause.

Gideon's Uncle Lazar picks up the narrative in 1939, describing Gideon's troubled adolescence that resulted in his enlistment in the Marines at age seventeen. Lazar's story portrays Leah as a selfish, manipulative woman who nearly ruins Gideon's life before he flees into the Marines. This section ends with Lazar's describing in graphic detail the reality of battle, preparing Gideon for what lies ahead.

The final section of the book, "Just Before the Battle, Mother," returns readers to Mitla Pass in 1956. Gideon, his story now complete, faces what may well be his final battle as the fanatical Colonel Zechariah defies orders from Central Command and insists on attacking the pass. The resulting battle is devastating to the Israeli forces. In passages that foreshadow the Gallipoli scenes in *Redemption*, Uris describes an impossible situation in which Israelis, including Shlomo, are mowed down by Egyptian fire. The battle is so fierce that Gideon is momentarily transported back to Tarawa in World War II, where he lost his friend and fellow soldier Pedro. In a rare instance of blaming an Israeli for a foolhardy and costly battle, Uris has Gideon rail against Zechariah. A memo from Central Command indicates that Mitla Pass is of no military value, underscoring the futility of the loss of life.

Having survived what he considers to be his ultimate test of manhood, Gideon returns for one last fling with Natasha before leaving her to resume life with his family. His introspection in the hours before and after the battle have led Gideon to conclude that, like Natasha, he too suffers from survivor's guilt. But unlike Natasha, he has conquered his fears of the past. The book closes with Gideon's offering a prayer of sorts to Miss Abigail, reveling in his newfound understanding of himself as a soldier, a writer, and a man.

CHARACTER DEVELOPMENT

Unlike other Uris novels in which the primary focus is on events, *Mitla Pass* is clearly the story of one man, Gideon Zadok. The battle that is reflected in the title of the book is simply the final hurdle Gideon must clear in order to fully realize his manhood. The other characters in the book are significant only insofar as they illuminate Gideon's character.

Gideon's similarities to Abraham Cady are many. Like Abe, Gideon experiences war at an early age, returning from battle wounded both physically and psychically. And like Abe, Gideon marries a woman whom he meets while recovering from his injuries. Both characters are also obsessed with writing, and both have been influenced by mentors who lost their lives in the Spanish Civil War. Both write first novels that reflect wartime experiences, and both struggle to avoid being sucked into the Hollywood quagmire after achieving some measure of fame. And both Abe and Gideon explore their heritage through a great novel about the Jews and the Holocaust.

What sets Gideon apart from Abe is that his awakening comes during his research for the novel, while Abe's occurs after it has been published, during his libel trial. As he immerses himself in Israeli culture, Gideon discovers that he is very much a part of his own research. This realization comes slowly, after a thorough exploration of his heritage and his life so far. While Abe Cady can only sympathize with Holocaust victims, Gideon becomes a part of the defense of Israel—he is a subject of his own book. Ironically, it is precisely that close identification with his subject that allows Gideon to look at his life objectively. To be able to make that assessment of his life is what allows Gideon to prevail in the end, whereas Abe is left consumed by doubts.

In assessing his life, Gideon comes to term with the unfairness of his treatment of Valerie. Uncertain of his own talent and ability to commit to writing, Gideon the young man blames his wife for his failings, insisting that it is her desire for stability that keeps him in Hollywood. This insistence that his wife is dragging him down is reminiscent of Abe Cady in *QB VII*. The young Gideon also blames Val for his many extramarital adventures. When she confronts him with her knowledge of his affairs, he responds, "You've known about this for a long, long time, Val. Why didn't you stop me?" (95). And when he finds evidence of her one brief affair, he plays the righteously indignant husband, refusing to forgive her and calling her "a slut, a whore, a tramp, a pig, scum" (324). It is only on the battlefield at Mitla Pass that he finally admits the truth, namely, that he has kept alive his grudge in order to justify his own behavior.

Gideon also comes to terms with his family heritage while on the battlefield. The long flashbacks to his own childhood and the early lives of his parents and grandparents help the reader, as well as Gideon, understand the anger and fear that compel him to risk his life in researching his book. Emerging from battle scarred but essentially whole, Gideon is finally able to rebuild his family.

The characters who help define Gideon Zadok include his extended family, his wife, his lover, and his friend Shlomo. His grandfather, Moses, epitomizes the small man who never sees beyond his own misery. Using his religion as an excuse to avoid the cares of the world, Moses makes his family's life so miserable that his wife and children leave him.

Moses's greatest crime, however, is turning the once sympathetic Hannah into a shrew. Using Moses as her example, Hannah teaches her daughters that men are worthless and brutal, especially Jewish men. And her daughter Leah learns the lesson well, manipulating three husbands, considering nothing but her own comfort.

In one sense, Leah and Nathan are well suited, neither capable of empathy with others. Nathan's propensity to blame his misfortunes and failures on others makes him as unsavory a character as his wife. That she has produced the sweet, patient Molly is nothing less than a miracle. It is not surprising that Gideon, Nathan and Leah's only child, becomes involved in a street gang at sixteen, attempts suicide at seventeen, and ultimately joins the Marines to escape his family. But Molly remains a steadying influence in his life, apparently immune to the influence of her mother and stepfather.

The only woman other than Molly whom Gideon trusts is Abigail Winters. Abigail is a larger-than-life character with virtually no human foibles. She approaches her teaching vocation with no less energy than she approaches her flying or her communist activities. And when she becomes disillusioned with the Communist Party, she maintains her ideals and fights, eventually losing her life, for the Loyalists in the Spanish Civil War. It is Abigail who meets Ernest Hemingway in Spain and shows him some of Gideon's work. And it is to Abigail that Gideon silently shouts when he has found his way out of his private Hell.

The man who guides Gideon through that Hell is his Israeli aide, Shlomo Bar Adon. Shlomo is a *sabra*, or native-born Israeli. He covers thousands of miles with Gideon, assisting him in thousands of interviews and enduring Gideon's arrogance and impatience. On the battlefield, Shlomo encourages Gideon to talk about his life and to come to terms with his love for Val and his need for Natasha. The death of the gentle Shlomo re-creates for Gideon the death of his friend Pedro on Tarawa, thereby freeing him from his survivor's guilt and allowing him to emerge from his psychic battle as whole as he emerges from the physical battle.

Natasha Solomon, Gideon's lover, is not so fortunate. She is not blessed with the capacity for introspection that allows Gideon to examine his life, nor does she have a friend like Shlomo for a guide. All she has is her nightmares and Gideon. That she remains unredeemed at the end of the novel is one of the novel's more unsatisfying features, for she has endured a far worse Hell than has Gideon. He may have had a difficult family life, but she has endured the Holocaust; she lives with the guilt of having been responsible, albeit unwittingly, for her father's death in the gas chamber. The ghosts that haunt Natasha are far stronger, far more frightening, than those that haunt Gideon. His parting words to her, "You and I are going to kill each other" (428), come off as smug, considering that he has always had a hope of redemption that will forever be denied her. Nonetheless, if Gideon is to experience a rebirth as a writer, a husband, and a father, he must do so without Natasha, the living reminder of all of his failures. It is Natasha who pays the price for Gideon's redemption.

THEMATIC ISSUES

While most of Uris's novels are plot driven, *Mitla Pass* focuses more on character, particularly the character of Gideon Zadok. The themes in the novel all relate to Gideon's character development, specifically, his finally coming to terms with himself. Secondary themes reinforcing this primary theme include the guilt of survivors, the special calling of the writer, and family relationships and responsibilities.

Gideon's own sense of family responsibility is shaped by his childhood. Alternately smothered and abandoned by his mother, and virtually ignored by his father, the young Gideon would be alone if not for his sister Molly and later his Uncle Lazar. His parents' dedication to the Communist Party blinds them to their children's needs. Nathan moves the family from city to city as the Communist Party dictates, and Leah exploits the children in order to gain credit from the grocer, the butcher, or the doctor. Suspicious of anyone other than Communist Party members who may have some influence on their children, Nathan and Leah attempt to isolate Molly and Gideon from what they consider fascist interests. The result is that the two children turn to each other for love and support.

To some extent, Gideon plays out the same scene with his own family. Instead of dedication to communism, Gideon's dedication is to his writing. That dedication at times keeps his family in poverty, and disrupts their lives every time Gideon feels that he must travel in order to research a book. By depriving his family of stability, by insisting that his needs as a writer supersede any other needs of the family, Gideon repeats the sins of his father. Even when he succumbs to Val's pleas that they settle in Hollywood rather than move to the unsavory Tenderloin district of San Francisco, he does so grudgingly, eventually blaming the failure of his Tenderloin novel on Val.

Unlike Nathan, however, Gideon struggles with his family responsibilities. Facing possible death in battle, he talks to Shlomo about his failings as a husband and father, acknowledging that his propensity to blame Val for his shortcomings is precisely the kind of behavior his father always exhibited. At the end of the novel, when Gideon returns to Val and the children, he returns a redeemed man, dedicated not only to his writing but to his family as well.

Gideon's struggle also involves his guilt over having survived the battle of Tarawa when so many of his fellow soldiers were killed. This is part of what draws him to Natasha, whose torment over having survived the death camps when her entire family succumbed forces her into self-destructive and violent behavior. Survivor guilt is in fact common among those who emerged from the Holocaust; Natasha's is simply more specific, given her unwitting responsibility for her father's death. What Gideon must appreciate if he is to heal himself is that, unlike Natasha, he was not responsible for the death of his friend Pedro on Tarawa. Ironically, it is Natasha, who will never be free of her guilt, who finally convinces Gideon that he was not responsible for Pedro's death. Gideon was doing his job; the radio message that he succeeded in transmitting saved an ammunition ship; he could not have saved Pedro and completed the transmission. When Gideon finally accepts the fact that he is not a "Jew coward" (428), he is freed from his demons.

It is only when Gideon is able to recognize his responsibilities to his family, to balance those responsibilities with the demands of his vocation, and to accept that he is not guilty of Pedro's death that he can finally come to terms with himself. In the final scene of the novel, he and Val reconcile, both of them recognizing that they will still have their battles and Gideon will still be consumed with the writer's passion. But having come through the battle of Mitla Pass—both the physical battle with the Egyptians and the emotional battle within himself—Gideon is finally able to escape his past and concentrate on living in the present and for the future.

A PSYCHOANALYTIC READING OF *MITLA PASS*

As a semiautobiographical novel, *Mitla Pass* lends itself naturally to a psychoanalytic reading, as described in Chapter 4. Within the novel itself the characters engage in pseudo-analysis of the motivation behind their behavior, most specifically when Gideon attributes Natasha's series of destructive love affairs to her guilt over having been responsible for her father's death. But the novel also serves as an accurate manifestation of the desires and fears of Americans, particularly men, in the second half of the twentieth century.

Like so many American men of his generation, Gideon saw combat in World War II. As Uris demonstrates in *Battle Cry*, the experience of that war forced innocent boys to grow up suddenly and brutally. The experience of battle, particularly hand-to-hand combat, is devastating to the psyche. But as many veterans of war reluctantly admit, those battles often remain the high point of their lives. The intensity of a life-and-death situation, coupled with the absolute dependence on fellow soldiers, creates an experience that can never be repeated. In Gideon Zadok Uris has created a man who craves that excitement he felt only while at war and who seeks to repeat his wartime experiences into middle age. Accompanying the Israeli forces into Mitla Pass allows Gideon to relive his battle days and to prove to himself once again that he is a real man. Through him, many readers can do the same.

The sense that nothing else in life can compare with the wartime experience is heightened in this novel by Gideon's response to the two jobs he takes after the war. The first, working as a newspaper distribution manager, represents the meaningless activity that men must pursue in peacetime. Compared with what he was doing several years earlier on Tarawa, this work seems demeaning to Gideon. His experience mirrors that of thousands of men who suddenly found themselves, ten or more years after the war, looking back on their lives and wondering what contribution they had made after discharge from the service. This sense of having nothing to contribute would be especially acute in the United States, with its comfortable standard of living and its stable social climate.

America's comfort and stability may have had a lulling effect on veterans, but far worse would be the sense of declining moral values since the war. For Gideon, the symbol of that decline can be found in Hollywood. The insincerity, the back stabbing, and the shallowness that characterize Hollywood in the novel serve as a sharp counterpoint to the honesty, the devotion, and the deep concern shared by soldiers on the battlefield. For those who did not remain in the military after the war, like Gideon, Hollywood and the pictures it produced might well be a painful reminder of the corruption of postwar American society. Gideon's Hollywood agent personifies the values of the town: "He liked *things*, lots of *things*, *things* with big engines, *things* that sparkled, furry *things* to drape on his tawdry wife and tawdry girlfriends, huge *things* to swim in" (71–72). The materialism of American culture, certainly present before the war, escalated in the decades following it, and that materialism demoralizes Gideon as it demoralized countless veterans who were seeking meaningful lives.

Gideon's affair with Natasha also reflects his dissatisfaction with his comfortable American life. Meeting her as he does in Israel, Gideon is able to make a connection with his collective past, with the Holocaust that cost him an extended family. At the same time the affair allows him to prove that he can move beyond that past. It is common for Americans who live in comfort and stability to feel the occasional pang of guilt at the thought of their less fortunate ancestors. This guilt would be particularly acute for Jewish Americans, who can thank the good fortune of having lived on this side of the Atlantic for the fact that they escaped the fate of their fellow Jews in Europe. When he encounters the sensual but volatile Natasha, Gideon feels both attraction and aversion to what she represents: she is at once a conquest, a beautiful woman who wants him as much as he wants her, and a nightmare of a past that Gideon did not share but cannot escape. It is significant that Gideon can only leave Natasha once he has faced his own survivor's guilt over losing Pedro on Tarawa; in leaving Natasha at that moment, Gideon frees himself from the guilt of both the real and the imagined experience.

Gideon's reconciliation with Val completes his, and the reader's, journey. Having proved his manhood and purged his guilt, Gideon is able to settle down as an ordinary American and enjoy the bounty of the United States. Readers who see in Gideon a reflection of themselves can be satisfied with this ending, because it tells them in essence that they are all right, that the comfortable lives they lead should generate no guilt. The past, both personal and collective, is past; once confronted, it can be put away.

Bibliography

WORKS BY LEON URIS

Novels

When Bantam paperback edition is listed after hardcover, references in the text are to the Bantam editions.

Armageddon: A Novel of Berlin. New York: Doubleday, 1964.
The Angry Hills. New York: Random House, 1955; New York: Bantam, 1972.
Battle Cry. New York: Putnam, 1953; New York: Bantam, 1954.
Exodus. New York: Doubleday, 1958; New York: Bantam, 1959.
The Haj. New York: Doubleday, 1984; New York: Bantam, 1985.
Mila 18. New York: Doubleday, 1961; New York: Bantam, 1962.
Mitla Pass. New York: Doubleday, 1988.
QB VII. New York: Doubleday, 1970.
Redemption. New York: HarperCollins, 1995.
Topaz. New York: Doubleday, 1967; New York: Bantam, 1968.
Trinity. New York: Doubleday, 1976.

Articles

"Girls Who Fought for Israel." *Ladies Home Journal* September 1967: 83–86.
"In Mencken's Hometown." *Nation* 5 November 1955: 374–375.

"The Legacy of Schindler's List." *TV Guide* 22–28 February 1997: 45+.
"Most Heroic Story of Our Century." *Coronet* November 1960: 170–178.

Collaborations (photo essays)

Exodus Revisited. Photographs by Dimitrios Harissiadis. New York: Doubleday, 1959.
Ireland: A Terrible Beauty. Photographs by Jill Uris. New York: Doubleday, 1975.
Jerusalem, Song of Songs. Photographs by Jill Uris. New York: Doubleday, 1981.

Play

Ari (Exodus: The Musical). Music by Walt Smith. Broadway production, 1971.

Screenplays

Battle Cry. Warner Brothers, 1954.
Gunfight at the O. K. Corral. Paramount, 1957.

Film adaptations

Battle Cry. Directed by Raoul Walsh. Warner Brothers, 1954.
The Angry Hills. Directed by Robert Aldrich. Metro-Goldwyn-Mayer, 1959.
Exodus. Directed by Otto Preminger. United Artists, 1960.
Topaz. Directed by Alfred Hitchcock. United Artists, 1969.
QB VII. Directed by Tom Gries. ABC-TV, 1974.
Mila 18. Directed by Jon Avnet. Forthcoming.

BIOGRAPHICAL INFORMATION

Christy, Marion. "Leon Uris: His Word Is Truth." *Boston Globe* 26 October 1988: 67, 70.
Kalb, Bernard. "Leon Uris." *Saturday Review* 25 April 1953: 16.
"Leon Uris." *Beacham's Popular Fiction in America*. 4:1395.
"Leon Uris." *Cyclopedia of World Authors*. 4th ed., rev. 5:2052–2032.
"Leon Uris." *Newsweek* 27 April 1953: 111.
"New Creative Writers." *Library Journal* 15 February 1953: 370.
Peckham, S. "PW Interview: Leon Uris." *Publishers Weekly* 29 March 1976: 6–7.
Tischler, Henry. "Leon Uris." "Authors Speak." 1995. http: www.authorsspeak. com/uris__1195.html
"Uris, Leon." *Authors in the News*. 1:477.
"Uris, Leon." *Contemporary Literary Criticism*. 7:490–493; 32:430–438.

"Uris, Leon." *Contemporary Novelists*. 3d ed. 652.
"Uris, Leon (Marcus)." *Contemporary Authors*. New Revision Series. 40:448–451.

REVIEWS AND CRITICISM

General

Downey, Sharon D., and Richard A. Kallan. " 'Semi'-Aesthetic Detachment: The Fusing of Fictional and External Worlds in the Situational Literature of Leon Uris." *Communication Monographs* September 1982: 192–204.

Battle Cry

Frank, Pat. "Tough Story of Transition from Hometown Boys to Men Trained to Kill." *New York Herald Tribune Book Review* 3 May 1953: 5.
Harrison, V. K. Review of *Battle Cry*. *Library Journal* 15 May 1953: 918.
McMillan, George. "Tension Never Eases." *New York Times Book Review* 26 April 1953: 5.
Miller, Merle. "The Backdrop Is Victory." *Saturday Review* 25 April 1953: 16–17.
"Tough Marines." *Newsweek* 27 April 1953: 111.
Weeks, Edward. "The Young Marines." *Atlantic Monthly* August 1953: 82, 84.

The Angry Hills

Cooney, Thomas E. "Love and Derring-Do in Greece." *Saturday Review* 19 November 1955: 46–47.
Dempsey, David. "Unwitting Go-Between." *New York Times Book Review* 16 October 1955: 32–33.
Hoey, Reid A. Review of *The Angry Hills*. *Library Journal* 1 October 1955: 2163.

Exodus

"Bestseller Revisited." *Time* 8 December 1958: 110.
Bresler, Riva T. Review of *Exodus*. *Library Journal* 15 September 1958: 2443–2444.
Coleman, John. "Proper Study." *Spectator* 10 July 1959: 44.
Geismar, Maxwell. "Epic of Israel." *Saturday Review* 27 September 1958: 22.
Gilroy, Harry. "The Founding of the New Israel." *New York Times* 12 October 1958: 32.
Godsell, Geoffrey. Review of *Exodus*. *Christian Science Monitor* 4 December 1958: 17.
Kupferberg, Herbert. Review of *Exodus*. *New York Herald Tribune Book Review* 28 September 1958: 5.

McDowell, "*Exodus* in Samizdat: Still Popular and Still Subversive." *New York Times Book Review* 26 April 1987: 13.
Wakefield, Dan. Review of *Exodus*. *Nation* 11 April 1959: 318–319.

Mila 18

Adams, Phoebe. "Warsaw Ghetto." *Atlantic Monthly* August 1961: 94.
Adelman, George. Review of *Mila 18*. *Library Journal* 15 June 1961: 2339.
"Back to *The Wall*." *Time* 2 June 1961: 94.
Decter, Midge. "Popular Jews." *Commentary* October 1961: 358. Reprinted in *The Liberated Woman and Other Americans*. New York: Coward, McCann & Geoghegan, 1971: 117–120.
Hope, Frances. Review of *Mila 18*. *Spectator* 27 October 1961: 598.
Pisko, E. S. Review of *Mila 18*. *Christian Science Monitor* 22 June 1961: 7.
Reynolds, Quentin. "In the Ghetto a Battle for the Conscience of the World." *New York Times Book Review* 4 June 1961: 5.

Armageddon: A Novel of Berlin

Barrett, William. "Big Canvas and Small." *Atlantic Monthly* July 1964: 135–136.
"Fresh Off the Assembly Line." *Time* 12 June 1964: 118.
"Hard to Digest." *Newsweek* 29 June 1964: 89.
Harlen, R. D. Review of *Armageddon*. *Library Journal* 15 May 1964: 2116–2117.
Levy, Alan. "War Is a Gold Mine." *New Republic* 11 July 1964: 24–25.
Mitgang, Herbert. "Problems and Perils of Berlin Airlift." *New York Times Book Review* 28 June 1964: 22–23.
Stern, Daniel. "The Letdown after the Airlift." *Saturday Review* 13 June 1964: 32.
Ware, Cade. "The Good Guys Win." *Book Week—The Sunday Herald Tribune* 14 June 1964: 16.

Topaz

Boucher, Anthony. Review of *Topaz*. *New York Times Book Review* 15 October 1967: 57.
Macklin, F. A. Review of *Topaz*. *America* 6 January 1968: 17.
Marsh, Pamela. "You Can't Tell Fact from Fiction." *Christian Science Monitor* 16 November 1967: 15.
Tannenbaum, Earl. Review of *Topaz*. *Library Journal* 1 October 1967: 3449.

QB VII

Duffy, Martha. "Bestseller Revisited." *Time* 28 June 1971: 80.
Lehmann-Haupt, Christopher. "How to Write a Leon Uris." *New York Times* 2 December 1970: 45.

Marsh, Pamela. Review of *QB VII. Christian Science Monitor* 11 March 1971: 7.
Neyman, Mark. Review of *QB VII. Library Journal* 1 December 1970: 4195.
Rogers, W. G. "Dr. Adam Kelno: Hero or Villain?" *New York Times Book Review* 15 November 1970: 70.

Trinity

Hamill, Pete. Review of *Trinity. New York Times Book Review* 14 March 1976: 5.
Moran, John. Review of *Trinity. Library Journal* 1 April 1976: 925.
Rowan, Diana. Review of *Trinity. Christian Science Monitor* 21 April 1976: 23.
Shuttleworth, Paul. "Do the Irish Need Uris?" *Pacific Sun Literary Quarterly* Summer 1976: 5.
Woods, William C. "Fighting Irish." *Washington Post* 25 April 1976: G7.

The Haj

Adler, Jerry. "The Unchosen People." *Newsweek* 21 May 1984: 84.
Hunter, Evan. "Palestine in Black and White." *New York Times Book Review* 22 April 1984: 7.
Leber, Michele. Review of *The Haj. Library Journal* 15 April 1984: 825.
Review of *The Haj. Kirkus Reviews* 1 February 1984: 113.
Spitzer, Jane Stewart. "*The Haj*, Uris's Richly Detailed Palestinian Portrait, Lacks Vitality." *Christian Science Monitor* 2 May 1984: 20.

Mitla Pass

MacDonald, Bob. "Uris Draws from Life for Latest Page-Turner." *Boston Globe* 13 December 1988: 70.

Redemption

Duffy, Malachi. Review of *Redemption. New York Times Book Review* 2 July 1995: 11.
Review of *Redemption. Publishers Weekly* 24 April 1995: 58.

OTHER SECONDARY SOURCES

The Holocaust

"Cybrary of the Holocaust." http://remember.org
Gutman, Israel. *Resistance: The Warsaw Ghetto Uprising*. Boston: Houghton Mifflin, 1994.

Kogon, Eugen. *The Theory and Practice of Hell*. Trans. Heinz Norden. New York: Berkley, 1980.

Langer, Lawrence L. *Admitting the Holocaust: Collected Essays*. New York: Oxford UP, 1995.

"Medical Experiments in Nazi Concentration Camps." http://www.luc.edu/ deps/modern_lang/holocast/medex.htm

"Polish Jews in World War II." http://cyberroad.com/poland/jews_ww2.html

Roland, Charles. *Courage Under Siege: Disease, Starvation and Death in the Warsaw Ghetto*. New York: Oxford UP, 1992.

Thomas, Gordon, and Max Morgan Witts. *Voyage of the Damned*. New York: Stein & Day, 1974.

Wyden, Peter. *Stella*. New York: Simon & Schuster, 1992.

Ireland

Bolger, Dermott, ed. *Sixteen on Sixteen: Irish Writers on the Easter Rising*. Chester Springs, PA: Dufour, 1988.

Caulfield, Malachy. *The Easter Rebellion*. Westport, CT: Greenwood, 1975.

Coogan, Tim P. *The Man Who Made Ireland: The Life and Death of Michael Collins*. Niwot, CO: Rinehart, Roberts, 1992.

———. *The IRA: A History*. Niwot, CO: Rinehart, Roberts, 1993.

———. *Eamon de Valera: The Man Who Was Ireland*. New York: HarperCollins, 1995.

DeRosa, Peter. *Rebels: The Irish Rising of 1916*. New York: Fawcett, 1994.

Israel and Palestine

Gerner, Deborah. *One Land, Two Peoples: The Conflict over Palestine*. Boulder, CO: Westview Press, 1991.

Kanafani, Ghassan. *All That's Left to You: A Novella and Other Stories*. Trans. May Jayyusi and Jeremy Reed. Austin: Center for Middle Eastern Studies at the University of Texas at Austin, 1990.

Literary History/Criticism

Bressler, Charles E. *Literary Criticism: An Introduction to Theory and Practice*. Englewood Cliffs, NJ: Prentice-Hall, 1994.

Cowart, David. *History and the Contemporary Novel*. Carbondale: Southern Illinois UP, 1989.

Howe, Irving. *Politics and the Novel*. New York: Horizon, 1957.

Feuchtwanger, Lion. *The House of Desdemona, or The Laurels and Limitations of Historical Fiction*. Trans. Harold A. Basilius. Detroit: Wayne State UP, 1963.

Index

About the Author

KATHLEEN SHINE CAIN is Professor of English at Merrimack College in North Andover, Massachusetts, where she has also directed the Writing Program and the Women's Studies Program. She is the author of articles on writing centers, detective novelists, and contemporary American writers, as well as several textbooks, the most recent of which is *Living in the USA: Cultural Contexts for Reading and Writing* (1994). Her research interests also include American women writers and the personal memoir as literary genre.

Critical Companions to Popular Contemporary Writers
Kathleen Gregory Klein, Series Editor

V. C. Andrews
by E. D. Huntley

Tom Clancy
by Helen S. Garson

Mary Higgins Clark
by Linda C. Pelzer

Arthur C. Clarke
by Robin Anne Reid

James Clavell
by Gina Macdonald

Pat Conroy
by Landon C. Burns

Robin Cook
by Lorena Laura Stookey

Michael Crichton
by Elizabeth A. Trembley

Howard Fast
by Andrew Macdonald

Ken Follett
by Richard C. Turner

Ernest J. Gaines
by Karen Carmean

John Grisham
by Mary Beth Pringle

James Herriot
by Michael J. Rossi

Tony Hillerman
by John M. Reilly

John Irving
by Josie P. Campbell

John Jakes
by Mary Ellen Jones

Stephen King
by Sharon A. Russell

Dean Koontz
by Joan G. Kotker

Robert Ludlum
by Gina Macdonald

Anne McCaffrey
by Robin Roberts

Colleen McCullough
by Mary Jean DeMarr

James A. Michener
by Marilyn S. Severson

Ann Rice
by Jennifer Smith

Tom Robbins
by Catherine E. Hoyser and Lorena Laura Stookey

John Saul
by Paul Bail

Erich Segal
by Linda C. Pelzer

Amy Tan
by E. D. Huntley

Leon Uris
by Kathleen Shine Cain

Gore Vidal
by Susan Baker and Curtis S. Gibson